Rationality and Ethics in Agriculture

Rationality and Ethics in Agriculture

Hugh Lehman

University of Idaho Press
Moscow, Idaho
1995

Copyright © 1995 the University of Idaho Press
Published by the University of Idaho Press,
Moscow, Idaho 83844-1107
Printed in the United States of America
All rights reserved

No part of this publication may be reproduced, stored in a
retrieval system, or transmitted in any form or by any means,
electronic, mechanical, photocopying, recording, or otherwise,
except for purposes of scholarly review,
without the prior permission of the copyright owner.

98 97 96 95   5 4 3 2 1

Lehman, Hugh
Rationality and ethics in agriculture / Hugh Lehman.
p.   cm.
Includes bibliographical references (p.   ) and index.
ISBN 0-89301-179-7 (pbk.)
1. Agriculture—Moral and ethical aspects.   2. Rationalism.
I. Title.

BJ52.5.L48   1995   94-45942
1974'.963—dc20   CIP

Library of Congress Cataloging-in-Publication Data

Contents

Introduction   vii

Part One: Rationality

1 Rationality of Agricultural Critics and Criticism   3

2 Reality, Objectivity, and Risk   21

3 Can Agricultural Policy Be Determined by Reason Alone?   35

4 Is It Rational to Attribute Beliefs or Desires to Animals?   51

5 Is It Rational to Deny That Animals Have Beliefs and Desires?   69

6 Is It Rational to Engage in Moral Reasoning?   83

7 Views of Rationality in Ethics   97

8 Does Rationality Require Holistic Thinking in Agriculture?   115

9 Rationality and Family Farming   129

Part Two: Ethics

10 Ethical Grounds for Sustainable Agriculture   147

11 Marginal Cases and Killing Animals   165

12 Speciesism and Confinement Rearing   183

13 Technoanxiety and Agriculture   199

Bibliography   215

Index   225

Introduction

My graduate studies led me to think of myself as an academic philosopher. While I occasionally read works of social criticism by philosophers, I tended to regard them as non-philosophical, as being of little relevance to philosophy itself. Conversely, I thought that the study of philosophy had little to contribute to such non-philosophical studies. I now believe that my former views concerning the mutual relevance of philosophy and social criticism were mistaken. Most of us think of ourselves as entitled to do most of the things that we do. This is especially true of the activities in which we engage in order to make a living. Further, we often think that some of the things people do are things that they ought not to do. Such thought (concerning our obligations and entitlements) invariably includes or takes for granted fundamental philosophical assumptions, assumptions about what is of value, about our moral obligations, about what we are justified in believing, about what sorts of beings we are, etc.

We appeal to such assumptions in attempting to justify our behavior in response to criticism or to justify our criticisms of others. Sometimes, of course, we are not fully aware of the assumptions we have made or of the controversial character of these assumptions. The assumption may be masked by reference to a particular term which we think we understand but which, in itself, is not a statement of principle. For example, recently there has been much talk about "sustainable development." Sometimes this term is explained as involving a commitment to equitable access to resources for all people. But such a minimal amount of clarification does not amount to a clear statement of any substantive principle. Terms such as "equitable access to resources" need to be interpreted by reference to statements of principle; further, the manner in which such statements are applied to concrete situations must also be made clear. In the absence of such explanation, terms such as "equitable access to resources," while not completely vacuous, are so vague that everyone can easily find reason to agree that everyone should have such access.

While we all make general philosophical assumptions, we do not always think carefully about these assumptions and rigorously analyze and evaluate them. We normally fail both to detect inconsistencies among the principles which we have assumed or to apply individual principles in a rigorously consistent manner. Careful philosophical study can contribute to reducing or eliminating both of these problems. In this way, philosophical thought can make a major contribution toward improving our thinking about our social practices and, ultimately, toward improving the practices themselves. Hopefully, these essays will make a contribution to improving thought about agricultural matters.

In recent years, agricultural practices have come under criticism, leading to forms of action ranging from discussion to boycotts to legislation and to the use of physical force to destroy property or to "rescue" animals. The criticism has also prompted discussion and other forms of action (though rarely, if ever, violence) from agrologists, agricultural producers, and others with strong interests in agriculture. Such criticism and discussion was the stimulus for my undertaking the investigations contained in this book. Each essay arises from remarks I have heard or read, remarks made by agrologists, philosophers, producers, etc.

I have not attempted to develop a coherent philosophical theory on the basis of which I could defend certain sorts of agricultural practices while condemning others. Development of such a theory would lead to an abstract philosophical work and, I confess, I am not optimistic enough to think that large numbers of agrologists or agricultural producers would be willing to read it. Rather, I have tried to produce a work which would be accessible to thoughtful agricultural scientists, producers, and others concerned more directly with agricultural practices. I have tried to enter discussions concerning the rationales for agricultural policies or practices in ways that are meaningful to agrologists as well as to philosophers, and I hope to move such discussions forward by applying philosophical criticism. I have not tried to have the last word on any issue; the discussions in these essays are not sufficiently thorough to achieve that. I hope that these discussions will challenge agrologists, producers, philosophers concerned with agriculture, etc., to think more carefully and deeply about their own views. That may lead ultimately to more sustained philosophical arguments. On a more practical level, if agrologists and critics are led to think more carefully about the philosophical assumptions underlying what they say, they may be led to discover points of agreement which, in turn, may help all of us to develop agricultural policies and practices of which we can all approve.

The development of a coherent framework for thinking about ethical questions of agricultural policy or practice requires more than simply advancing claims in support of one's own position. It requires participants on both sides of each issue to listen to their opponents, to search for areas of common ground, and to calmly investigate value and ethical assumptions over which there appears to be disagreement. While agricultural scientists and critics of agricultural practices have often advanced claims and, in some instances, have tried to support those claims with reasons and evidence, they have not yet achieved a sustained discussion of the issues with each other. Participants to such discussions have often tried to strengthen their own position by denigrating their opponents. They have not listened calmly to the viewpoints of their opponents. They have not been willing to patiently explore controversial matters. In preparing these essays I hope that I have made some steps toward changing these attitudes. I have tried to explore the elements of and possibilities for developing a coherent framework within which ethical questions concerning agriculture can be investigated calmly.

In trying to focus attention on basic philosophical assumptions which enter into many discussions of agricultural issues, I noticed that in practically any discussion in which someone is questioning the wisdom or moral acceptability of an agricultural policy or practice, a question is raised about rationality. Rationality is the unifying theme of the chapters of part one of this book. Often agrologists perceive the critics of agriculture as irrational. Although this charge is obviously not true, I regard it as substantive. If and where it is true, that truth must be shown by presenting reasons or evidence. Presentation of such reasons presupposes a coherent framework of thought within which reference to rationality makes sense. In this work I discuss elements of such a framework. I try to point to the kinds of reasons that must be established in order to justify the charge that some people, be they agricultural scientists or critics of agriculture, are irrational.

Roughly the first two-thirds of this book is concerned explicitly with aspects of rationality. Much of the material of the last part, which is directly concerned with ethical questions, is concerned with rationality also. For example, speciesism may be regarded as an irrational ethical perspective; some people would regard technoanxiety as a kind of irrationality as well. Resolutions of ethical controversies may prompt questions concerning the rationality of ethical arguments, for example, arguments involving the use of the principle of parsimony or arguments over where the burden of proof rests.

The use of the term "rationality" and related terms such as "reason" and "rational," throughout this book should not be taken to imply that I think that there is one form or essence of rationality which is manifest in many particulars. A number of different sorts of things are said to be rational or irrational. Among these are beliefs, recommendations, actions, policies, other people or animals, ethical principles, etc. I have not tried to elicit a core meaning which applies in all such uses of the terms "rational" or "rationality." Rather, in each essay in which there is concern about rationality, I have tried to make it clear what the subjects of the discussion are, whether they are beliefs, actions, people, etc. I have been concerned with whether the beliefs, actions, attitudes, ethical theories, etc., are rational or not; with reasons for claiming that some actions are rational or not; with ways to challenge such claims, etc. I do not believe that efforts to find a core meaning of "rationality" and related terms would add to the clarity of my discussions, nor do I think that the absence of such a general definition is reason to think that it is inappropriate to use the term "rationality" in the title of this work.

Questions concerning rationality in agriculture arise in a number of contexts. Critics of agricultural practices or policies are often accused of being irrational or emotional. I have approached this accusation from a number of respects, which may be regarded as attempts to elicit the concept or concepts of rationality underlying the agrologists' thoughts. In particular, rationality is often contrasted with emotion. This issue is considered in the chapter on reason and emotion. Again, some agrologists and others seem to think that it is irrational to act on moral principles as opposed to acting so as to maximize one's own gain or to maximize one's profits. This issue is considered in the chapters on moral cynicism and on views about the rationality of ethical principles. Further, one chapter is devoted to considering the rationality of supporting family farms. Wendell Berry has raised some significant issues in this regard, and we have considered a criticism of Berry by an agricultural economist who appears mainly to have failed to understand Berry's perspective.

Much of the criticism of agriculture is motivated by concern for safety—safety of farm workers, consumers, etc. Agrologists' claims that these safety concerns are irrational may be understood as a criticism, in turn, of the critics' mode of expression, beliefs or actions. This has led to our consideration of rationality in these regards in two chapters, namely the chapter on rationality of agricultural critics and criticism and the chapter on objectivity, rationality and risk. Concern about safety also underlies the discussion in the chapter concerned with "technoanxiety." The specific issue concerning the rationality of attributing beliefs or desires to animals is considered in two separate chapters.

The chapters of part two of this work concern matters in which critics of agriculture have alleged that agricultural practices are unethical. Several chapters concern our moral obligations to or regarding animals, specifically chapters eleven and twelve; there we have considered the marginal cases argument and claims about speciesism which have been very effective in motivating people to condemn intensive animal production. We have also considered arguments which underlie the claims that animals have important moral rights, namely the claim that animals are subjects-of-a-life.

Questions have been raised concerning whether agriculture is sustainable. This issue is considered in one chapter in which we focus both on defining the concept of sustainability and on considering the principles which underlie our (alleged) obligation to make our agricultural practices sustainable. Often, those in the vanguard of challenging the sustainability of agriculture have been ecologists who allege that the major problems of agriculture arise from agrologists taking reductionist rather than holistic approaches to solving problems; this criticism is considered in one chapter. Others, Wes Jackson in particular, are particularly alarmed by the prospect of widespread application in agriculture of techniques derived from molecular biology, that is, they are alarmed by the prospect of the implementation of genetic engineering. We have addressed this matter in a chapter on technoanxiety.

Since I hoped to address scholars and scientists as well as other philosophers, I have tried to organize the material under consideration into relatively small parcels. Each chapter of this work is an essay in itself and, in general, the chapters can be read independently of each other. There is no need to start with the first chapter and march dutifully through to the end, although in some cases, to avoid repetition, material in some chapters is relevant to material in others. I have tried, in the introduction of each chapter, to give a clear sense of the content of that chapter.

Part One
Rationality

I. Rationality of Agricultural Critics and Criticism

AGRICULTURE IN MODERN times has been criticized on a number of different grounds. For example, critics have said that contemporary animal production practices should be modified since, under current practices, many animals are subjected to spatial restrictions that are too confining, or to frustration of drives to display various behaviors, or to diets which are unsatisfactory from the perspective of the animal's health, etc. Other critics have asserted that the use of herbicides or pesticides in production of food or other crops should be drastically reduced or eliminated, on the grounds that residues are potentially harmful to human health, or because the toxic substances contained in the pesticides contaminate water supplies from which humans obtain water for drinking, or because the pesticides destroy not only the intended pest but also many other creatures and consequently contribute to other harmful effects such as elimination of populations of beneficial insects.

Agricultural scientists, put on the defensive by such criticisms, often respond by claiming that the critics, or the positions they take in regard to the disagreement, are irrational. Apparently the scientists' response is intended as a reason in support of the position that the agricultural practices in question ought not to be changed in accord with the critics' recommendations. The scientists are maintaining, in effect, that the practices are acceptable and that we may dismiss the critics' reasons and recommendations because either the critics or their reasons or their recommendations are irrational. What does this mean?

Sometimes when agricultural scientists claim that critics are irrational, what they mean is that the critics are appealing to emotion. Emotion, as understood here, is opposed to reason. The scientists may allege that the critics' position is based purely on emotion and thus that we should conclude that their objection does not reflect anything real concerning the herbicide or the circumstances of its use. The implication is that the critics' objection reflects only their internal mental attitude or feeling. If the critics' claims reflect only their feelings, then—the scientists seem to be suggesting—we should disregard their arguments as unsound and their position as mistaken while, on the contrary, the scientist's position, being based on reason should be taken as correct.

This view, which we have attributed to scientists, presupposes a distinction between reason and emotion. We shall investigate this matter in another chapter, where we will see that this attitude toward reason and emotion is oversimplified: reason is not necessarily opposed to emotion. However, the suggestion that action should be based on reason rather than emotion may mean that certain beliefs, which enter into the rationalization of action, should be justified by sufficiently strong evidence. I evaluate this idea in section two of this chapter. Alternatively, the charge of irrationality might mean that the rationalization of action requires certain assumptions about rational behavior. I discuss this idea in section three of this chapter. I shall try to show that the critics of agricultural practices are neither always irrational nor that it would always be wise to disregard their recommendations. Let us turn to this task.

RATIONALITY OF TACTICS, CLAIMS, AND RECOMMENDATIONS

We shall start by considering briefly whether the deployment of certain tactics to attempt to change public attitudes or social practices is rational. Let us consider an example. Suppose that some agricultural scientists are advocating the general acceptance of the use of some agricultural chemical, while the critics are opposed to the use of the chemical. As has been the case, we may suppose that the chemical is being widely used. The critics are trying to get a governmental regulatory body to ban the use of the chemical, or to get a law enacted to achieve that effect. The scientists have ample evidence that the use of the chemical achieves the purposes for which it is used, e.g., it increases productivity through reducing weed infestations. Further, let us suppose that evidence that the chemical, when used with appropriate care, causes any serious harm, is inconclusive. Nonetheless, the critics object to the use of the chemical on the grounds of possible harms to human health or to parts of our environment. They may make claims about possible harms which are unsubstantiated. Further, we suppose that the critics resort to tactics designed to attract attention. They may resort to various forms of political action, or campaigns through the media, picketing, letter-writing campaigns, and perhaps even to the destruction of property.

With respect to an example such as this, we can distinguish four aspects of the critics' position, namely, certain claims that they make as to what the facts are, certain arguments that they advance in behalf of the conclusions they support; the recommendations that they make as to what ought to be done; and finally, the tactics that they employ to attract attention and to influence social policies or practices. The charge of irrationality might be directed at the evidence for the alleged facts, at the recommendations based on those alleged facts, or at the tactics used in the attempt to win support for those recommendations.

Critics of agriculture often use tactics designed to call attention to their concerns. The tactics may involve violence, boycotts, marches, political pressure, etc. The resort to such tactics is indicative of strong or passionate feelings concerning the use of the pesticide. The charge that the critics are irrational may be essentially a reference to those feelings. If that is so, we should ask whether it is necessarily irrational to resort to such tactics. Here, I wish to take issue with the idea that passionate or emotional defense of action or social policy is necessarily irrational.

The critics are trying to effect change in social practices. If one is trying to attract attention to his views in order to influence social policy, it may be quite reasonable to act in ways which are noisy and attract attention to oneself. Such ways of acting may strike scientists as irrational. Scientists may see themselves as dispassionate and therefore rational. However, this judgment is often unwarranted. After all, scientists are not trying to change social practice. In this context, they have no reason to display passion on behalf of a cause, such as the cause of changing social practices in regard to herbicide use. However, this is not to say that they are any less emotional about the position they support. It is rather that in the circumstances where they wish to maintain the status quo, it is better tactics for them not to attract attention. Indeed, in some cases where scientists have resorted to public relations campaigns in defense of policies that they favor, their appeals are often just as emotional as the tactics employed by critics of agricultural practices. In any case, concern with the rationality of the critics' views is not a concern with the tactics they may use to change social practice. Let us now turn to consideration of the rationality of the critics' position.

RATIONALITY OF BELIEFS ABOUT HARMS AND POSSIBLE HARMS

Agrologists often suggest that critics are irrational for accepting as true some claims about the properties of agricultural chemicals which have not been scientifically established. Let us consider as an example a claim that residues of a particular herbicide in fruits or vegetables are harmful to the health of consumers. We allowed above that the evidence for such a claim may well be inconclusive. We may, however, assume that there is some indirect evidence for the claim. For example, farm workers have been harmed through exposure to agricultural chemicals.[1] Let us assume that some farm workers have become ill and that there is strong evidence that they became ill through long exposure to this or similar chemicals. We may further assume that some animals have developed serious illness after exposure to relatively large doses of the chemical. Yet it is not clear that the type of exposure to such chemicals to which consumers are subjected causes disease. Let us agree that it is irrational to be strongly committed to a belief, such as that eating fruits and vegetables containing residues will lead to cancer, if the belief is not strongly confirmed by all relevant available evidence.[2] In consequence, let us agree that it would be irrational for a consumer to be firmly convinced that he will get cancer or some other serious disease as a result of consuming fruits and vegetables containing residues of this herbicide, where the residues occur at or below socially established levels. The evidence does not strongly support the conclusion that the residues cause serious disease.

However, critics of the use of herbicides, whose concern arises out of worries about getting cancer, need not be strongly committed to the belief that by eating fruits or vegetables containing small residues of this chemical they will get cancer. Such individuals might be saying no more than that in light of the fact that the herbicide is known to be toxic to humans, there is some risk of getting cancer or other serious disease even from a minimal exposure, that is, exposure at the socially accepted levels. In other words, all that the critics need to be saying is that there is some probability that eating fruits or vegetables containing residues will lead to the occurrence of cancer.

If that is all that the critic is asserting, then we cannot accuse him of being irrational on the grounds that his commitment to a belief is stronger than the evidence warrants. Let us briefly explain why this is so.

Assessing the rationality of beliefs about what is probable is more difficult than assessing the rationality of beliefs about what is actual. To see this we must first comment briefly on the sense of the term "probable" as it may be understood in this context. When the critic says that there is some probability that consuming residues of the pesticide will lead to cancer (or some other serious harm), I believe that he means that he has some evidence on the basis of which it is reasonable to suspect that consuming the residues may cause cancer. The evidence is not necessarily strong enough to say that he knows that consuming the residues will cause cancer. Rather, he believes that he has evidence which indicates that he should be alert to the possibility that consuming the pesticide could cause him to get cancer.

The statement about what is possible in this context is not a report of merely abstract or purely logical possibilities. It is a claim about what is possible given the nature of physical reality and given actual prior states of affairs. There is no possibility, in this sense, that the hypothetical herbicide being considered in this example will be transformed after its use into wine or even into pure water. Similarly no such possibility exists for the actual herbicides currently in use. When we say that it is possible that a consumer of herbicide residues will get a serious disease, we are talking about a possibility which, given the current state of our scientific knowledge, has some, albeit small, probability of occurring. The possibility that a consumer of residues will get a serious disease as a result is a real possibility, unlike the possibility that some herbicide will be turned into wine or pure water. Given this assumption, we can ask whether there is adequate evidence, in some cases, for the critic's belief that it is possible that by eating fruits and vegetables containing herbicide residue he will get cancer. If there is such evidence, then we should conclude that it is rational for the critic to subscribe to that belief.

It is perhaps worth noting at this point that sometimes, on the basis of evidence and reasoning, scientists are able to arrive at measures of the probability of rare events. Through such procedures, scientists may estimate that the probability of getting cancer or some other serious disease from the low level of exposure to which consumers are subjected to be very small indeed, for example, one in a million or one in ten million. It appears that some scientists concerned with the rationality of beliefs about getting serious illness from exposure to pesticide residues take the position that such a small probability of illness is equivalent to no probability of illness at all. People who took this position would maintain that on the basis of the evidence there is no possibility of becoming seriously ill as a result of such exposure. However, this judgment, namely that a sufficiently small probability is equivalent to no probability at all, is unwarranted. If the probability of cancer (or some other serious illness) due to exposure to a herbicide is one in ten million and ten or more million people are exposed to the herbicide, then there is a high probability that a small number of the exposed people will get cancer from the exposure.[3]

What evidence does the critic have concerning the possibility that exposure to a pesticide residue will cause him to get cancer? In a way, this question is too general. The defender of pesticide use will want to narrow the question down by making reference to a particular pesticide, or at least to a particular scientific class of pesticides. Ultimately, we might indeed have to do just that. However, consideration of the general question is, I believe, sufficient in this context.

According to some careful scientific analyses, approximately 10,000 cases of cancer occur per year in the United States as a result of exposure to pesticides.[4] Pimentel cites numerous studies which link cancer in human beings, at least indirectly, to exposure to various pesticides. As a result of scientific analyses, the carcinogenicity of various herbicides, and other substances used to protect food or to facilitate its production, has been established.[5] However, while the carcinogenicity of the active ingredients of many agricultural chemicals is known, there is much that we don't know concerning adverse consequences of long-term exposure to these substances. In addition, there is much that we don't know concerning adverse consequences of exposure to combinations of agricultural chemicals. Further, while we have been discussing cancer as an example, exposure to powerful chemicals is known to cause other serious diseases, such as neurological disorders, and serious allergic reactions as well.[6]

Given this knowledge, the claim that it is irrational for a person to believe it possible that he will get cancer (or some other serious illness) as a result of exposure to pesticide residues is often unwarranted. It is rational for the critic to believe that there is a significant possibility he will get cancer as a result of his exposure to pesticide residues; that is, that there is some probability that the type of exposure to residues we have been considering will lead to his getting cancer. The critic's belief, properly qualified, is not merely an expression of his internal emotional state. Rather, it is based on scientific evidence.

Thus far, our discussion of the rationality of the beliefs of agricultural critics has focussed on an example concerning the belief in the disease-causing effects of an herbicide which leaves a residue in food products. Other critics of agricultural practices are more concerned with the treatment of animals. The critics may base their criticism on the grounds that agricultural animals suffer frustration of desires, pain, etc. Scientists may wish to maintain that such a belief is irrational. Let us defer consideration of the rationality of the beliefs of these critics: we shall take up that issue in another chapter, in which we focus on the rationality of beliefs which attribute feelings or desires to animals.

As we have noted, some critics of the use of pesticides might justifiably be charged with irrationality in regard to their belief, providing that their belief is that they definitely will get cancer as a result of their exposure to pesticide residues. Other, more sophisticated critics, who maintain only that there is some probability that such exposure will lead to cancer, cannot necessarily be charged with being irrational on this count. I have suggested that a reasonable person might have evidence which, while not strong enough to prove that exposure to a pesticide through consuming a residue causes cancer, is strong enough to warrant the belief that there is a significant probability that such exposure will cause cancer. It would be equally reasonable, at this point, to wonder how much evidence one must have for this belief to be reasonable. This is a difficult question. Indeed, while I can say something about the nature of this evidence, I cannot say how the strength of such evidence should be measured. Philosophers and scientists have speculated for years on the nature of scientific evidence and on ways of assessing the strength of evidence.[7] This continues to be a controversial matter.

Some scientists might wish to dismiss the distinction to which I have appealed, that between evidence which shows that a hypothesis is true and evidence which only strong enough to indicates that there is some probability that a hypothesis is true. However, it is not hard to see that this is a distinction that scientists must make themselves, because it underlies their acceptance of beliefs as they conduct their scientific work. For example, a scientist trying to solve a problem may have to consider which hypothesis is worth further consideration. In such a context, the scientist may decide to conduct further research on a hypothesis for which there is evidence indicating some probability of its truth. Many other examples which illustrate this distinction could also be given.

Clearly, some reasons that people might offer in support of the claim that there is some probability that exposure to a pesticide causes cancer should not be accorded any weight. For example, if a person refers to an article in a disreputable tabloid, one known to publish claims that have been created in the imagination of the writer, reason does not require that article to be taken seriously. One can readily envisage other alleged reasons which are not worthy of serious consideration. However, there are some types of reasons which should not be dismissed as easily as the tabloid example. Suppose, for example, that a substance has been tested to determine whether it is carcinogenic. Animals of one or two species are exposed to high doses of the pesticide. Suppose that a considerable number of the animals do get cancer following exposure, but the incidence is not strong enough to warrant the conclusion that the substance causes cancer. Suppose also that the substance was not tested in conjunction with other substances to which humans are often exposed as well. If a person is aware of these factors in regard to the alleged carcinogenicity of a substance, he or she has some evidence that there is some probability that consuming the residue will cause cancer. It is impossible to say how strong that evidence is. Similarly, if a person concludes that he or she would rather not be exposed to that substance because there is some probability that the substance causes cancer, we are not entitled to conclude that the person's acceptance of this belief is irrational. It is not as if the person accepted the belief without any regard for what the evidence is. Further, it is not as if the person accepted the belief on the basis of worthless evidence.

Sometimes, instead of claiming that critics of agricultural practices are irrational, scientists express a closely related view by claiming that whereas scientific estimates of risk are "objective," the estimates of those concerned about the dangers of pesticides are mere perceptions. In order to pursue our consideration of rationality we shall defer consideration of this idea until the next chapter.

There is a third way in which the agricultural critics may be irrational; namely, in regard to the recommendations that they make. Defenders of pesticide use may wish to maintain that when they say that the critics are irrational, they say it not because of the critic's belief that exposure will possibly cause cancer, but because of the recommendations the critics make (or the conclusions they accept) on the basis of the claim that there is some probability of cancer due to exposure to pesticide residue. Let us turn to consideration of this claim.

RATIONAL RECOMMENDATIONS AND ALAR: CRITICISMS AND REPLIES

At this point we shall have to postulate another concept of rationality. In the discussion above, we agreed that beliefs are irrational if they are held even though there is not sufficient evidence to support the belief. However, here we are considering not the rationality of accepting particular beliefs, but the rationality of recommendations which may be based, at least in part, on beliefs.

Let us agree, then, that it is rational to believe that exposure to pesticide residues may cause cancer. On the basis of his belief in the possibility of getting a serious illness as a result of exposure to a herbicide, the critic may make any of a number of recommendations. He may recommend that all use of pesticides that leave residues in food products be eliminated. Or, he may recommend that pesticide residues in food be permitted only for pesticides that have been tested for carcinogenicity far more rigorously than is currently the case in countries such as the United States, Canada, Sweden, etc. Alternatively, he might recommend that the amount of residue that should be tolerated be reduced to lower levels, or that only residues of certain pesticides should be tolerated.

Of course, whether the critic's recommendations are rational will depend to some extent on the particular recommendations that he makes. However, our judgment concerning the rationality of the recommendations will also reflect our theoretical beliefs regarding the conditions under which recommendations for action are rational. No doubt, we should not regard recommendations as rational if the reasons given in support of the recommendations are claims about facts for which there is no significant evidence of their truth.[8] However, recommendations can be irrational even if they are based on rigorously established factual claims. This is a consequence of the fact that the rationality of recommendations is determined in part by the rationality of acting in accordance with those recommendations. We would not say that recommendations are rational if it were irrational to act in accordance with those recommendations.

We can distinguish two sorts of assumptions which enter into the assessment of the rationality of recommendations. On the one hand, there are assumptions about how values should be utilized to judge the rationality of acting in accord with a recommendation. On the other hand, there are assumptions concerning how valuable or disvaluable, i.e., how good or bad, the consequences of acting in accord with some recommendations will be. We shall explain these assumptions briefly.

One theory concerning the rationality of action implies that it is rational to employ a technology if its expected value is greater than the expected value of alternative actions. This theory of rationality appeals to the concept of expected value. Let us briefly explain this concept. We shall oversimplify in order to keep matters simple.

Let us suppose that we are considering acceptance of the use of a chemical or herbicide, such as Alar or Alachlor, in food production. We shall assume that there are only two possible courses of action, namely, either allow use of the chemical or ban its use. Clearly, in reality, there are more than two alternatives. One could ban use of the chemical, allow its use without restriction, or allow its use subject to various restrictions. In many discussions this third possibility is ignored even though consideration of the third possibility will have profound effects on assessing the expected value of various possible actions.

One possible action, then, is to allow use of the chemical. Let us represent this by "allow C." Now, if we allow C, any of several outcomes may occur with varying degrees of probability. For example, we may find that we increase profitability and that a certain number of serious illnesses occur. Call this outcome O(1). The probability of this particular outcome is, let us say, p. Let us assume that we can arrive at an overall value of this outcome and that the value is V(1). However, if we allow C, there is some probability, let us assume it is (1 - p), that outcome O(2) will occur and that the value of O(2) is V(2). By assuming that the probability of O(2) occurring is (1 - p), we have assumed that O(1) and O(2) are the only two possible outcomes. The expected value of the action allow C is the sum of p x V(1) and (1 - p) x V(2). Having determined the expected value of the action "allow C," we can, hopefully, determine the expected value of the alternative action, which action might be called "prohibit C". One assumption widely made is that action in accord with recommendations is rational if, and only if, such action will tend to maximize expected values in the circumstances.

However, some thinkers would not agree that it is always rational to act so as to maximize expected values. To see why they might be right, consider the following hypothetical example. Suppose that the expected value of the act allow C is higher than the expected value of any possible alternative action. Suppose further that the probability of some terrible outcomes is greater given that one has followed the act allow C than if one has followed the act prohibit C. Some people would maintain that rationality requires that one reduce, as much as possible, the probability of certain relatively horrible outcomes. These people would say that if the possible terrible outcomes of following the act allow C are sufficiently horrible then it is not rational to follow this course of action even if its expected value is greater than any alternative. In assessing the rationality of acting in accord with recommendations, one must consider whether it is rational to maximize expected value or to minimize the probability of horrible outcomes.[9]

These distinct theories about the rationality of action don't always conflict. Sometimes actions which are irrational on one view are irrational on the other view, as well. Further, it should be noted that it is possible to consistently hold some combination of these theories of rationality. One could hold, for example, that normally it is rational to act so as to maximize expected values, but that in circumstances involving particularly horrible possible outcomes, it is rational to act so as to minimize the probability of such outcomes.

Whether it is rational to act on certain recommendations is also influenced by assessments of the value of the consequences, or possible consequences, of such action, as well as by assumptions concerning relations between the value of possible consequences and the rationality of action.[10] Use of many agricultural chemicals has led to consequences which many people judge to be beneficial. For example, use of synthetic pesticides increases the quantity and quality of agricultural products such as corn. Of course, there are costs associated with these benefits. The producer must pay for the pesticide and perhaps also for its application. However, reliable estimates indicate that the increases in profits to the producer exceed increased producer costs.[11] Agrologists maintain that increased profits to the producer yield further benefits, including reduced prices of agricultural products for the consumer, and reductions in the quantity of land required for agricultural production. There are also additional costs, such as accidental poisoning of farm workers and animals, destruction of honeybees and other beneficial insects, depletion of natural resources from which the pesticides are produced, contamination of both rural and urban water systems, etc. A complete determination of the profits and costs, financial and otherwise, to society requires taking all these additional benefits and costs into account, a complex undertaking indeed. To explore the ramifications of these ideas briefly and simply, with respect to the rationality of recommendations concerning use of herbicides, we need to make a number of assumptions. To explain these we shall consider the case of a hypothetical consumer.

Let us assume then that we are dealing with a consumer who is not in a position to produce his own food. To survive, he must purchase food at a market. Further, to maintain a condition of good health (rather than mere survival) he needs a variety of foods, including fruits and vegetables. In modern times, in the industrialized world, most of us, even farmers, are in this position. Indeed, even if we could, most of us have no desire to make the drastic changes in lifestyle which would be required were we to become producers of all the foods we would need for a healthful, well-balanced diet. In consequence of his position and his awareness of his needs and desires, our consumer has a strong desire to eat fruits and vegetables. Further, he has a strong desire to avoid serious illnesses such as cancer or neurological disorders. Is it rational for him to recommend that food production practices which leave pesticide residues be reduced or eliminated, and to take political action accordingly?

To answer this question, one assumption we shall make is that it is rational for a person to accept food production practices which leave residues if they are necessary for him to have a well-balanced diet. Moreover, we would agree that such practices are necessary if, in the absence of such practices, either the range of foods necessary for a well-balanced diet would not be available at all or if, while the foods were available, they would be too expensive. A related assumption we must make concerns what prices count as too expensive. Let us assume that foods are excessively expensive if the consumer does not have enough money to buy all he needs or if he will have enough money only by sacrificing other basic needs or important goals in his life.

Given these assumptions, let us consider whether it would be irrational for consumers such as we have been considering, to recommend that use of an agricultural chemical such as Alar, in production of apples or some other fruit, be eliminated. We assume that there is significant evidence that the chemical may be carcinogenic and that residues of the chemical remain in the fruit or other products (such as apple sauce or apple juice).[12] Given the assumptions that we have made regarding the rationality of actions, to determine whether this recommendation is rational we have to learn whether use of the chemical is necessary for production of sufficient quantities of foods which are important components of a healthful diet. In the case of Alar, while apple producers favored the use of the chemical, it is clear that elimination of the chemical did not result in apples or apple products becoming inaccessible or prohibitively expensive. Thus, we cannot conclude that it was irrational to make this recommendation, in the case of Alar, on these grounds. Those making this recommendation were not advocating actions that were self-defeating, that is, incompatible with achieving the basic objective of obtaining a nutritious diet at an affordable cost. Conceivably, objections to the use of Alar were based on the theory of maximizing expected values. But even if this is not the case, that is, even if using Alar had a greater expected value, the fact that it is reasonable to think that such use increases the risk of cancer, particularly in children, involves envisioning a horrible outcome, one that it might be rational to try to avoid even though this may lead to acting in ways not consistent with maximizing expected value. In any case, it would be difficult or impossible to show that the costs of acting on the critic's recommendation outweighed the gains.

Often, agricultural scientists have suggested that while the chemical residues in food products are carcinogenic, the consumer's exposure to the chemical is so slight that the risk of cancer is very small. However, even supposing that the risk of getting cancer from exposure to a pesticide residue is small, it does not follow that it is irrational to take steps to avoid the risk. Indeed, whether it is rational to avoid a particular risk depends, in part, on the seriousness of the harm which may result from taking the risk. As we have noted, if the harm is a very great harm, such as is involved in dying from cancer (possibly after a long period of debilitating and perhaps painful illness), then it may well be rational to take steps to reduce or eliminate even a small risk.

Sometimes, the scientists' argument is not simply that it is not rational to try to avoid very small risks; it is rather that we often freely accept many other risks of harm, even serious harm, in which the risk of harm is greater than the risk of harm from the pesticide residue. For example, it has been suggested that the risk of getting cancer from eating peanut butter is greater than the risk of getting cancer from pesticide residues in other food products, and thus that it is irrational for consumers to eat peanut butter but object to the use of carcinogenic chemicals which leave residues. (Peanut butter contains aflatoxin, which is a carcinogen.)

Let us suppose that somehow we know that the risk of getting cancer from eating peanut butter is greater than the risk of getting cancer from consuming some food product which contains residues of a carcinogenic agricultural chemical. Does it follow that it is irrational to recommend that use of the chemical be banned? The answer to this question is negative. To see this, let us suppose that it is possible for a consumer to enjoy a particular fruit or vegetable without being exposed to a chemical, since the food in question can be produced at moderate cost without the chemical. The consumer chooses to eat peanut butter, which he enjoys, even though doing so involves a very small risk of cancer and, at the same time, chooses not to be exposed to some additional cancer risk through exposure to the chemical, since it is possible for him to have the fruit or vegetable he enjoys without exposure to the residue in question. It is not irrational to accept some risk in doing something one enjoys while not wishing to expose oneself to additional risk where the gain from this additional exposure is, at most, marginally cheaper food.[13] Saying that it is irrational to accept the risk of cancer from eating peanut butter while not accepting the risk of cancer from exposure to the agricultural chemical is mistaken because there is a significant difference between the cases. Whereas it is possible to have the fruit or vegetable, e.g., apples, without the risk, it is not possible, given present technology, to have peanut butter without the risk. Conceivably, for a consumer, eating peanut butter while avoiding some additional risk maximizes his or her expected value.

A similar argument advanced by scientists who support maintenance of the status quo in regard to pesticide use is that it is irrational to oppose the use of synthetic pesticides in agricultural production because people are exposed to a range of natural pesticides, that is pesticides produced by the plants themselves which enable them to resist attacks of pests. However, one may reply to this argument in the same manner as we replied to the above argument. If we are unable to avoid some risk of cancer or other serious disease as a result of exposure to natural pesticides in the foods that we choose to eat, it does not follow that it is rational to accept unnecessary exposure to additional pesticides, given that we can have the foods (which are now produced with synthetic pesticides) at slight increase in cost, without the additional pesticides (or with less of them).

Indeed, this rebuttal can be put in even stronger terms. Whereas we can choose not to eat peanut butter and still find a fully nutritious diet, we cannot have a fully satisfactory diet if we exclude all fruits and vegetables. We have to eat, and there is good reason to think that a diet which includes sufficient quantities of vegetables and fruits is best for us; thus it is rational to eat such a diet. If we must tolerate some exposure to natural pesticides in order to have the diet which is best for us, then it is rational for us to accept such exposure. It does not follow that it is rational to accept additional exposure where there is no prudential reason for doing so.[14]

Some agrologists may attempt to respond to the above defense of the critics on the grounds that the critic who recommends that we avoid exposure to some risk is irrational on the grounds that the critic's view presupposes that it is always irrational to take any risk. However, the critic need not be taking this position. To assume reasonable the demand that social policies (such as accepting the use of pesticides) involve no risk of harmful consequences would indeed be an irrational position to take. However, the critic need not make this presupposition; he may be well aware that in many cases every action open to a person may involve some risk. The critic need only believe that, when engaging in some course of action, it is not rational to avoid some act if the alternative involves a greater risk of harm. In some cases, every alternative action open to a person would involve greater risk to him than the risk associated with a given action.[15] In the above example, the critic did not need to base his objection to the use of Alar on the grounds that use of Alar is unacceptable because it involves some risk. The critic needs to contend only that the use of Alar involves unnecessary risks.

In considering this last objection we have accepted a distinction between synthetic and natural pesticides. Synthetic pesticides are pesticides produced through human technological processes; natural pesticides are pesticides produced as a consequence of the activity of genetic processes in plants. Consideration of this distinction suggests that those who maintain that it is irrational to oppose use of synthetic pesticides given that we are exposed to natural pesticides anyway may be making an assumption about the reasoning of the critics of pesticide use. In particular, those who advance this objection may be assuming that the critics naively believe that whereas synthetic pesticides are possibly carcinogenic to humans, natural pesticides are free of risk.

Of course, it may be that some of the critics of the use of synthetic pesticides have indeed opposed such use on the grounds that what is synthetic is potentially harmful whereas what is "natural" is safe and good. If there are such critics, we should agree that their belief about pesticides is irrational in that it is based on an assumption which is known to be false in many instances. Substances produced as a consequence of the genetic activity of plants (or as a consequence of the environment to which the living plant is exposed) may indeed cause serious injury to humans who ingest the substance. For example, some mushrooms are known to produce substances which are highly toxic to humans. Many other examples could be given. Further, since many natural pesticides have not been tested for carcinogenicity, it is irrational to believe with great confidence that such substances are not carcinogens.

However, opposition to the use of synthetic pesticides, for reasons having to do with human health, is not, in general, based on the assumption that only human-made pesticides are harmful. There are indeed more rational grounds for thinking that long-term exposure to residues of synthetic pesticides may be harmful to human health. We have given a brief indication of the nature of these reasons above. The critic's beliefs, on which he bases recommendations that synthetic pesticide use be reduced or eliminated, have not, in many cases, been shown to be mere expressions of emotion. Further the critic's recommendations have not been shown to lead, in many or all cases, to actions which cost (lose) more than they achieve (gain), or to be self-defeating.

SUMMARY

In this chapter we have considered the claim that many people who criticize agricultural practices, such as those involving use of synthetic pesticides, are irrational. The argument may be that the tactics the critics use to try to persuade people to oppose use of pesticides are irrational because they appeal to emotions. Another criticism may be that the beliefs of the critics about the possibility or probability of harm from pesticide use are not based on a rational assessment of the evidence. A final criticism may be that even if the beliefs about possible harms are evidentially warranted, the recommendation that the use of pesticide be curtailed is self-defeating. We have presented arguments to challenge these claims that the critics' tactics, beliefs, or recommendations are irrational.

NOTES

1. See David Pimentel et al., "Assessment of Environmental and Economic Impacts of Pesticide Use," in *The Pesticide Question*, ed. Pimentel and Lehman, 50; Janet S. Hathaway, "Alar: The EPA's Mismanagement," in *The Pesticide Question*, ed. Pimentel and Lehman; and Gary Comstock, "Genetically Engineered Herbicide Resistance."

2. As we shall see in another chapter, this assumption is not the same as claiming that it is irrational to be strongly committed to a belief which has not been strongly confirmed according to scientific criteria. A belief may be strongly supported by all available evidence in cases where the available evidence does not satisfy scientific criteria. This distinction does not affect the discussion in this chapter.

3. The view we are criticizing here is sometimes expressed by saying that "hazards whose probabilities... are below a given level... are unimportant or insignificant." K. S. Shrader-Frechette, *Risk Analysis and Scientific Method*, 127. Shrader-Frechette discusses this view in considerable detail and raises serious objections to the main reasons for accepting such a view. See chap. 5.

4. Culliney, Thomas, W., Pimentel, David and Pimentel, Marcia H., "Pesticides and Natural Toxicants in Foods," *The Pesticide Question: Environment, Economics and Ethics*, ed. David Pimentel and Hugh Lehman, p. 136.

5. Pimentel, David, Acquay, H., Biltone, M., Rice, P., Silva, M., Nelson, J., Lipner, V., Giordano, S., Horowitz, A., D'Amore, M., "Assessment of Environmental and Economical Impacts of Pesticide Use," *The Pesticide Question: Environment, Economics and Ethics*, ed. David Pimentel and Hugh Lehman, p. 49

6. For some discussion of testing, see Vincent T. DeVita Jr. and Harriet P. Kennedy, "Of Mice and Men: What Animal Tests of Carcinogens Mean to Us," 581–83.

7. One introductory discussion of this issue is John Earman and Wesley Salmon, "The Confirmation of Scientific Hypotheses," in *Introduction to the Philosophy of Science* by Salmon et al., 42–103.

8. This is not to say that it is rational to believe only statements which have been rigorously proved by scientific methods. Some statements are not candidates for such proof and it may be rational to believe them anyway. For more on this see William James, "The Will to Believe" in James, *The Will to Believe.*

9. Other views concerning the rationality of acting in accord with recommendations might be considered here. However, I believe that the above discussion is sufficient to make the main point.

10. In the following paragraphs it becomes clear that considering the rationality of action involves consideration of risk, i.e., expectation of undesired outcomes. There are many complexities which enter into thinking about risks. I take up some of those considerations in the essay on objectivity, rationality and risk.

11. "Investment in pesticidal controls has been shown to provide significant economic benefit through increased crop yields. Dollar returns for the direct benefits to farmers have been estimated to range from $3 to $5 for every $1 invested in the use of pesticides." David Pimentel et al., "Environmental and Economic Impacts of Reducing U.S. Agricultural Pesticide Use," 679.

12. Hathaway, J.S., "Alar: The EPA's mismanagement of an Agricultural Chemical," *The Pesticide Question: Environment, Economics and Ethics*, ed. David Pimentel and Hugh Lehman, p. 337.

13. For discussion concerning the carcinogenic risks of herbicides, see Gary Comstock, "Genetically Engineered Herbicide Resistance, Part Two," 114–46. For a discussion concerning rationality in regard to acceptance of risks associated with pesticides, see K. S. Shrader-Frechette, "Pesticide Toxicity: An Ethical Perspective."

14. See Paul B. Thompson, "Risk: Ethical Issues and Values," 211.

15. For a discussion of methods for determining acceptable risk, see Shrader-Frechette, *Risk Analysis and Scientific Method*. This matter is also discussed at length in K. S. Shrader-Frechette, *Risk and Rationality: Philosophical Foundations for Populist Reforms.*

2. Reality, Objectivity, and Risk

WHILE MANY PEOPLE are strongly disposed to employ new, scientifically based forms of technology, there has been increasing recognition of the harms that have resulted from the use of such technology in the recent past. Consequently, people have devised methods to evaluate the technology and to determine whether society should permit newly developed technologies to be deployed. Further, sometimes, older technologies are also scrutinized to determine whether their continued use should be allowed. Some of the methods used for such purposes involve evaluation of risks associated with the technologies in question. In our discussion of the rationality of critics of agricultural practices we noted that some scientists have claimed that whereas the critic's references to alleged harms or dangers of technologies were references only to perceptions, scientists' claims about risks referred to real or actual risks.[1] In contexts in which there is concern about possible harm from some technology, this claim is advanced as part of a rationale for accepting the assessments of scientific experts as to the real danger associated with the technology, rather than the assessments of those critical of the technology. The use of the term "perception" to describe the assessments of the critics is supposed to imply that the assessments of the critics are based on illusions, for example, seeing dangers where there are none; or, at the very least, distortions of the real risks, for example, exaggeration of the probability or severity of harm. The defender of the technology is dismissing the assessments of the critics as mere appearance. It is taken for granted that it is irrational to guide one's actions on the basis of mere appearance or illusion as opposed to reality. In this chapter I try to evaluate this rationale through consideration of some basic assumptions on which it rests. I then offer two arguments which purport to show that this rationale is not warranted. Finally, I consider an alternative view concerning the "objectivity" of risk assessments, and conclude with a few reflections on ethical concerns about risk analysis.

RISK AND REALITY

Talk of real risk as opposed to perception of risk suggests that real risk, like mass or volume, is some quality or relation found among the objects of the universe. Perception of risk, on the contrary, is not a quality of objects or a relation among objects, but is a mental state which may describe or represent real risk. We should start, then, by asking what risk is.

According to a commonly accepted definition of the term "risk," the use of a technology involves some risk if and only if there is some probability that such use will lead to some harm or other negatively valued outcome.[2] When I have tried to discover what scientists mean by the term "risk," it appears that this is the definition they have in mind. If the reference to a distinction between real risk and mere perception of risk makes sense, then given the assumption that the scientists who refer to risk would accept this definition, we can ask whether they are entitled to assume that risk is something real. Scientists who refer to the beliefs of members of the public as mere perceptions of risk may be taken either as implying that the probabilities of negative outcomes with which the beliefs are concerned are either too high or too low, or as implying that the magnitude of the negative value is either too great or too little.

By the above definition, the risk associated with a technology is the probability that it will lead to an outcome with negative value. If risk is something real, then the probability of various outcomes must be real, and so also must be the negative value of the outcomes. Thus, we must ask whether probabilities of outcomes or negative values of outcomes are real; this, in turn, should lead us to ask for definitions of "probable" and of "negative value."

The concept of probability continues to provoke considerable controversy.[3] In some views the probability of an event is a person's confidence that the event will occur. If the person has a high degree of confidence that the event will occur, then the probability of that event is high. However, if probability is understood as a degree of confidence, then risk also is essentially a degree of confidence. If this is the case, then we may well wonder what the distinction between real risk as opposed to perceived risk amounts to. If probability is a degree of confidence, then risk essentially involves some sort of judgment or perception. At the very least, the contrast between alleged real risk and perceived risk is misleadingly described.

However, probability in some views is regarded as a property of things or events in the world or as a relation among such events. One such view, which is widely accepted among scientists, is that probability is a relative frequency. On this view, the probability of an event of a certain kind is the relative frequency of events of that kind within a larger class of events. For example, one could think of the relative frequency of disease or injury among the class of all consequences of the use of a pesticide. Since a risk associated with a technology is a certain sort of outcome arising from the use of that technology, the probability of that outcome would be the relative frequency of that kind of outcome among all the outcomes. A relative frequency of certain consequences or outcomes among all consequences or outcomes is a relation among events of the world. References to probability, construed as relative frequencies, are references to relations among real events. Given such a view of probability, we could understand perceived risk as some sort of judgement or expectation of relative frequencies as opposed to the relative frequencies themselves. Perhaps then we should regard those scientists who appeal to this distinction as assuming that the probability of an outcome is a relative frequency.[4]

Since risk, as we have assumed, is a probability of outcomes with negative value, then for risk to be something real, as opposed to a mere perception, both probability and negative value must be real. Now, I suspect that some scientists might begin to feel uncomfortable at this point since many scientists assume that value, whether positive or negative, is not real; that is, it is not simply a property of events or a relation among events. A person who holds that risk is a combination of a probability and a value and that risk is real (as opposed to a perception) and that value is not real, holds views which must be mistaken since they are logically inconsistent. A person who holds such views commits himself to an assertion and a denial of the same proposition. To eliminate the inconsistency, such a person must either abandon the assumption that risk is real or abandon the view that value is not real.

The view that value is something real, some aspect of, or relation among, things or events of the world, could be true. However, I shall not try to resolve that question in this book. Rather, I shall return to considering whether the scientists, who wish to defend the use of various agricultural technologies, are entitled to hold that their claims of the risks associated with those technologies are reports of the real risk whereas the claims of the critics reflect mere perceptions. I shall offer two arguments in opposition to this claim. The first argument is based on a dichotomy: values are either real or they are not. The second argument is based on the assumption of the incommensurability of values.

Values are either properties of or relations among events, or they are not. Let us first assume that values are not properties of or relations among events. In this case, risk is not real, and the claim that the risk assessments of scientists are descriptions of real risk whereas the risk assessments of others are not is incorrect. At best, given this assumption combined with the relative frequency interpretation of probability, the scientists' claims about the probability of certain outcomes of the use of technology could be correct. If the scientist went beyond making assertions about the probability of outcomes, he or she would no longer be describing some feature of the real world. Thus, given this assumption, the claim that the scientists' description of risk reports the real risk is unwarranted. The scientist is not entitled to make this claim.

Next, let us assume that values are properties of or relations among events, that is, that values are real. Given this assumption we may ask whether the scientist is entitled to claim that his or her assessments of risk are descriptions of real risk. To respond to this question we have to consider whether the work that the scientist undertakes enables him or her to discover the values inherent in the events or processes which are under investigation. If the scientist's work is not suited to reveal these values, then even though values might be real, the scientist's judgments about the magnitude of these values would not be warranted by scientific evidence or reasoning.

It is commonly assumed that scientific work does not serve to reveal the values inherent in events or processes. Further, there are reasons for thinking that this assumption is correct. For one thing, we might ask which scientists specialize in uncovering the values in things. It does not appear that physicists do, or chemists, or biologists, etc. Indeed, it does not appear that any of the scientific disciplines yield knowledge of values. For another thing, if one reflects about the nature of scientific reasoning, it appears that scientific methods could not yield knowledge of values. For scientific methods to be capable of yielding knowledge of values, either value would have to be an observable quality or else the assumption that something possessed positive or negative value would have to play an essential role in explanations of what we do observe. However, apparently value is not observable and does not enter into explanations of observations.[5] Finally, even if it turns out that there is a science which is capable of yielding knowledge of value as it is in itself, there is no reason at this point to believe that that science is chemistry or crop science or any of the other agricultural sciences.

These arguments about the possibility of scientific knowledge of values are certainly not conclusive. However, as this is a rather speculative and specialized matter, I shall not pursue it further. I strongly suspect that most readers of this book would accept the assumption that scientific method does not yield knowledge of what is either positively or negatively valuable. If this assumption is granted then again, the claim that scientists are entitled to claim that their accounts of risk describe risk as it is in itself is not warranted. Value is either real or it is not real. In either case, it appears that scientists are not entitled to say that their views of risk reveal real risk, whereas non-scientific views of risk are only perceptions.

The claim that agricultural scientists' assessments of the risks of agricultural technologies present the real risks arising from those technologies may be challenged on other grounds. Let us continue to assume that risk is a function both of the probability of certain outcomes and of the negative value of those outcomes. When considering something complex, such as the deployment of some agricultural technology, there are many outcomes which derive from the application of the technology. It appears that these outcomes have many different values. Some of the values are positive and some are negative. For example, in discussing the value of pesticides in corn production, one might cite such outcomes as cheaper food, the aesthetic value of fields free of weeds, less tedious farm labor, and less use of land per volume of product, as positively valuable. Further, one might cite outcomes such as pesticide runoff in groundwater, elimination of beneficial insects, loss of jobs of farm workers, destruction of populations of organisms dependent on insects, etc., as negatively valuable. No doubt, other positively and negatively valued outcomes of pesticide use might be cited also.

If one were to try to compare the overall risk of using pesticides with the overall risk of not using pesticides, presumably one would have to find some way of meaningfully combining all these values to arrive at the overall risk of using pesticides and similarly for not using pesticides. However, an assumption to which many people would subscribe is that there is no meaningful way to combine these values to arrive at the overall value. In support of this assumption consider trying to add the positive aesthetic value of weed-free fields to the negative value of lost jobs to the negative value of loss of populations of wild animals etc. I do not see how these values can be combined in any way that may be construed as representing the real value of the use of pesticides. (Of course, one could arbitrarily assign positive or negative numbers to the various values and then combine the numbers. However, such arbitrary combining of values could not be justifiably said to represent the real value of pesticide use.) The various components that would enter into the determination of the overall value are said to be incommensurable, that is, there is no common measure by reference to which all these values can be compared and combined.[6]

While I have challenged the claim that scientists are entitled to claim that their accounts of risk are descriptions of real risk, as opposed to mere perceptions, there are some things which scientific knowledge can reveal which should be of great importance in making risk assessments. First, given that probabilities are relative frequencies, properly conducted scientific investigations of the use of technologies can yield reliable information on the probabilities of specific outcomes from the use of technologies. For example, scientific investigations can yield reliable knowledge of the probability of getting some type of cancer from exposures of certain magnitudes to certain pesticides. Some people might suggest that such knowledge might be expressed as knowledge of the risk of getting that type of cancer from that type of exposure. However, to speak this way would be unwarranted, since the use of the term "risk" implies not only a judgement about probability but further a judgement about negative value.[7]

OBJECTIVITY OF SOME RISK ASSESSMENTS

We have been considering the theory that scientific assessments of risk are desriptions of real risks, whereas non-scientific assessments are merely perceptions. We have found that theory unwarranted. The basic problem is that, given that risks combine some degree of chance in regard to future outcomes with a negative evaluation of those outcomes, the claim that assessments, conducted by scientists, of the degree of risk of some technology reflect only relations among real events, is untenable. Perhaps, however, when defenders of technology refer to some risk assessments describing the real risk, they were speaking loosely. Perhaps what they meant was that scientific risk assessments are objective, whereas risk assessments not based on the work of scientists are not objective. To consider this suggestion we must first try to determine whether the meaning of the term "objective" is clear enough.

The term "objective" is not clear. Of course, it is opposed to "subjective," but that term is equally unclear. In one sense of the term, a description or assessment of the value of an object which is valid or correct from any possible point of view might be said to be objective. Subjective descriptions are valid only from certain points of view. For example, a description of an object as looking square is very likely a subjective description, since if one looks at the object from various oblique points of view it will not look square. Similarly, a value assessment accepted only by people who held a certain point of view might be said to be subjective.

However, given that statements about risk are statements about values, it is not clear that statements about risk can be "objective" in this sense of the term. It is not clear that there are objective assessments of values; however, even if there are, it seems most unlikely that the value assessments of either those favoring or those opposing the use of some technology are objective. Very often opponents in such controversies differ radically in regard to what value assessments they will accept. Thus the value assessments to which such disputants appeal are not acceptable from every point of view, and consequently are not objective assessments.

The term "objective" can also be understood as implying independence from individual bias or from the bias of special interest groups, for example, human races, nationalities, ethnic groups, social classes, religious groups, etc. An assessment of the degree of risk of a technology could be said to be objective in this sense if the method of arriving at the evaluation did not automatically favor the interests or value preferences of some individual or interest group. "Objective" in this sense of the term is roughly equivalent to "impartial."

Given that this is a satisfactory explanation of the term "objective," we may suppose that the defenders of the agricultural technology were claiming that scientific assessments of the risks associated with a technology are objective. We may wonder, of course, what reason we could have to think that we should be disposed to accept objective risk assessments rather than risk assessments which are not objective. This question is appropriate given that we are supposing that the appeal to objectivity is offered as a reason for favoring the risk assessments which allegedly have this quality.

To try to show that the objectivity of a risk assessment is a sufficient reason for assenting to that risk assessment would involve extensive considerations. The scientists who were trying to defend the use of an agricultural technology by telling us that they were describing the real risks were assuming that we would regard knowledge of the real risk as knowledge of great value in making decisions which would realize purposes which are important to us. It is reasonable to wonder whether risk assessments which are objective would yield the same sort of instrumental value. However, it is not clear that we would be able to show that the objectivity of a risk assessment is a sufficient reason for anyone to accept that assessment. The reason for this is that some people might have a distinct and strong interest in rejecting that assessment in favor of some alternative assessment which would yield a decision of greater benefit to themselves. However, while we cannot show that it necessarily would be rational for any person to assent to an objective risk assessment, it may be that there are sufficient ethical reasons why we ought to be willing to assent to objective risk assessments. Whether this is true is itself a complex question of ethical theory.

Rather than pursue these complex theoretical issues, let us raise another question which is clearly appropriate at this point. Are the risk assessments of agricultural technology, undertaken by good scientists, objective or unbiassed? There is some reason to expect that such risk assessments would be unbiassed. After all, a good scientist is a person who would rigorously employ scientific methods in the effort to discover something concerning the nature of the real world. Rigorous deployment of those methods is free of bias, is it not? Unfortunately, the answer to this last question may well be negative. To illustrate this claim I shall refer to an example.

A group of scholars has presented a detailed discussion of the proceedings of several agencies of the Canadian government regarding the registration for use of the pesticide Alachlor, which had been used in production of corn and soybeans. The authors of this study note that experts who were parties to the dispute concerning the registration of this pesticide reached incompatible conclusions regarding the magnitude of the risks associated with the use of this pesticide. Further, the authors conclude, the existence of the divergent conclusions cannot be explained as a result of errors in scientific methodology. Rather, the divergencies result from the appeal to different value assumptions, or criteria, in the determination of the magnitude of the risks. They claimed "our analysis of the risk estimations shows that these criteria are not objective and value-neutral. . . ."[8] There are many examples in which experts who disagreed as to whether Alachlor should be registered appeal to different criteria. Those opposed to the registration of Alachlor, for example, scientists from the branch of government concerned with protection of health of human beings, believed that Alachlor should not be registered unless it could be proved not to cause disease. Those who favored the registration of the pesticide, for example, scientists from the branch of government concerned about the competitive position of Canadian corn and soybean producers, argued that the burden of proof rested with the opponents, that is, that Alachlor should be registered unless it could be proved to cause disease.[9]

Does this show that scientific risk assessments inevitably fail to be objective? This question is more complex than it might appear to be. To proceed let us first consider whether objectivity in this context requires that risk assessment be free of all assumptions regarding what is valuable, that is, be value-neutral. If objectivity of risk assessments requires that methods of risk assessment be value-neutral, and if scientific risk assessments are not completely value-neutral, then scientific risk assessments are not objective.[10]

There are strong arguments in support of the conclusion that scientific investigations are not value-neutral, that is, that application of scientific procedures must appeal to value assumptions. This is true even where the objective of the the investigation is strictly theoretical as opposed to practical.[11] (A theoretical investigation is an investigation aimed solely at describing or understanding some event or process. A practical investigation is aimed at some further objective, such as finding a cure for a disease or increasing the efficiency of the use of a resource.) Such assumptions enter into the determination of what data is relevant, what hypothesis to test, and whether the data confirms the hypothesis. The value assumptions that are required in the deployment of scientific methodology for theoretical purposes may be called epistemic values. If making any value assumptions compromises objectivity, then scientific risk assessments are not objective.

However, it may be argued that appeal to epistemic value assumptions does not compromise objectivity. Objectivity is compromised when the value assumptions that enter into an investigation inevitably predispose the outcome of that investigation to favor the interests of some individual or interest group. It can be argued that appeal to strict scientific criteria, such as that observations should be carefully made, measurements should be precise, descriptions of data should be accurate, reports of data should not be vague, causal claims should be established on the basis of results that are statistically significant to a high degree, etc., do not inevitably bias the outcome of investigations so as to favor individuals or sub-groups of human beings. If this argument is sound, then even though science may fail to be value-neutral it still may succeed at being objective.

Can risk assessments, such as those undertaken to determine the magnitude of the risk of disease from use of the pesticide Alachlor, be objective? It is apparent, if the study to which I referred above is correct, that the scientists undertaking this risk assessment went beyond strictly epistemic value assumptions. For example, scientists made distinct assumptions concerning the burden of proof, which data are relevant, and many other factors. For example, in regard to testing the exposure of human applicators to the chemical, there was disagreement as to whether the tests should be conducted on research subjects wearing protective clothing or not.[12] There was disagreement concerning what standard for evaluating risks and benefits should be applied. There was disagreement over the relvance to the final conclusion (whether Alachlor should be considered as potentially a human carcinogen) of data concerning cancer in an animal species. In general, those who were opposed to registration of the chemical were biassed in favor of the interests of the applicators. They were concerned about risks to the applicators' health. Those in favor of the registration of the pesticide were biassed in favor of the interests of the people of Monsanto chemical company and also of Canadian corn and soybean producers.

Could such bias be eliminated? Could it be shown that the appeal to bias in the above study could have been eliminated? While it is conceivable that all disputed questions could have been resolved by undertaking further scientific investigations, careful consideration suggests that this is not the case. For one thing, it appears that some of the disagreements concern the appropriateness of certain value judgements, a matter which, as we have indicated above, cannot be resolved by scientific investigation. If we accept the assumption that scientific methods do not yield knowledge about values at all, it follows that scientific methods do not yield such knowledge in an objective manner. An example of a matter of this sort is the issue of the burden of proof. Further, in other cases, while some investigations could have resolved other issues, such as the issue of which method of measuring exposure of applicators is more reliable, investigation to resolve all such issues would have extended the time required for the investigation to such an extent that were efforts made to complete the investigation the outcome would have been purely academic. Monsanto would have argued that they could not afford to wait so long for a decision. It appears, then, that bias cannot be eliminated from scientific assessments of risk. Scientific assessments of risk do not give us an account of real risk, and they are not objective.[13]

Given that assessment of risks fails to achieve objectivity, significant questions must be faced concerning ethical requirements in management of risks. It is commonly accepted that risk cannot be avoided. Deployment of any technology involves risk. One can see that this must be true, given that some concequences of the use of any technology are certain to be negatively valued by some people. Given that risk is inevitable, we cannot agree that we ought to utilize only those technologies which avoid all risk. What needs to be considered is how to determine what technologies are acceptable on ethical grounds.

Another ethical principle which is clearly unsound is that a technology is acceptable on ethical grounds if someone benefits from the use of that technology. It is hard to envisage anyone appealing to this principle to try to show that he or she is entitled to utilize some technology. Some people seem to think that a sound ethical principle is that a technology is acceptable providing that the overall benefits of use of that technology outweigh the overall harms which result from that use. However, even if there were no other objections to this ethical assumption, it is clearly incomplete. Given that assessment of harms and benefits is inevitably biassed, at the very least this principle needs to be supplemented by further ethical assumptions regarding methods of assessment of risks and possible benefits. If investigators are always biased then procedures must be used to correct for such bias. Further, it is arguable that even if an ethical method of assessing risks and benefits is obtained, it is not sufficient simply to weigh overall costs and benefits. Fairness in the distribution of costs and benefits ought to be considered also.[14]

SUMMARY

In this chapter we have explored the claims that scientific risk assessments yield descriptions of the real risks from use of a technology, and that scientific risk assessments are objective or unbiassed. We have argued that both of these claims are unwarranted. Finally, we have pointed out that the failure of both of these claims regarding scientific risk assessments has important implications for ethics.

NOTES

1. In several talks, Homer LeBaron of Ciba-Geigy used a slide in which he contrasted the "actual level of risk" with risk as ranked by various groups of people. See Comstock, "Genetically Engineered Herbicide Resistance." Scientists invited to lecture to my class concerning ethics and agriculture have appealed to the same distinction. Further, Chauncey Starr also appeals to a distinction between real risk and perception of risk. Starr is quoted in Paul B. Thompson, "Risk Objectivism and Risk Subjectivism: When are Risks Real?" 3.

2. Rescher defines "risk" as the "chancing of some negativity—of some loss or harm." Nicholas Rescher, *Risk: A Philosophical Introduction to the Theory of Risk Evaluation and Management*, 5. Lowrance defines "risk" as "a compound expression of likelihood and severity of deleterious effect." William Lowrance, *Modern Science and Human Values*, 118. Paul Thompson criticizes Rescher's views about risk but, in the end, accepts this definition as appropriate. See Paul B. Thompson, "The Philosophical Foundations of Risk," 285. Thompson has devoted a number of papers to contrasting this analysis of risk, which he calls the "event-based concept of risk," with other concepts of risk, particularly a concept which he calls the "action-based concept of risk." See Paul B. Thompson, "Agricultural Biotechnology and the Rhetoric of Risk: Some Conceptual Issues," 316–26. See also Paul B. Thompson, "Collective Action and the Analysis of Risk," 23–42.

3. The topic is discussed in Earman and Salmon, "The Confirmation of Scientific Hypotheses," 66.

4. The interpretation of probability as relative frequency is not the only interpretation which implies that probability is something real or objective. Another interpretation which has this implication is the propensity interpretation. For explanation of this see ibid.

5. One philosopher who might disagree with this claim, that values don't enter into the explanations for the existence of the universe, is John Leslie. See John Leslie, *Value and Existence*. Some philosophers, called intuitionists,

have maintained that while value is not observable by the senses, we become aware of it directly through another mental faculty. Some philosophers have argued that value is identical to some qualities of objects, qualities which could enter into explanations of what we observed. One such philosopher was Ralph Barton Perry, who said, "An object is *good* in the generic sense when it is the object of a positive interest." See Ralph Barton Perry, *Realms of Value: A Critique of Human Civilization*, 104. For Perry, the term "object of a positive interest" was a theoretical psychological term. Perry's colleague at Harvard, Clarence Irving Lewis, disagreed with Perry concerning the meaning of value. Lewis maintained that goodness, like redness, can be directly experienced. This experience can be reported in a self-verifying judgment, in other words, a judgment which we know, without further need of proof, to be true. In Lewis's view, such knowledge is analogous to our knowledge of the color of an object we are presently observing. Lewis, then, might be taken as saying that value is an observable quality of things. In saying that scientific methods do not serve to yield knowledge of values, I have taken a position contrary to that of Lewis or Perry. Lewis also described the immediate apprehension of value as something which is felt. This, I think, is closer to the truth. However, since feelings are not evidence for scientific knowledge, I would argue that science does not yield apprehension of values. Lewis' thought is found in Clarence Irving Lewis, *An Analysis of Knowledge and Valuation*, chaps. 12 and 13.

6. This argument is made in Rescher, *Risk: A Philosophical Introduction*, 24.

7. Paul Thompson reaches a similar conclusion. He said, "Risk is not a real entity or relation that yields its secrets to objective scientific analysis." See Thompson, "Risk: Ethical Issues and Values."

8. Conrad Brunk et al., *Value Assumptions in Risk Assessment: A Case Study of the Alachlor Controversy*, 5.

9. For further discussion, see Hugh Lehman, review of *Value Assumptions in Risk Assessment*, by Brunk et al., 110–12.

10. For purposes of this discussion, scientific risk assessments are assessments conducted by scientists.

11. See Hugh Lehman, "Are Value Judgements Inherent in Scientific Assessment."

12. Brunk et al., *Value Assumptions in Risk Assessment*, 85.

13. For an extended discussion of problematic strategies in assessment of risks, see Shrader-Frechette, *Risk and Rationality*, part two.

14. For more on this see ibid., part three.

3. Can Agricultural Policy Be Determined by Reason Alone?

IN THE INTRODUCTION to the first chapter, we suggested that many agricultural scientists argue that the views of critics of agricultural policy should be rejected because those views are based on emotion rather than reason. In the development of that chapter we challenged this claim: in some cases, the beliefs of agricultural critics are based on evidence, and their recommendations are rational also. In this chapter we shall pursue another issue which is posed by the reply of the agricultural scientists. In particular, the agricultural scientists' position presupposes that we understand the nature of reason and emotion, and further, that it is possible for agricultural policy to be based on reason alone. In this chapter we challenge these presuppositions. We briefly review a number of distinct views concerning the nature of reason and emotion and the relations between them. Awareness of these distinct views should indicate to agricultural scientists and others that their argument, that the critics' views are unsound because those views rest on emotion, rests on some obscure assumptions. For the argument of the agricultural scientist to be strengthened, these obscurities need to be eliminated.

TWO CONTRASTING THEORIES

We are concerned with the claim that our agricultural practices or policies ought to be determined on the basis of reason rather than emotion. To investigate the possibility that reason alone, in the absence of emotion, is sufficient to determine agricultural policies (or anything that we do), we shall have to consider briefly the nature both of reason and of emotion. The question, whether agricultural policy should be determined by reason rather than emotion, is an ethical question, and we shall address it briefly near the end of this chapter.

Let us start by calling attention to two contrasting theories concerning the nature of reason. The first theory is that of Plato. In *The Republic*, Plato outlines a theory, according to which the human soul has three parts: reason, appetite, and a spirited part.[1] In Plato's view, it is because of the spirited part of the soul that we experience emotions such as anger and love. According to Plato, each part of the soul has its proper function. The proper function of reason is to determine the proper course of action in one's life. The proper function of emotion or passion, the spirited part, is to keep the person on the right course, especially in the face of temptation arising from his or her appetites.

Plato's view is an early expression of an idea that still has considerable influence amongst agricultural scientists; the idea that one's actions in regard to agricultural policies or practices should be governed by reason, rather than by emotion.[2] But, we may ask whether it is possible for reason to determine our agricultural policies or practices. That is, we may ask whether it is possible for reason alone to determine what we do. To see that there are grounds for rejecting Plato's view, let us briefly consider an alternative view, that of David Hume. Hume explicitly denied an assumption on which Plato's view rests, namely the assumption that it is possible for reason alone to govern our behavior.

According to Hume, through the use of our reason we can discover either matters of fact or principles of logic and mathematics. For example, we can discover that such and such plants contained such and such toxic substances or that if cows are injected with bovine somatotropin their milk production is increased. However, in Hume's view, reason is not a motive; that is, in itself, it cannot cause us to do one thing rather than another. Reason, Hume said, "is and ought only to be the slave of the passions, and can never pretend to any other office than to serve and obey them." He also said, " 'Tis not contrary to reason to prefer the destruction of the whole world to the scratching of my finger."[3]

To understand this view, consider to what we refer when we make reference to human reason. Are we not making reference to our capacity to make observations and to interpret these observations so as to detect causes, patterns, or trends? If this is correct, then the products of our reasoning capacity are knowledge or beliefs that such and such is the case, that so and so is a consequence of such and such, that such and such sequences of events manifest such and such a pattern, etc. While any such information might be very useful to us in regard to our decisions as to what to do, such bits of information are not motives. In Hume's view, actions are products of motives, and our reasoning capacity does not yield motives. Consequently, our actions cannot be determined by our reason alone. According to Hume, if we decide to use genetically engineered bovine growth hormone in milk production, our decision is itself a product of reason plus emotion. The emotion is reflected in the desire to have increased milk production (without having increased herds of dairy cattle). It is this desire, combined with beliefs about the efficacy of growth hormone, that leads to the actions. Reason alone is impotent.

If Hume is correct, then it is impossible for our actions to be determined purely by reason. If we further agree that we are not morally obligated to do what is impossible to do, namely to govern our behavior by reason alone, then the agriculturalists' claim that our actions should be determined by reason is mistaken. Can the agriculturalist make a satisfactory reply to this objection?

Apparently, one approach for the agriculturalist would be to argue that Hume was mistaken concerning the limitations of human reason. The agriculturalist could argue that while reason enables us to discover matters of scientific and mathematical fact, it also enables us to discover moral principles and further motivates us to act in conformity with the requirements specified in such moral principles. (We shall consider, in a subsequent essay, whether it is reasonable to hold the view that through the use of our reasoning capacities we can discover correct moral principles.) However, in light of attitudes commonly expressed by many contemporary agriculturalists, it would be surprising to find many agriculturalists taking this approach. Specifically, it is not unusual to find agriculturalists, in conversations, expressing the idea that moral judgments express and rest on emotions. Such a theory of moral judgments may be called an emotive theory of ethics.[4] Indeed, Hume's ethical theory may be called an emotive theory of ethics. I suspect that, rather than trying to refute Hume's views concerning the relations of reason and ethics, agriculturalists would be inclined to agree with him.

WHAT IS THE AGRICULTURALIST'S VIEW?

Another approach for the agriculturalist to take in reply to the above objection would be to maintain that he or she did not intend the statement that our actions should be determined by reason rather than emotion to be interpreted by reference to the Platonic theory concerning relations of reason and emotion. Let us consider this suggestion further. How should the agriculturalist's claim that our actions should be determined by reason be interpreted?

The agriculturalist may say that agricultural practices or policies are not ends in themselves. Rather, such policies are adopted as means toward other objectives, such as having an ample supply of nutritious and palatable food and having supplies of wood, oils, and other agricultural materials which enter into our manufacturing processes. In saying that our agricultural policies should be determined by reason, rather than by emotion, the agriculturalist can say that he or she did not mean that these other objectives should be determined by reason. Rather, what he or she meant is that we should rely on reason, rather than emotion, to determine the method we will follow to achieve these other objectives.

The basic idea here is that, given our objectives, we can discover, through the use of scientific methods, the means for achieving those objectives. The agriculturalist understands the term "reason," we assume, as refering to our capacity for employing scientific methodology. The moral claim that the agriculturalist is making is that we should adopt methods to achieve our objectives which have been tested and shown to work by scientific means. We should not be influenced in our choice of methods by such emotions as fear or sentimental attachments to tradition. The agriculturalist can make this claim without presupposing Plato's psychological or moral theories, theories with which he or she is not in agreement. Rather, the agriculturalist can maintain that he or she is in agreement with Hume. Reason does not tell us what we ought to do; it tells us only what means will or will not work to do whatever we determine, on other grounds, is morally right or appropriate.

While this reply may be correct, it is not consistent with the initial position taken by the agriculturalist. According to that position, it is possible that agricultural practices or policies are determined by reason alone. According to this reply, the decision to adopt agricultural practices, such as use of herbicides, is determined by reason plus something else. Suppose that we wish to grow a certain plant crop, and further suppose that, as a result of our scientific investigations, we discover that the only means available to us to reduce the incidence of a certain weed is through use of a certain herbicide. We may decide to use the herbicide; we may decide not to grow the plant crop; or we may decide to grow the plant crop without using the herbicide. What is the additional factor which determines which course of action we follow? Consider these three alternative actions, namely, use herbicide and grow the crop, grow the crop without herbicide, or don't grow the crop. I suspect that the course of action which is chosen will be determined by a combination of desires, by the relative strength of those desires, and by beliefs about the most effective way to achieve those desires. To allow that desires must enter into the determination of our action is to allow that emotion must have some role in the determination of our actions.

Of course, when Hume denied that our decisions or actions are determined by reason alone, he did not deny that our actions are determined by a combination of mental states which includes both emotion and reason. For example, our decision not to use pesticides on a particular occasion is a result both of a desire which is determined by an aversion to certain effects, that is, a desire determined by an emotion, and of our belief that using pesticides on that occasion would yield the effects.

TWO FURTHER THEORIES CONCERNING REASON AND EMOTION

The agriculturalist, we have claimed, maintains that agricultural policy must be based on reason rather than on emotion. We have also suggested above that the agriculturalist, in modern times, is likely to accept a Humean view of human reason, according to which reason, i.e., science, can discover the properties of or relations among objects, but can neither discover valid moral truths nor, indeed, provide any motives for action. Given his or her acceptance of the Humean view of reason, how can the agriculturalist maintain that agricultural policy must be based on reason as opposed to emotion?

Again we can turn to Hume for part of the answer to this question. We have interpreted the term "reason" to refer to the use of scientific method. Possibly "reason" should not be so understood. Hume suggests that while there is no opposition between reason and emotion per se, there could be opposition between calm passion or emotion and emotion which is violent. A common error, according to Hume, is to refer to calm passions, such as the love of truth, benevolence, etc., by the term "reason."[5]

However, we don't have to agree with Hume that reason is not a motive. Perhaps reason is a calm passion or emotion. Perhaps when the agriculturalist maintains that agricultural policy should be determined on the basis of reason, what he or she means is that agricultural policy should be determined on the basis of calm emotions. The opposition, which is presupposed by the initial position taken by the agriculturalist, is not an opposition between an emotion and something which is not an emotion. Rather, it could be an opposition between one sort of emotion, namely rationality, and other sorts of emotions, namely sentimentality, fear, etc. This does not lead us to Plato's view, since Plato, like Hume, would not have admitted that reason is an emotion. (On this point Plato and Hume agree.) Thus, it should be considered as a third view concerning reason and emotion. The three views can be summarized as follows: according to Plato's view, reason can be or can yield motives which determine our actions, but reason is not an emotion. According to Hume's view, reason is not an emotion and (consequently) it cannot yield motives. The third view is that reason is a kind of emotion, a calm passion, and can provide motives.[6]

Initially, the agriculturalist's position often is that it is irrational to act on the basis of emotion. While this position resembles Plato's view, in allowing for an opposition between reason and emotion, it differs in one important way. Plato did not hold that acting on the basis of emotion is necessarily irrational. Acting on the basis of emotion, according to Plato, would be rational providing that the emotions, in turn, were directed by reason. The third view which we have identified resembles Plato's view since it allows that it can be rational to act on the basis of certain emotions: calm emotions.

What would it be like for our agricultural practices to be adopted on the basis of the passion of rationality? To see what it might be like, let us consider a society in which people, prior to making a decision regarding some practice such as the use of a certain pesticide, carefully try to discover what biological systems will be affected by the use of that pesticide, and the consequences in each of the affected systems. They then carefully consider the benefits and losses in each system and try to arrive at a decision based on maximizing benefits or minimizing losses or both. A society which proceeded deliberately and calmly, as in this hypothetical example, might be contrasted with our own societies in North America, wherein the decision to apply pesticides and herbicides on a large scale has proceeded, to a great extent, without the benefit of such extensive and calm deliberation.

There is a fourth possible view concerning reason and emotion which we have not yet mentioned. This view may be revealed by reflecting on another presupposition made (at least initially) by the agriculturalist: the assumption that whereas reason has the capacity to yield information about the external world, emotion does not have this capacity. According to this presupposition, emotion is simply a reflection of some internal or "subjective" state. However, this presupposition is open to serious question.

Consider how use of reason can yield information about the external world. We believe that such information is achieved because our sensory perceptions are determined, in part, by properties of and relations among external objects. For example, we see that the sky is blue because of the wavelengths of light which strike our retina after passing through the Earth's atmosphere. The sensory stimulation, on which such a perception is based, is an internal state which is caused by some external states of affairs. Now, sometimes the causes of our emotions, such as anger, fear, and love, are caused in part by external states of affairs. Thus, it is possible that the emotions to which a person is subject yield information about the external world just as the mental states which attend closely with sensory stimulation yield such information. This, in turn, suggests that emotions can be a kind of rational capacity or a part of our capacity to reason. Whereas in the third view reason is conceived as a kind of emotion, in this fourth view emotion is conceived as a kind of reason. Sensory perception, properly carried out, can be a reliable source of information about the external world. However, sensory perception is not always reliable: witness the various possibilities for sensory illusion or false belief based on observation. Similarly, even if emotion is often unreliable as a source of information about the external world, subject to appropriate restrictions it could possibly be a source of valid information. For example, is it not possible that a feeling of fear can be a valid indicator of an external threatening state of affairs? Given the possibility that emotion can, in some circumstances, yield information about the external world, it is not rational to exclude emotion *a priori* as a part of the basis for determining what our agricultural policies should be.

EMOTION AND RATIONAL ACTION

The view which we have been critically considering in this essay, that actions should be determined solely by reason, reflects a distinction which appears to have some validity, namely that between actions which are rational and actions which are not rational. The theory that some actions can be determined solely by reason may be regarded as an effort to explain how this distinction arises. It suggests that actions which are rational are caused solely by reason. However, this theory is, as we have seen, a psychological theory, further, it is a theory which appears to be overly simple. Reason, as conceived by Hume, is not the sort of thing which can cause actions. However, Hume may be mistaken. Reason may be a kind of emotion. That is, reason and emotion, as we have seen, may not be entirely distinct capacities. If reason is our capacity for discovering the nature of the external world, then emotion may be part of that capacity.

Rather than pursuing very complex questions about psychology which would, no doubt, take us far afield, let us return to the distinction between actions which are rational and actions which are not rational. We shall assume that actions are determined by desires and beliefs, and that actions are rational if they are determined by rational desires and rational beliefs. Making this distinction should help us to resolve questions such as whether it is rational for a person to purchase food only if it is produced without pesticide use. I will suggest a way of making this distinction by reference to concepts of rational belief and rational desire. Let us attempt to explain these concepts briefly.

We shall say that a person's beliefs or opinions about what is the case are rational providing that there is strong scientific evidence, of which the person is aware, that the beliefs are correct, and that they have not been disconfirmed by such evidence, or even though the person makes reasonable efforts to keep abreast of such matters, he or she was not aware of the evidence which disconfirms the belief. Some people might prefer to say that it is irrational to subscribe to a belief about the world unless the belief is conclusively proved. We shall not adopt this position because: there are casesin which accepting a belief, even in the absence of conclusive proof, will be beneficial for a person. I would not want to say that it is irrational for aperson to have a belief if the person would be better off if he or she had that belief.

We shall say that a person's belief is irrational if it is accepted in spite of the fact that there is strong scientific evidence that the belief is false and the person is aware that there is such evidence or is aware of the evidence. Clearly, the categories of rational and irrational belief do not exhaust all possibilities. There may well be beliefs which are non-rational, that is, neither rational nor irrational.[7]

Our notion of rational desires is more complex. Let us try to explain this notion by reflecting on Hume's view of reason. Hume, as noted above, maintained that reason does not yield motives. To emphasize this point he made the remark, quoted above, that it is not contrary to reason to prefer the destruction of the world to the scratching of one's finger. Some people might take issue with this remark. They might maintain that a preference for the destruction of the whole world, or even of oneself in most circumstances, to the scratching of one's little finger is an irrational desire. This view does not seem unreasonable. Why is that so?

To answer this question, let us assume that there is a distinction in each of our lives between basic desires (or preferences) which are basic and desires which are not basic. Basic desires are those which are not explained by reference to other desires and which, in turn, play an essential role in explaining other non-basic preferences. Generally, our basic desires determine the large or overall patterns of our motivation. We can say that one way in which a desire is irrational is if satisfaction of that desire is incompatible with satisfaction of some basic desire. Hume's remark seems unreasonable because we would assume that, for most of us at least, the satisfaction of a desire for the destruction of the world would frustrate virtually all of our basic desires, and so the desire for the destruction of the world is an irrational desire. The desire to scratch your finger is probably not irrational (though it could be in some circumstances). Having desires which are irrational in this first way is probably often due to the presence of certain emotions; for example, if a person has a desire because of his or her anger, and the satisfaction of the desire will frustrate the person's basic desires, then we would say that that desire is irrational.

This theory about basic desires does not stray far from Hume's view. We have not placed any restrictions on what basic desires are possible and we have not said that any basic desires are necessarily irrational. We might define "irrational person," rather than "irrational desire," so as to say that a person is irrational if his or her basic desires are incompatible with each other. If we did say that it could well turn out to be the case that we are all irrational. Conceivably, there are people whose basic desires include a desire for the destruction of the world. Clearly there are people whose basic desires include religious desires, for example a desire for the salvation of one's immortal soul. Whether those desires are regarded as rational will depend in part on how the corresponding religious beliefs are regarded. Again, we shall consider the issue of the rationality of belief in the next chapter. For the purposes of this chapter, we do not need to consider any limitations on the rationality of basic desires.

To describe another way in which desires can be irrational, let us note that many of our desires are caused in part by our beliefs. If we desire X and we believe that to achieve X we must first achieve Y, then we come to desire Y. Let us say that a desire is irrational if a person has that desire because he or she irrationally subscribes to some belief. Often, I suspect, people irrationally subscribe to certain beliefs because of their emotions. Their emotions may lead them to ignore evidence of which they are aware or to be unable to evaluate that evidence in a logical or rational way. Thus, emotion can give rise to irrational desires of either sort. However, it does not follow from this that whenever emotion gives rise to desires or to beliefs that those desires or beliefs are irrational. Emotion can give rise to rational desire or belief. For example, the love of truth may give rise to a person having beliefs which are accepted only after intensive scrutiny of scientific evidence.

With these ideas on the rationality of beliefs and desires in mind, let us consider what is necessary for an agriculturalist to justify a claim that someone's desire is irrational. Suppose we consider, as an example, the desire of many people to have fresh vegetables or fruit which is free from pesticide residues. Is this an irrational desire?

In order to show that this desire is irrational, given what we have said above, the agriculturalist would have to establish either that the realization of this desire is incompatible with the realization of other more basic desires, or that the people who have this desire would not have this desire if certain of their irrational beliefs were eliminated or replaced by rational beliefs. While it might be possible to establish these claims for some people, in general neither claim will be easy to establish.

To see this, let us consider a person who is, in my view, typical of many people in the general public of industrialized nations and who desires to have fresh vegetables which are free of residues of synthetic herbicides and pesticides. Is this desire incompatible with the person's basic desires? Of course, this will depend on what those basic desires are. The agriculturalist may assume that among the person's most basic desires is the desire to have his or her food as cheaply as possible. Indeed, for many people this may be a basic desire. If the desire for food free of residues of synthetic pesticides is incompatible with the desire for the cheapest possible food, and if the desire for the cheapest possible food is a basic desire, then the desire for food free of pesticide residues is an irrational desire, according to our account above. However, for many people, the desire for cheap food is less basic than the desire to have food that does not contribute to serious illness or than the desire to have water and air free of residues of synthetic herbicides or pesticides. For such people, the desire to have food free of such residues is not incompatible with their most basic desires.

However, the charge that the desire to have food free of residues of synthetic pesticides may be one of those desires which arises because of the belief that such residues contribute, or may contribute, to serious illness. Here, to establish the claim that the desire is irrational, the agriculturalist would have to show that there is very strong scientific evidence that this belief is false (and that the person is aware of the existence of such evidence). Now, with respect to beliefs about some pesticides, such evidence might be available, but often it is not. (Indeed, sometimes there is scientific evidence that the belief is true.) In these cases, where the evidence is insufficient to show the falsehood of the belief that consuming food containing some residue will cause serious illness, the agriculturalist will not be able to show that the desire to have residue-free food is irrational.

In spite of such difficulties, the agriculturalist may sometimes succeed in showing that certain desires concerning agriculture are irrational and thus that practices based on those desires are based on irrational rather than rational desires. Given what we have said concerning irrational desires, the fact that an agricultural practice has been determined on the basis of an irrational desire is a good reason for thinking that it is unwise and that a society would be ill-advised to adopt that practice. Since the practice is either based on false beliefs or will lead to the frustration of basic desires of people in the society, it is reasonable to expect that the adoption of the practice will lead to consequences which are, on the whole, unsatisfactory. For this reason also, it is likely that the society morally ought not to adopt practices based on irrational desires. However, it does not follow that practices based on rational desires are morally justifiable.[8]

OUGHT AGRICULTURAL POLICY TO CONSIST ONLY OF RATIONAL ACTIONS?

I began this essay by mentioning the claim that agricultural actions and policies ought to be adopted on the basis of reason rather than emotion. We can now see that this question presupposes a distinction between reason and emotion which is not valid. Reason should not be conceived as opposed to emotion. Certain emotions, such as the love of knowledge or truth, may enter into the very nature of reason. We might try to reformulate the claim as follows: agricultural actions and policies should not be adopted unless they are not irrational, that is, unless they are based on beliefs and desires which are not irrational. Is this a valid claim?

This claim is readily defensible. Beliefs are irrational if there is strong evidence that the beliefs are false and if those who subscribe to the beliefs in question are aware of that evidence. Desires are irrational if they are either caused by irrational beliefs or are incompatible with basic desires. If agricultural policies and actions are based on irrational beliefs or desires, they will very likely fail in their objectives. Since we have allowed that a person's beliefs may be neither rational nor irrational, it does not follow that it is morally wrong for the society to act on desires or beliefs which are not rational. Consider, for example, a society which accepts certain metaphysical or religious beliefs as the basis of its agricultural policies. Suppose, for example, that the members of the society believe that there is a divine creator and that the creator commanded human beings to observe a day of rest and prayer. Such a belief cannot be conclusively proved to be true; however, such a belief need not be irrational, either. The desire to obey the alleged commands of a creator described in one's religious beliefs could be among the basic desires of members of that society. It is hard, in the abstract at least, to see why it would be morally wrong for such a society to act in accord with its beliefs even if such beliefs are regarded as non-rational.

MUST AGRICULTURAL POLICY BE ADOPTED ONLY AFTER CALM DELIBERATION?

Possibly when the agriculturalist maintains that agricultural policies should be determined on the basis of reason, he or she might mean that such policies should be determined only after calm deliberation. This claim is distinct from that considered previously and is worth considering in its own right. This claim may be taken in one of two ways, either as a bit of advice or as a moral injunction. If we interpret the claim as a moral injunction, what it says is that we (the people to whom it is addressed) are morally obligated to act on the basis of calm deliberation rather than under the influence of more violent passions. However, taken in this way, the claim is too general. Taken as a moral injunction, the claim is mistaken. A person is not always morally obligated to act calmly; he or she may be unable to do so. Further, even assuming that one is able to be calm, one may not have sufficient time or resources to act on the basis of calm deliberation. Taken as a bit of advice, the claim may be incorrect also, and for similar reasons. Acting on the basis of cool deliberation may not be in a person's self-interest in all circumstances.

Consider an example. Suppose that you are a recently-elected member of a town council, and you discover that a developer is preparing to develop a parcel of land in a way which, in your judgment, will lead to a destruction of an area of wetlands, with a consequent reduction in variety of life forms in the area. In your judgment such a loss in variety would be harmful, not only for the creatures that will be extinguished but also for the human residents of the area. Must you act deliberately and do a thorough study of the situation prior to taking action to prevent the development? Surely, in some such circumstances, it could be argued that you must not act calmly and deliberately. If you do, it may be too late. Even if you have time, undertaking the research necessary for a careful analysis of the situation may be too expensive for your town. It could be better, on the whole, for you to risk the consequences of rash action rather than proceeding in a more deliberate manner.

Here is another example. If we calmly investigate for too long a period the consequences of burning coal to produce power, we may lose, due to acid rain, large areas of valuable forests which might have been saved had we acted less calmly. It is not as if calm deliberate action avoids all serious risks whereas rapid less deliberate action is very risky; there are risks in either case. One must use judgment to determine which risks it is wiser or better to take.

The claim that all agricultural practices must be determined on the basis of calm passions (plus reasoning) may be challenged for another reason. Action which is calm and deliberative is not necessarily directed to morally acceptable objectives. It is easy to envisage a group of people acting deliberately, on the basis of their collective self-interest, to implement agricultural policies which, while beneficial to those individuals, will cause widespread suffering or inconvenience to others, for example, by damaging the environment on which these others depend. In some ethical theories, support could be offered for the claim that agricultural practices should be determined on the basis of *some* calm passions rather than certain other violent or agitated emotions. But, as we have indicated by the above examples, agitated motivation may be sometimes morally justifiable.

SUMMARY

In this chapter we have evaluated the claim that agricultural policies ought always to be based on reason rather than emotion. We have argued that this claim is obscure in consequence of there being a number of distinct views concerning the nature of reason and emotion and their relationships. Following a description of Plato's view on this matter, we have briefly described a Humean view on these matters and also considered some modifications of that view in order to allow for the possibility of irrational desires. Finally, we have argued that there are good reasons for saying that agricultural policy should not be based on irrational beliefs or desires. Further, there are good reasons for thinking that both prudence and ethics may require that we take action in some situations even though there has not been time or opportunity for calm deliberation.

NOTES

1. See *The Republic of Plato*.

2. This idea is expressed frequently. One statement is, "Ignorance, fear and emotions must be replaced by education, reason and rational thought and action." See Homer M. LeBaron, "Herbicide Resistance in Plants," 102. Clearly, LeBaron presupposes that fear (and other emotions) are irrational. However, sometimes fear is rational; for example, if a person is really put in jeopardy by something, then it is rational for him or her to fear that thing.

3. These quotations are from David Hume, *A Treatise of Human Nature*, vol. 2, part 3.

4. A classic statement of an emotive theory of ethics is found in Charles L. Stevenson, *Ethics and Language*.

5. "Now 'tis certain there are certain calm desires and tendencies, which, tho' they be real passions, produce little emotion in the mind, and are more known by their effects than by the immediate feeling or sensation . . . When any of these passions are calm, and cause no disorder in the soul, they are very readily taken for the determinations of reason. 'Tis evident passions influence not the will in proportion to their violence, or the disorder they occasion in the temper; but on the contrary, that when a passion has once become a settled principle of action . . . it commonly produces no longer any sensible agitation . . . . We must, therefore, distinguish betwixt a calm and a weak passion; betwixt a violent and a strong one . . . . But notwithstanding this, . . . when we would govern a man, and push him to any action, 'twill commonly be better policy to work upon the violent than the calm passions, and rather take him by his inclination than what is vulgarly called his 'reason'." Hume, *A Treatise of Human Nature*, vol. 2, part 3, sections 3 and 4, pp. 417–419.

6. For a view of reason and emotion similar to this third view, see William James, "The Sentiment of Rationality," in *The Will to Believe, Human Immortality and Other Essays on Popular Philosophy*. The essay was formed

by combining parts of two papers by James. The first appeared in *Mind* in 1879 and the second appeared in the *Princeton Review* of July 1882.

7. The nature of rational belief is taken up again in chapter four, where we consider whether it is rational to attribute desires or beliefs to any farm animals.

8. For more on reason and emotion, see Ronald de Sousa, *The Rationality of Emotion*.

4. Is It Rational to Attribute Beliefs or Desires to Animals?

IN OUR DISCUSSION in chapter three we maintained that a person's belief is a rational belief if there is strong scientific evidence, of which the person is aware, that the belief is correct while the belief has not been disconfirmed or refuted scientifically (or if it has, then, even though the person makes reasonable efforts to keep abreast of such matters, he or she has not learned of the disconfirming evidence). We also said that a person's belief is an irrational belief if there is strong scientific evidence that the belief is false and if the person is aware that there is such evidence. The above statements about rational belief do not say that a person's belief is irrational if he or she accepts it, even though he or she is aware of the evidence and the evidence does not strongly confirm the belief. It may be rational for a person to accept a belief which has not been established as true on scientific grounds. Conceivably it could also be rational for another person, who is aware of the same evidence, to reject the same belief. (It is not self-contradictory for me to maintain that while it is rational for one person to think that animals have beliefs and desires, it is not irrational for another person, with the same evidence, not to accept this belief. One person can think the belief true even though he or she knows that the evidence does not prove it, while the other person knows that the evidence does not prove the belief and does not think it true.)

As a reason for agreeing with what we have just said, consider the case of a scientist who (a) accepts a belief on the basis of some evidence even though the belief has not been scientifically established and where (b) the scientist's acceptance of the belief subsequently plays an essential role in the scientist's motivation to try to find evidence which would establish the belief and where (c) the scientist ultimately succeeds in getting the required evidence. In my view we would not want to say that the scientist's acceptance of the belief, which had such useful consequences in regard to knowledge, was irrational.[1] However, we would not want to say either that some other scientist was necessarily irrational if he or she, while aware that the evidence was inconclusive, rejected the same belief.

In the first chapter we observed that some scientists have alleged that people, who believe that domestic animals (and certain wild animals as well) have feelings, desires, or beliefs, are irrational. We deferred consideration of this claim at that point in order to pursue considerations regarding the rationality of accepting risks. Now, let us pick up that thread and consider whether it is rational to attribute beliefs or desires to animals? I shall not be much concerned with the question of whether domestic animals are sentient, that is, feel pain or pleasure. While some people have tried to raise doubts as to whether animals feel pain or pleasure, most agricultural scientists, veterinarians, etc., readily accept that such creatures are sentient.[2] Another way of asking part of this question is to ask whether animals have ideas about the features of their environment which they accept, ideas which lead them to anticipate experiences. An alternative way of asking whether animals have desires is to ask whether they are conscious or aware of being motivated to have certain objects, e.g., food, or to be in a state other than the one they are in, e.g., free of a certain restraint.

Some scientists have implied that it is irrational to attribute beliefs or desires to animals because the evidence that can be brought to bear on this question is insufficient to establish scientifically that animals have such mental states.[3] I have frequently heard scientists refer to the attribution of beliefs or desires to animals as anthropomorphism, an attitude which they regarded as some sort of fallacy. I shall consider anthropomorphism in the first section of this chapter.

Do we have sufficient scientific evidence or reasons to warrant attributions of desires and beliefs to animals? Following the discussion in the first section of this chapter, I shall proceed by describing the kind of scientific reasons which would be sufficient to warrant or refute attributions of beliefs or desires to animals, and then consider whether such reasons are available. I shall conclude that such reasons are not yet available. However, I shall ultimately argue that it does not follow that it is irrational to attribute beliefs or desires to animals. The claim that it is irrational to attribute beliefs or desires to animals, where the evidence or reasons are not sufficient, on scientific grounds, to warrant accepting such a claim as true, is mistaken. In part, the basis for this conclusion rests on our assumption that it may be rational to accept beliefs even though one is aware that such beliefs have not been scientifically proven.[4]

RATIONALITY, ANTHROPOMORPHISM, AND QUESTION-BEGGING

Many animal scientists, veterinarians, and others have implied that the attribution of beliefs or desires to animals is irrational. They have referred to such attributions as "anthropomorphism." Taken literally in this context, the term "anthropomorphism" connotes the attribution of human traits to animals; however, this attribution is not necessarily fallacious. Animals may have some traits that humans have. For example, humans and some animals both have reflexes. Possibly, then, we should not hold that anthropomorphizing is irrational or fallacious. Perhaps anthropomorphizing is irrational at some times but not at other times.

In reply to our suggestion that anthropomorphism is not necessarily fallacious, an animal scientist might maintain that I have misunderstood the term "human traits." I have taken this term as equivalent to "traits which human beings have." Perhaps however, the term "human traits" should be understood as referring to the set of traits that are distinctively human, i.e., to the set of traits that all and only human beings have. If there is such a set of traits, then anthropomorphism would be a fallacy.

But perhaps there is no such set of traits.[5] At the very least, to claim that there is such a set is to make an assumption. (Let us call such a set "a set of essential traits.") Further, given that all biological species emerge by natural selection from other species there is good reason to believe that, at least for many species, there is no such set of essential traits. According to gradualist views of species emergence, which are widely accepted among biologists, while at any time the individuals of a species may share a cluster of traits, over time descendants (or ancestors) of these individuals can be found which lack some traits of the cluster (or which have additional traits). Further, at any particular time, for many species of biological organisms, there will be abnormal individuals, that is, individuals which have traits which are not part of the cluster or which lack traits which are part of the cluster. Thus, given widely accepted beliefs about biological species, the assumption that for every species there is a set of essential traits is probably false. This assumption, that for every species there is such a set of traits, has been called essentialism. Since this assumption may be false, essentialism may be a fallacy.

Even if there is a set of essential traits for *Homo sapiens*, it is possible that having desires or beliefs are not a part of this set. Even if humans do have desires and beliefs, it is possible that animals do also. The question at issue is whether it is irrational to attribute such traits to animals. To assume, without thorough consideration, that these traits are essential human traits would be to commit the fallacy of begging the question.[6]

Of course, some scientists may be sure that animals do not have desires or beliefs. Such scientists may hold that attribution of desires or beliefs to animals, i.e., anthropomorphizing, is a fallacy and thus irrational. However, we may challenge the assurance of such scientists. We do not believe that they are entitled to be sure on the basis of scientific evidence and reasons. The claim that no farm animals have desires or beliefs (and that humans do have such psychological states) is a very broad negative universal generalization. Establishing such generalizations on scientific grounds is, at best, a very difficult matter and, to my knowledge, has not been accomplished in this case. To maintain that farm animals have no desires and beliefs given the evidence and reasons available at the present time is again to commit the fallacy of begging the question. While anthropomorphizing may be a fallacy, it may equally be a fallacy to confidently assert that no farm animals have desires or beliefs.

SCIENTIFIC EVIDENCE: EMPIRICISM AND PRAGMATISM

Our problem is not simply that of reviewing the available evidence or reasoning to determine whether it is sufficient to warrant attribution of beliefs and desires to animals. The question is complicated by there being a number of assumptions that many scientists make which have a bearing on the possibility of establishing the claim that animals have beliefs or desires. For example, many animal scientists, ethologists, etc., accept a philosophical assumption concerning the nature of evidence in accordance with which one cannot observe the beliefs or desires of creatures other than oneself. A second, widely made philosophical assumption is that one can observe one's own beliefs, desires, or other mental states. Both of these assumptions are reflected in the following quotation from Tinbergen: "We feel there are, in principle, two types of observables when dealing with behavior. One type, which includes the movements of animals, can be shared by different observers; . . . The other observables are the subjective phenomena that coincide with behavior, which we observe, each of us, in ourselves; and these are, by definition, observable only to the subject."[7]

The above quotation and the philosophical assumptions it reflects are obscure. Must we agree that we can observe our own beliefs or desires? There are objections to this assumptions. For one thing, there may not be any cognitive states of the sort to which the term "belief" ostensibly refers. Stephen Stitch, in his article "Do Animals Have Beliefs?" presents challenging arguments against the claim that there are beliefs. Further, even if such cognitive states exist, they may not be observable.[8]

In spite of the fact that the assumptions cited by Tinbergen are questionable, we shall accept them for the sake of argument here. The importance of that will be obvious immediately, given what we say concerning the nature of scientific evidence below. Granting Tinbergen's assumption means that we cannot have evidence for the existence of beliefs or desires of others, regardless of whether the others are animals or human beings.[9]

In order to discuss the nature of scientific evidence, we need to make some stipulations regarding the understanding of words. To this end, we stipulate now that by "evidence" we mean observations and observations only. Reasons which enter into purported justifications of statements or theories about unobserved entities do not count as evidence in this sense of the term. Statements which are considered as interpretations of scientific data are not evidence even though such statements are often offered as reasons in support of scientific conclusions. We shall call statements other than observation reports, which are offered as reasons in support of scientific conclusions, scientific reasons rather than evidence. As an example of an interpretation which might be offered as a reason for accepting a scientific conclusion, consider a situation in which a scientist makes an appeal to the claim that some species had evolved as a reason for accepting some conclusion. The claim that the species evolved from a species that existed earlier is not a statement of evidence, since this event is not observed. However, it could be a scientific reason for accepting some conclusion about the species. We shall agree with the above philosophical assumptions, for the sake of argument, namely that we have observations of movements and that we do not have observations of the beliefs or desires of other creatures. Granted these assumptions, we have evidence for the existence of movements, but we do not have evidence for the beliefs or desires of animals or of people other than ourselves. However, perhaps we can have scientific reasons for thinking that animals have beliefs or desires.

A third philosophical assumption often made in conjunction with the above two assumptions is that there is a clear distinction between observations, on the one hand, and inferences based on (or interpretations of) observations, on the other. This assumption has also been challenged. It has often been pointed out that reports of scientific observations always tacitly appeal to theoretical assumptions. If this is true, then the distinction between observations and interpretations is, at the least, fuzzy. However, it can be argued that this last point indicates more than the existence of a fuzzy distinction. If observation reports presuppose theoretical assumptions, then reports of observations can be rejected or modified if those underlying theoretical assumptions are rejected. Such rejection has happened frequently over the course of the history of science. In the course of this century the theoretical assumptions of physics, chemistry, biology, sociology, economics, etc., have changed radically. Since these sciences underlie the agricultural sciences, I expect that a careful study of the history of agricultural sciences in this century would reveal many occassions where what was once accepted as observed fact is ultimately rejected, and rejected in part because of changes in underlying theory. Again, while the assumption that there is a clear distinction between observations and interpretations is subject to serious challenges, we shall accept it here. We want to show that even if these assumptions are granted, the claim that scientists or others who attribute beliefs or desires to animals are necessarily irrational is mistaken.

At this point it is useful to make a distinction between two epistemological theories, both regarding the nature of rational belief. We shall call one of these theories "extreme empiricism" and the second "pragmatism." The question of whether we have sufficient evidence to attribute beliefs or desires to animals, may be considered within the context of either theory.

The extreme empiricist maintains that it is not rational to accept a statement as true unless what the statement asserts to be the case has been observed to be the case. For example, consider a statement such as "This pig has four legs." Assuming that one had observed the pig in question and had observed that it had four legs, then it would be rational to accept this statement as true. Similarly, it would be rational to accept of a particular calf the statement that it was displaying care-soliciting behavior. However, assuming that one could not observe the desires of the calf, it would not be rational, according to the extreme empiricist, to accept the claim that the calf desires to eat. Indeed, even if one observed the calf displaying characteristic forms of behavior which regularly occur just prior to normal feeding times, and observed the calf eating vigorously as food was presented, it would still not be rational, according to the extreme empiricist, to accept as true any statement referring to the calf's desire to eat. According to an ultra-extreme form of empiricism, it is not rational to accept any statement as true unless one can verify that statement by making the appropriate observations oneself. In such a view, it is not rational to accept statements about the past as true or, in general, to rely on the testimony of others which one cannot verify oneself.

To see the limitations of extreme empiricism, let us consider a claim that animal scientists would, I believe, be disposed to accept as a report of observations. The claim is, "That calf is displaying care-soliciting behavior." Is this a report of observations? It might be argued that it is not an observation report since an assumption underlying this claim is that the behavior serves a biological function; it serves to arouse the care-giving animal to provide attention which contributes to the well-being of the calf. The assumption regarding the function of the behavior is a theoretical assumption. We can envisage, at least as a possibility, that at some time in the future, when there is greater knowledge of calf-cow relationships, this assumption will be modified. Perhaps certain instances of behavior which is now regarded as care-soliciting will come to be seen as having a different function. Given that this report rests on theoretical assumptions, it may be argued that it is not an observation report. If it is not an observation report, then in an extreme empiricist view, this is not a statement which a scientist should accept as true. It is rather merely a hypothesis or interpretation.

Reflection upon many episodes from the history of science has led many people concerned with proper scientific methodology to adopt a less rigorous form of empiricist theory of knowledge. Such thinkers have observed that scientists frequently make assumptions which refer to the existence of unobserved entities. Such assumptions often play a significant role in directing scientific research. Subsequently, as our powers of observation have been extended, the entities to which reference was made in such assumptions are observed. Probably the most well-known example of this phenomenon concerns the assumption that there are planets beyond the orbit of Saturn, namely, Uranus, Neptune, and Pluto. Deviations in the orbit of known planets had been observed. One possible explanation for such deviations was that Newton's theory of gravity was mistaken. Another possible explanation was that there were additional as yet unobserved planets acting on the masses of the known planets. Scientists regarded the second assumption as more plausible and searched for the additional planets, which were subsequently observed using telescopes.[10] Another example in which an assumption of unobserved entities was subsequently confirmed involves the postulation that blood in many creatures circulates. In Harvey's time there were observations which led scientists to deny that blood circulates, for example, the observation of the different color of the arterial and venous blood. Further, no one had been able to observe connections which would allow blood from arteries to flow into veins (capillaries). The understanding and observations that ultimately provided a resolution of the objections to Harvey's theory were not achieved until long after the theory was generally accepted as correct.[11]

One may ask whether, at some point in time prior to the first observation of Neptune or Pluto, scientists were warranted in accepting as true the assumption that there are trans-Uranic planets. Similarly, one may ask whether scientists were warranted in accepting Harvey's views as true prior to the time at which capillaries could be observed. An affirmative answer to these questions reflects the assumption that one can have reasons for a belief which are strong enough to rationally warrant accepting the belief as true, even though one has not made observations which strictly verify the belief. One theory, that under some circumstances one can have reasons which are strong enough even in the absence of verifying observations, is called "pragmatism." According to this theory, if a theoretical assumption is essential for explaining observational data, or if the use of the theory is essential in anticipating observations, then one has reasons which, if they are strong enough, warrant acceptance of the theory as true.[12] While the theoretical assumption may refer to unobserved entities, according to the pragmatist the assumption is corroborated by the data which, with its help, one was able to anticipate.

Further examples of assumptions which were accepted as true even though the objects or processes to which they refer were not observed at the time, may be given. For much of this century, most biologists have regarded some version of genetic theory as true, even though no one had yet observed genes. Similarly, the fundamental theory of biology, the theory of evolution of species by natural selection, has been widely regarded among biologists as true, even though the creation of a new species by this process has not been observed.[13] Apparently many scientists are pragmatists in regard to theory of knowledge.

Pragmatism should not be confused with ancient views on methodology, which implied that we could have scientific knowledge of the existence and nature of objects with no (observational) evidence at all. According to the pragmatic theory of knowledge, the evidence for all scientific assertions consists of observations. Pragmatism and extreme empiricism agree on that. However, whereas the extreme empiricist maintains that we can have knowledge only of what we have observed, the pragmatist maintains that we can have knowledge, under some circumstances, of properties of, or relations among, entities which we have not observed.[14]

Even if the pragmatist theory of knowledge is accepted, and we grant that we have knowledge about entities which we have not observed, it does not follow that it is rational to accept the claims that some animals have desires or beliefs. We must first briefly consider the conditions under which it is rational, according to pragmatists, at least, to accept as true statements about unobserved entities or processes. Then we must consider whether statements which attribute desires or beliefs to animals satisfy such conditions.[15]

RATIONALITY OF BELIEFS ABOUT UNOBSERVED STATES OR PROCESSES

Above, we discussed assumptions made by Tinbergen and other scientists regarding our knowledge of beliefs and desires. According to these assumptions, we each know that we ourselves have beliefs and desires because we observe our own beliefs and desires. However, we do not observe the beliefs and desires of others. How do we know that other creatures (other humans or other animals) have beliefs or desires? The quotation from Tinbergen suggests that our own beliefs and desires coincide with particular behaviors. This correlation is observed in ourselves. In others we observe only the behaviors. How then do we know that others have beliefs and desires?

Tinbergen's statement suggests a view which has been called the "analogical theory" or the analogical argument for the existence of other minds. This argument has been expressed as follows: "I observe . . . that there are a number of bodies which resemble my own fairly closely in their shape, size and manner of movement; I conclude by analogy that each of these bodies is animated by a mind more or less like myself."[16] Clearly, to a scientist, this argument is very problematic. Even if this argument were sound, it would not yield sufficiently strong reasons in support of the statement that there are minds other than our own to justify claiming to know that this statement is true. Even if it is correct that we observe a correlation between the movements of our own bodies and our own beliefs and desires, we would have observed this correlation in only one case. Clearly, observation of only one case cannot discriminate between a general correlation and a coincidence which obtains only in the observed case. If our belief that others had beliefs and desires rested on the analogical argument, it would be nothing more than a mere guess. The analogical theory is not a correct account of the kind of reasons which, even in pragmatist views of knowledge, would warrant attribution of beliefs or desires to animals.

Some farm animal ethologists appear to believe that the only basis for justifying the attribution of beliefs and desires to animals is the analogical theory.[17] However, this claim is mistaken. Underlying this claim is a false dichotomy, namely the assumption that either we are justified, on the basis of the analogical argument that animals have beliefs or desires or we are not justified in this belief at all.

Training as a scientist is training to be at least moderately skeptical with respect to beliefs about objects in the world. Even the pragmatist, while being more tolerant in regard to the acceptance of claims to knowledge than the radical empiricist, remains a moderate skeptic. For a hypothesis to be acceptable, it must survive rigorous testing in accordance with methodological criteria. According to pragmatism, a hypothesis, such as that animals have certain beliefs and desires, must provide an explanation for a number of observed phenomena. Prior to its acceptance, the hypothesis must be rigorously checked in controlled observation or experiment. Alternative hypotheses must be checked and ruled out through careful observations. If, in the course of such experiment, a hypothesis is not confirmed to a high level of statistical significance, the hypothesis will be rejected.

SCIENTIFIC ADEQUACY OF EVIDENCE FOR ANIMAL BELIEFS

Is there sufficient evidence to warrant our claiming to know that animals have beliefs or desires? Of course, we are not asking this question with respect to all animals. We are concerned here primarily with farm animals, e.g., cows, sheep, chickens, etc. We are asking whether there is sufficient evidence to warrant attribution of beliefs to such animals. Further, we are concerned only with whether such animals have some beliefs. We are not concerned about very general or abstract beliefs. We wonder, for example, whether we could have sufficient reason to accept as true assertions such as that some chickens have such beliefs as "That is something to eat," and such desires as "I want to eat that."

We have accepted (for the sake of argument) the assumption that we cannot observe an animal's (or a person's) beliefs or desires. According to a pragmatic theory of knowledge, the only alternative way of establishing that animals have beliefs or desires is via a theoretical explanation of the animal's (observable) behavior, one which includes assumptions specifying animal beliefs and desires. To establish sufficient grounds for accepting such an explanation as true, the purported explanation must explain the relevant observations better than any other alternative. This, in turn, requires that there be no significant patterns of behavior which are anomalous relative to the purported explanation; further, it requires that there be no alternative explanation of the animal's behavior (which makes no reference to beliefs or desires) which is as satisfactory or more so.

Some ethologists attribute desires to chickens, for example, the desire to lay an egg in a nest.[18] Suppose we have observed the movements (behaviors) of the hen which we associate with nest building and preparing to lay an egg. We know from experience that when a hen performs those behaviors she shortly afterwards will build a nest (if she is able to do so) and normally will lay an egg. Are we justified in saying that the hen has a desire to build a nest or to lay an egg? Presumably such a desire would be a cause of the observed movements. Thus, the attribution of such a desire to the hen would explain our observations. However, we may ask, is this the best explanation? Are there observed anomalous behaviors which do not agree with the attribution of the desire to the hen? Are there alternative assumptions regarding the causes of the observed behavior which yield better explanations of the behavior that we have observed? Should we deny that the hen has this desire and hold out for some alternative motivation for the observed behavior? Rather than saying that the hen desires to build a nest, should we speak of stimuli which release nest-building behavior or stimuli which inhibit such behavior?

Again, some scientists attribute expectations to hens.[19] We may ask whether such expectations are beliefs. If expectations are beliefs then hens have beliefs, at least according to these scientists. Should we say that expectations are beliefs?

These questions are difficult to answer, and the difficulty does not arise simply from our inability to get a sufficient number of observations of hen behavior. Whether we should say that expectations are beliefs depends on our understanding of our concepts of "expectation" and of "belief." Similarly, whether we say that the motivations that underlie the hen's behavior are desires depends on our understanding of our concepts of "motivation" and of "desire." The difficulty in getting the evidence to resolve these questions arises, I suspect, because our theories of both human and animal motivation and intelligence are too incompletely developed. In consequence, the differences between the observational implications of alternative theories are unclear, and we don't yet know how to design research programs to find or confirm answers to the above questions. We haven't yet accumulated enough evidence to decide whether hens (or other animals) have beliefs or desires because we do not yet know what to do to get such evidence. In other words, there are explanations of the animal behaviors which include posits that the animals have beliefs and desires and there are alternative explanations which do not appear to include these posits (though the alternatives may include other posits). We haven't yet done the scientific work to determine whether explanations of either pattern are scientifically warranted or disconfirmed.

Donald Griffin argued that it is reasonable to suppose that animals sometimes engage in conscious thinking.[20] The question of whether animals engage in conscious thinking is not the same as that of whether animals have desires or beliefs. On some psychological theories it makes sense to speak of a being's desires and beliefs as being unconscious but as influencing his or her thinking nonetheless. However, considerations which Griffin maintains are indicative of conscious thought may also be taken as indicative of desires and beliefs. Griffin says, "If the animal does much the same things regardless of the state of its environment or the behavior of other animals nearby, we are less inclined to judge that it is thinking about its circumstances or what it is doing. Consciously motivated behavior is more plausibly inferred when an animal behaves appropriately in a novel and perhaps surprising situation that requires specific actions not called for under ordinary circumstances."[21] We might cite the same consideration as a scientific reason for asserting that the animal has desires or beliefs. However, we would not be justified in saying that this reasoning is strong on scientific grounds since we have not done the conceptual and observational work to clarify and rule out alternative explanations of the animal behavior—explanations which do not posit animal desires or beliefs.

Similar remarks apply to Tom Regan's arguments that Fido (a dog) has beliefs. Regan argues that Fido has a belief about the flavor of bones, namely, that they have a flavor which he desires to experience. Attribution of this belief to Fido allegedly explains the choices Fido makes with regard to what he chews.[22] However, many scientists would disagree with Regan. While allowing that the animal is motivated to chew the bone and that the animal has expectations in respect to the bone, they would deny that such motivations are desires or that such expectations are beliefs. They propose patterns of explanation of the dog's behavior which they allege to not imply that the animal has desires and beliefs. Until the contrasts between the belief-desire explanations and the alternatives are more fully developed, we have to agree that the claim that animals have desires or beliefs has not been scientifically established.[23] There is strong evidence which supports this claim. I have made efforts to keep abreast of this matter, and am not aware of any scientific evidence or reasoning which refutes the claim.

RATIONALITY OF BELIEFS ABOUT ANIMAL BELIEFS AND DESIRES

Let us return then to the question with which I started this essay, that of whether it is irrational to attribute beliefs or desires to animals. We have allowed that we do not have sufficient scientific reason to establish the truth of the attribution of beliefs or desires to animals. Does this admission imply that it is irrational to attribute beliefs or desires to animals? There are several reasons for answering this question in the negative.

First, the justification for the admission that we do not have sufficient reason to attribute beliefs or desires to animals was predicated on taking "sufficient reason" in accord with strong standards of scientific reasoning. We don't have sufficient reason given either radical empiricist or pragmatist theories of scientific knowledge. The same reasoning implies that we do not have sufficient reason to attribute beliefs or desires to human beings. Our scientific theories of human motivation are not sufficiently well developed to confirm or refute attribution of beliefs or desires in rigorous scientific ways. However, given the more tolerant standards of evidence and reasoning acceptable in everyday practices, there is ample reason to warrant attribution of beliefs and desires to human beings and other animals. Indeed, for much of the behavior of animals with which we are familiar in our common practices, there is really no alternative theory by reference to which animal behavior can be described or explained. There are numerous anecdotal accounts of the behavior of pets or farm animals which clearly imply that these animals have desires and beliefs, e.g., cows have no trouble recognizing each other. Such recognition implies that they have beliefs which enter into their capacity to distinguish conspecifics, and into other capacities also. Unless we are willing to conclude that absence of strong scientific reason for attribution of beliefs and desires in the case of human beings implies that such attribution is irrational, we should be equally reluctant to draw this conclusion in regard to animals.

Second, even though there is not sufficiently strong scientific reason to warrant the attribution of beliefs and desires to animals, we would be entitled to conclude that it was irrational to attribute beliefs and desires to animals only if we knew that for any claim C (such as the claim that animals have beliefs or desires) it is rational to accept C as true only if we have strong enough scientific reason to accept C. However, this assumption regarding rationality is unwarranted, even with respect to beliefs that scientists accept in regard to their scientific work. A scientist who accepts the assumption that animals have beliefs or desires is not thereby irrational. As we argued at the start, let us hypothesize that there is a scientist who is working on the overall problem of understanding animal motivation. Making this assumption may underlie the design of experiments. Experiments designed on the basis of this and other assumptions serve, of course, to test those assumptions. If those assumptions are strongly confirmed by the evidence then the assumption regarding beliefs or desires of animals may come to form a part of a more completely developed theory of animal motivation which is strongly confirmed by (yet to be obtained) scientific evidence. We do not know that this assumption is false. To maintain that it is irrational to make this assumption could be to block a direction of scientific work that could ultimately yield a strongly confirmed theory.

With respect to other beliefs it is even clearer that it may be rational to accept as true beliefs which have not been established on scientific grounds. Sometimes we must make up our minds as to what is the case in the absence of sufficient scientific evidence. Such is the case when we must take some course of action to achieve some (important) objective. In such circumstances it may well be irrational to withhold acceptance of appropriate beliefs merely because one does not have scientific proof of the truth of such beliefs. In such circumstances rationality may require that we accept as true the belief which is most strongly supported on the basis of the available evidence, regardless of whether that support is strong enough to satisfy scientific standards.

SUMMARY

In this chapter I have argued that attribution of beliefs or desires to animals need not be fallacious. We have considered two theories of scientific reasoning, extreme empiricism and pragmatism. We have agreed that on either theory, we cannot conclude that we have proof that domestic animals have beliefs or desires. However, I have also argued that it is not irrational to accept as true some beliefs which have not been scientifically proved, and further that the claim that it is irrational for a person to attribute beliefs or desires to animals is unwarranted.

NOTES

1. An early statement of a view similar to the one we are defending here is expressed in William James, "The Will to Believe," in *Essays in Pragmatism*.

2. An extended discussion of whether animals are sentient is found in Bernard Rollin, *The Unheeded Cry: Animal Consciousness, Animal Pain and Science*. Two reviews of this book are available: Evelyn Pluhar, review of *The Unheeded Cry* . . . by Bernard Rollin, and Hugh Lehman, review of *The Unheeded Cry* . . . by Bernard Rollin. One philosopher who raises a question concerning whether animals feel pain is Peter Carruthers. His views are briefly described in *The Ag Bioethics Forum* and at greater length in *The Animals Issue*.

3. Donald Griffin refers to a number of scientists who have held views which imply that animals do not have beliefs or desires. See Donald Griffin, *The Question of Animal Awareness: Evolutionary Continuity of Mental Experience*, chap. 4.

4. For more on the question of whether animals have beliefs, see Stephen Stich, "Do Animals Have Beliefs?" For a deep consideration of whether animals or anything else has beliefs see Stephen Stich, *From Folk Psychology to Cognitive Science: The Case Against Belief*.

5. David Hull has argued against the view that biological species, e.g., *Homo sapiens*, are sets of organisms unified by a set of characteristics which all and only members of the set possess. For some discussion of this matter see David Hull, *Philosophy of Biological Science*, 47. See also David Hull, "The Effects of Essentialism on Taxonomy."

6. Begging the question is sometimes called arguing in a circle. Roughly, someone commits this fallacy if in the course of trying to establish some conclusion C on the basis of evidence or reasoning E, one includes C or something obviously equivalent to C, as part of E. In some cases someone tries to establish a conclusion and in the course of doing so offers as evidence something which is merely a reformulation of that conclusion. Sometimes the assumption which renders the reasoning circular is not obvious.

7. S. Tax and C. Callender, *Evolution After Darwin* vol. 3, p. 185.

8. This claim depends on getting clear on conditions necessary for something to be observable. We might say that something is observable if a term that refers to that thing can be learned ostensively, like the term "green." The term "belief" does not appear to be such a term. Alternatively, something might be said to be observable if any of a group of suitably trained and suitably situated observers would all agree on whether the thing in question is present. Again, beliefs do not seem to be the sort of things that are observable. This view of observation is discussed in W. V. Quine and J. S. Ullian, *The Web of Belief*, 2d ed. For more on observation, including debates over views such as that expressed by Tinbergen, see Robert J. Swartz, ed., *Perceiving, Sensing and Knowing*.

9. I have challenged some of these views in Hugh Lehman, "Anthropomorphism and Scientific Evidence for Animal Mental States."

10. For brief discussion of the discovery of planets, see Gerald Holton and Duane Roller, *Foundations of Modern Physical Science*, 195.

11. For interesting discussion regarding the development of views regarding circulation of blood see Mark Graubard, *Circulation and Respiration: The Evolution of an Idea*.

12. The pragmatic theory was expressed at the end of the nineteenth century; see William James, "What Pragmatism Means" and "Pragmatism's Theory of Truth," in *Pragmatsim and Four Essays from The Meaning of Truth*.

13. William James gave credit for the pragmatic theory to Charles S. Peirce. See Charles S. Peirce, "The Fixation of Belief"; also "A Theory of Probable Inference." These essays and other essays of Peirce have been collected in many anthologies. One such anthology is Justus Buchler, *Philosophical Writings of Peirce*.

14. For a review of criticisms of extreme empiricism, see Israel Scheffler, *The Anatomy of Inquiry*, parts 2 and 3.

15. R. G. Frey has argued that animals do not have desires or beliefs. See R. G. Frey, *Interests and Rights: The Case Against Animals*. Frey's arguments have been criticized in S. F. Sapontzis, *Morals, Reason and Animals*.

16. Henry H. Price, "Our Evidence for the Existence of Other Minds," 617.

17. This seems to be the view taken in G. C. Brantas, "Interpretation of Behaviour Observations," in *Proceedings of the First European Symposium on Poultry Welfare*, 45.

18. V. G. Kite, "Does a Hen Require a Nest," in *Proceedings of the Second European Symposium on Poultry Welfare*, 120.

19. See D. M. Broom, "Stress, Welfare and the State of Equilibrium," in *Proceedings of the Second European Symposium on Poultry Welfare*, 73.

20. Donald R. Griffin, *Animal Thinking*, chap. 2.

21. Ibid., 37.

22. Tom Regan, *The Case for Animal Rights*, chap. 2.

23. Perhaps the strongest case to be made for the claim that animals have beliefs is in the work of the psychologist Irene Pepperberg, who claims to have shown that parrots can communicate referentially. Her work is described in "Referential Communication with an African Grey Parrot." This article includes references to a number of scientific articles by Pepperberg.

5. Is It Rational to Deny that Animals Have Beliefs and Desires?

WHEREAS WE ARGUED, in chapter four, that rationality does not require that we abstain from attributing beliefs and desires to animals, the question might be raised as to whether it is rational to deny that animals have beliefs and desires, that is, whether rationality requires that we accept this belief. While we have answered this question in the negative in our discussion in chapter four, there are some arguments which we have not yet considered to which some people might appeal in support of an affirmative answer. In this chapter we shall consider those arguments.

Let us start by briefly reviewing what has been called the belief-desire pattern of explanation. Often, at least in non-scientific contexts, we explain people's actions by reference to their beliefs and desires. For example, suppose that Jack put on his jacket and Jill wonders why Jack did that. One possible answer is that Jack wanted to be warmer and he thought that by putting on his jacket he would soon be warmer. This answer is allegedly an explanation of his action, that is, of his putting on his jacket. In this explanation there appears to be a reference to one of his desires, namely his desire to be warmer and to one of his beliefs, namely his belief that if he put on his jacket then he would be warmer. Construing the answer as an explanation implies that the combination of these two psychological states, the belief and the desire, causes Jack to put on his jacket. Explanations which refer to beliefs and desires have been called "belief-desire explanations."[1]

In his recent book Tom Regan concluded that "we are rationally entitled to believe that" animals have beliefs and desires.[2] To support this claim

Regan advanced what he called "the cumulative argument." The conclusion of the cumulative argument taken together with some rebuttals of philosophers who have argued that animals may not have desires or beliefs, is that we are rationally entitled to believe that domestic animals have beliefs and desires. This conclusion is consistent with the conclusion we accepted in the last chapter. However, Regan needs to establish a stronger conclusion. He needs to show not simply that we are rationally entitled to believe that animals have beliefs and desires, but that we are rationally required to believe this. Regan's objective is to produce arguments which show that we have obligations to respect many kinds of animals, including domestic animals; in his view, it appears that this entails that, other things equal, we ought not to kill them merely to satisfy our desire for food or other products, given that there are alternative ways for us to satisfy our desires. If we are not rationally required to believe that animals have beliefs and desires, then human omnivores can reply to Regan that while you are rationally entitled to believe animals have beliefs and desires, we are rationally entitled to believe the contrary. If the omnivores are entitled to think this, then they are entitled also to reject the basic value and moral principles to which Regan appeals in his effort to show that we have an obligation not to kill animals merely to satisfy our desire for food, etc. In this chapter we shall not investigate the moral and value principles to which Regan appeals. Rather, we shall argue that the cumulative argument does not succeed in establishing the stronger conclusion which Regan's moral conclusions require.[3]

THE CUMULATIVE ARGUMENT

The cumulative argument may be stated as follows:
    According to both our common sense and to ordinary language, animals, such as mammals, have beliefs and desires. "The behavior of those animals is consistent with attributing beliefs and desires to them; evolutionary theory supports the view that animals frequently behave as they do because they desire what they desire and believe what they believe. . . Griffin observes. . . it is unparsimonious to assume a rigid dichotomy of interpretation which insists that mental experiences have some effect on the behavior of one species of animals but none at all on others."[4]

Apparently Regan regards this as a collection of arguments, each of which supports the conclusion that animals have beliefs and desires. Taken together they constitute the cumulative argument. He is suggesting that each of them lends some support for the conclusion and that this support is cumulative so that taken together the cumulative argument provides strong support for this conclusion. Actually, he doesn't say that the cumulative argument shows that the conclusion is true. Rather, he maintains that the cumulative argument establishes that those who would deny that animals have beliefs and desires must bear the burden of proof, that is, they should believe that animals have beliefs and desires unless they present strong enough counterarguments to undermine the evidence which supports this belief. To show that we are rationally entitled to hold that domestic animals have beliefs and desires, Regan bolsters the cumulative argument by criticizing arguments advanced by some philosophers which purport to show either that animals cannot have beliefs or desires or at least that it is very doubtful that animals have such psychological states. I take this to mean that, at this point in time, reason requires that we attribute beliefs and desires to animals. I shall challenge this claim. I shall argue that the separate arguments that constitute the cumulative argument are not strong and that it is not clear that such strength as they have may be added together to yield a strong argument. Further, I shall argue that reason does not require those people who would deny that animals have beliefs or desires to shoulder the burden of proof.

The first sub-argument which Regan uses is that common sense and ordinary language each imply that animals have beliefs and desires. I take it that this means that it is quite common for ordinary people to think that animals have beliefs and desires. This is very likely true; that is, people commonly think that animals have beliefs and desires. Even scientific articles sometimes contain statements which may imply that animals have beliefs and desires. For example, in a recent work on bonding, a scientist said that wolves seek close human contact.[5] The scientist in question might readily deny that it was his intention that his remark should be taken literally as implying that the wolf had beliefs and desires. The scientist could maintain that such a statement is to be understood as describing certain aspects of the wolf's behavior, aspects which would be worth explaining. The behavior is *as if* the wolf were searching for a human. What the causes of this behavior are is another matter. Perhaps the wolf desires human companionship; perhaps it does not. The scientist would, most likely, remain noncommittal about that.

However, I don't think that the fact that people commonly think that animals have beliefs and desires is a good reason at all for thinking that the belief-desire pattern of explanation is true. People commonly think all sorts of things which probably are mistaken. It would be easy to give examples of widely held views which are false or, at any rate, not true. For example, many people believe that they are not responsible at all for the circumstances in which they find themselves. They attribute everything to bad luck. Many people believe that homosexuals deliberately set out to engage in immoral behavior. Many people have false beliefs about causes of many phenomena.

Bernard Rollin refers to cases in which science, allegedly through departing significantly from "common sense," is led into error.[6] Many examples could be given in support of Rollin's claim on this point. Others have defended common sense also. Early in the twentieth century, G. E. Moore defended common sense views about the nature of the external world.[7] One can envisage someone suggesting that in cases in which science and common sense come into conflict, it would be wiser to trust the claims of common sense than to trust the claims of science, that a person would be more likely to have true beliefs if he or she trusted common sense or ordinary language. Conceivably, Regan, in formulating this first part of the cumulative argument, is making some such presupposition. I, for one, do not find that suggestion very plausible. If we assume that common sense views about the nature of things are grounded on experience and have "worked" for people, that is, have led them to results which were satisfactory for them, then we should grant that there is some evidence in favor of common sense theories. There is presumably evidence for the scientific theories also. Where there are conflicts between common sense and science, we certainly should conclude that one or the other is mistaken. However, I don't think that we are entitled to conclude that it is science which is more likely to be mistaken. Just as examples can be given in which the scientific claims ultimately turned out to be mistaken, examples can be given, as I have done above, in which common sense is mistaken.

The second stage of the cumulative argument is that animal behavior is consistent with attributing desires and beliefs to animals. Let us assume that what Regan meant here is that we are able to find some beliefs and desires that we can attribute to animals such that the observed behavior of the animal does not lead us to say things which contradict this attribution. Again this is true, but it is not clear that this argument has any strength at all. The behavior of plants is consistent with attributing desires and beliefs to them. The behavior of some inanimate objects is consistent with attributing desires and beliefs to them. Suppose, for example, that one attributes to the water on the Earth the desire to reach the sea. The behavior of the water on Earth is consistent with this hypothesis, i.e., in spite of obstacles, such as evaporation, the water tends to return to the sea.

This argument, that attribution of beliefs and desires is consistent with animal behavior, could be reformulated in a way which leads to a stronger argument. We would be required to attribute beliefs or desires to animals providing that the attribution of such states of mind was essential for the best explanation we could have for the animal behavior we observe.[8] This is the strongest argument which Regan could give. Properly construed, it amounts to the kind of evidence for animal beliefs and desires which we discussed in the last chapter. I have already argued that at best such an argument does not amount to a proof according to scientific criteria.

In elaborating this second argument, Regan considers a hypothetical dog Fido. He claims that in light of Fido's behavior we know that the dog believes that bones have a flavor he or she desires.[9] However, this argument is question-begging. Regan has not described experiments regarding dogs and bones which have been carefully carried out under controlled circumstances. Further, Regan has not reviewed alternative explanations of the dog's behavior or carried out carefully controlled experiments to determine whether other possible explanations are more satisfactory than the belief-desire explanation. Regan's argument amounts to a thought experiment. What we need here is careful descriptions and then carefully formulated hypotheses and experimental tests. A thought experiment will not serve to establish that Fido really has the belief which Regan says Fido has.

A scientist who has argued that animals engage in conscious thought is Donald Griffin. In his book *Animal Thinking*, Griffin argues that "versatile adaptability of behavior to changing circumstances and challenges" is scientific evidence of animal thinking.[10] It is fairly clear that when Griffin speaks of conscious thinking he is thinking of belief-desire explanations of behavior. For example, in his discussion of animals learning that food will be available in a certain place at a certain time of day he says ". . . it seems reasonable that these animals really do expect food at a certain time or place and that they experience disappointment, annoyance, or other subjective emotions when their expectations are not fulfilled."[11] Another sort of example to which Griffin calls attention are cases in which animals learn a new behavior through watching and imitating other animals.[12] These are examples in which an explanation of observed behavior, by reference to beliefs or expectations and desires related to basic emotions, explain the behavior. Griffin obviously thinks they are good explanations. However, many other scientists disagree. Whether the belief-desire explanations are the best explanations is an open question. Thus, we cannot say that in examples such as these we have scientific proof that animals have beliefs and desires.

In defense of the view that we have attributed to Griffin (and of Regan's view), someone might charge that those scientists who refuse to accept the conclusion that animals have beliefs and desires are being irrational. In elaboration of this charge, it may be suggested that these scientists fail to accept this conclusion because their thought is biassed by behaviorist prejudices. However, the charge that these scientists are irrationally biassed is one that needs to be established itself by reference to strong evidence. Furthermore, it is hard to see how such a general charge could be substantiated in this case. Scientists who are reluctant to appeal to belief-desire explanations could maintain that they are appealing to strong methodological principles of science, such as that explanatory assumptions should be able to deal with a wide range of phenomena without having to make ad hoc adjustments, a weakness to which belief-desire explanations are notoriously subject. I shall return to this point below.[13]

The third part of the cumulative argument is that in light of evolutionary theory it is unparsimonious to assume that while some animals have beliefs and desires, other animals do not. This argument rests on the assumption of the principle of parsimony, which affirms that in developing explanations of what we observe, it is rationally preferable to favor explanations which rest on the smallest number of independent assumptions. Regan is saying that we use belief-desire explanations for understanding human behavior. If this principle works for animal behavior, then if we attribute beliefs and desires to animals we won't have to make additional explanatory assumptions. Thus, we ought to attribute beliefs and desires to animals in understanding their behavior. This argument is open to numerous criticisms.

The appeal to the principle of parsimony, if it had any strength, would tend to show that all animals (even insects or flatworms) have beliefs and desires, that plants have beliefs and desires and perhaps even that inanimate objects had beliefs and desires. Animals evolved from plants, and perhaps all forms of life evolved from inanimate objects. If we assume that Regan would not accept the claim that inanimate objects have desires or beliefs, then, by virtue of the logic of this argument, he should conclude, by appeal to the principle of parsimony, that neither plants nor animals nor people have desires or beliefs.

The principle of parsimony is only one of a number of methodological principles which enter into the evaluation of scientific explanations. Another principle is that we should prefer explanatory schemes which can be applied to wide ranges of phenomena. A major problem with belief-desire explanations is that particular explanations have very limited generality. A belief-desire explanation that applied to one sort of animal behavior might well not apply to another sort of behavior. For example, in the article by Fentress referred to above, the author observed that it was easy to teach a wolf to present a paw but difficult to teach it to sit. If one had explained that the wolf readily learned to present a paw because it desired to please and believed that this behavior would please the human, then one will have to invent some other explanation for the difficulty in teaching the wolf to sit. Again, belief-desire explanations that apply to dogs will often not apply to closely similar animals such as coyotes or wolves.

Due to the lack of generality of the explanatory assumptions in such explanations, there are serious questions as to whether it is possible to get observational evidence which strongly confirms them. Another methodological principle is that explanatory assumptions should be subject to confirmation or disconfirmation through rigorous observational methods. Even if the principle of parsimony did lend support to the assumption that animals have beliefs and desires, the lack of generality and the concomitant problems in getting evidential support would tend to undermine that support.

I have reviewed each of the three arguments contained in the cumulative argument, and have claimed that each argument is weak at best. Thus, even if I agreed that we could combine the strength of these arguments, I would not agree that the cumulative argument is a strong argument. However, it must be admitted that claims about what arguments are strong or weak do not rest on a consensus amongst epistemologists or scholars concerned with methods for achieving knowledge of what counts as a strong argument. During the period of early modern philosophy, roughly speaking, early in the seventeenth century, a number of thinkers tried to formulate rules of method. Most notable among these were Francis Bacon and Rene Descartes.[14] Work in these areas continues, and while it is of great interest among students of scientific methodology, there is no consensus on many major issues. Regan's claim about the strength of the cumulative argument would itself be a strongly warranted claim only if there were an established theory which clearly distinguished strong from weak arguments. There is no such theory.

This last point bears some further scrutiny. Many scientists may think that within science itself there is an established method which clearly distinguishes strong scientific arguments, arguments which serve to prove scientific claims, from relatively weak arguments. I do not believe that this is correct. Of course, there are widely accepted statistical criteria which scientists regularly employ in evaluating the strength of observational or experimental support for hypotheses. If the data which support a hypothesis are not statistically significant to a high level, the hypothesis is not accepted. However, the appeal to such criteria does not, by itself, determine what pieces of scientific reasoning amount to strong support for a hypothesis. The hypothesis must itself satisfy other criteria having to do with generality, plausibility, parsimony, etc. A number of these concepts are obscure. For example, one may ask how simplicity or generality of hypotheses are to be compared. Thus, it is not clear how all these factors are to be taken into account to yield a uniform measure of strength of arguments.

BURDEN OF PROOF

Regan does two things in support of his view that the burden of proof lies with those who deny that animals have desires and beliefs. First, he offers the cumulative argument in support of his claim, and second, he severely criticizes the arguments of Stich and Frey, who had maintained that animals do not have desires and beliefs.[15] In my judgment, Regan's criticisms of Stich and Frey are sound. Is this sufficient to support his conclusion regarding the burden of proof? I shall argue that it is not.

It is perhaps worth noting that there are no clear, well-established logical guidelines regarding the burden of proof. Indeed, if one turns to contemporary works of logic one will find virtually no guidance in this regard. Regan cannot appeal to contemporary authorities in logic in support of his claim. Perhaps there are authorities from earlier times of whom I am unaware, however, he gives no references in this regard and formulates no general guidelines himself regarding the burden of proof. Let us attempt to formulate of a position on this matter.

Regan's position regarding burden of proof appears to be that if one has presented a strong argument in support of a position and has refuted the strongest objections to that position, then the burden of proof rests on those who reject that position. Let us tentatively accept this assumption for the sake of getting on with the argument. Given what we have tentatively accepted, to challenge his views regarding the burden of proof we must show either that he has not presented a strong argument in support of the contention that animals have desires and beliefs or we must show that there are strong objections to that view which he has not refuted. We shall attempt to show that Regan's argument fails in both these respects.

We have already argued that the cumulative argument for the conclusion that animals have desires and beliefs is not a strong argument. Regan claimed that "The cumulative argument provides defensible grounds for viewing Fido and other mammalian animals as being like us in having beliefs, understood as functional or psychological states, and their behavior provides us with the needed basis for saying what they believe."[16] In light of what we have said above, while the cumulative argument is defensible, it is not a strong argument. Scientists are not rationally compelled to admit that animals have beliefs and desires which serve as causes for their behavior. Nor are they compelled by this argument to agree that they know what desires or beliefs animals have.

Nor do I think that Regan has refuted the strongest objection to the claim that animals have desires and beliefs. In my judgment, the strongest objection to the claim that animals have desires and beliefs is that desire-belief explanations do not satisfy scientific criteria such as criteria of generality and of freedom from *ad hoc* qualifications. Thus, even if we accept the above suggestion regarding the burden of proof, Regan has not shown that those opposed to attributing beliefs and desires to animals must prove that animals do not have these psychological states.

ON ATTRIBUTION OF FEELINGS OR EMOTIONS TO ANIMALS

In this chapter we have focussed our attention on the question of whether we are rationally compelled to accept the claim that domestic (or some other) animals have desires and beliefs. We have argued that scientists who refused to accept this claim are not necessarily irrational for doing so. At this point someone might ask whether the same is true in regard to feelings, such as feelings of pain, frustration, satisfaction, or comfort. Further, someone might ask whether the same is true in regard to emotions, such as fear, affection, boredom, or curiosity.

In regard to feelings, the scientific community is close to a consensus that animals do indeed have both feelings of pain, discomfort, or frustration, as well has feelings of comfort or satisfaction. There continues to be some disagreement as to how these feelings should be described.[17] In my judgment, this near unanimity is a result of it being the case that it is indeed rational to affirm (and irrational to deny) that domestic and some other animals are sentient, that is are conscious of feelings of comfort, discomfort, etc. Of course, there is behavioral evidence of the presence of those feelings, e.g., animals may cry out or moan when injured, they tend to avoid stimuli of sorts which have injured them or which they apparently perceive to be threatening. Similarly, some stimuli which are normally beneficial to the survival of the animal serve as positive reinforcers. Such evidence is abundant. Further, there is considerable understanding of the physiology of feeling, especially of unpleasant or painful feelings. The neurological structures which give rise to pain in human beings are present in many types of animals also. Animals as well as humans possess both motor and afferent neurons. Veterinarians have no trouble distinguishing substances, such as curare, which merely immobilize a creature, from analgesics or anesthetics.[18]

A primary objection to the attribution of beliefs or desires to animals has to do with the lack of generality of belief-desire explanations, and with difficulties in conducting experiments to confirm hypotheses about these intentional psychological states. However, in regard to feelings the same is not the case. Hypotheses concerning processes which are painful or pleasant to experience are, in many instances, of broad generality. Relations both between feelings and behavior and between feelings and underlying physiological states are simpler. There is widespread agreement that opportunities to fulfill motivations which apparently arise normally as a result of the animal's fundamental genetic constitution yield comfort or pleasure for the animals.[19]

A significant objection to attributing beliefs and desires to domestic animals arises from the difficulty of determining the content of the animal's beliefs or desires. This is the objection discussed at length by Stich, to which we referred above, and which was criticized by both Regan and Sapontzis. Even though Regan's and Sapontzis' criticisms of this objection are strong, scientists continue to display widespread unease in attributing content to the cognitive or motivational states of domestic or other animals. Regardless of the force of this problem in regard to the rationality of attributing beliefs or desires, it is not a problem in regard to attributing feelings. Feelings, unlike desires or beliefs, are not intentional states: that is, feelings, such as a feeling of pain or comfort, do not necessarily refer to anything beyond themselves. They are not internal representations of an external reality. In light of these considerations, I would be willing to affirm that scientists and others acquainted with the evidence are irrational if they reject the claim that animals experience feelings of pain, contentment, etc., and similarly for positive or negative feelings associated with motivations.

SUMMARY

The discussion in this chapter has focussed on criticizing the claim that we are rationally required to hold that domestic animals have desires and beliefs. While Tom Regan did not make this claim, he needed to do so to justify a premise essential for conclusions he drew concerning our moral obligations to animals. Regan used the cumulative argument in support of his claim. We have shown that the cumulative argument is logically weak. Only one part of the argument has any rational force; so, even if it is possible to accumulate the strength of the parts, the total logical or rational force of the argument is, at most, small. Finally, we have argued that scientists are rationally required, in light of the evidence and our understanding of the matter, to agree that animals have certain feelings.

NOTES

1. Of course, belief-desire explanations have been used by scientists in many works of sociology and psychology also. Thus the pattern should not be dismissed as unscientific. Some thinkers have suggested that explanations of the belief-desire pattern are remnants of psychological assumptions which should now be regarded as myths. See Stich, *From Folk Psychology to Cognitive Science*.

2. Regan, *The Case For Animal Rights*, 78.

3. Actually, Regan argues for much more than that animals have beliefs and desires. He argues that they have an awareness of their own psychophysical identity as a being with a future. He calls beings who have this awareness "subjects-of-a-life." He argued that being subjects-of-a-life, animals are possessors of "inherent value" and so are entitled to be treated in ways that show respect for the inherent value they possess. This principle of respect for inherent value is the basic moral principle of Regan's theory. See Regan, *The Case for Animal Rights*, 74, 81 and chap. 8.

4. Ibid., 34.

5. John C. Fentress, "The Covalent Animal: On Bonds and their Boundaries in Behavioral Research," 47.

6. Bernard Rollin, *The Unheeded Cry*, 20. Of course, Rollin does not say that whenever science conflicts with common sense science is in error. Nor does Regan make this assumption.

7. G. E. Moore, "A Defense of Common Sense." Moore was not defending common sense against critiques on the basis of scientific views. He was defending the view that there are objects, such as our bodies, which exist independently of anyone thinking of them—a view Moore thought was contrary to the views of philosophers known as idealists. Moore appealed to much scientific knowledge in support of his position.

8. Formulated in this way, the argument that animals have beliefs and desires could be said to satisfy pragmatist criteria for knowledge. Pragmatism was briefly discussed in chap. 4.

9. Regan, *The Case for Animal Rights*, 74.

10. Griffin, *Animal Thinking*, 37.

11. Ibid., 137.

12. Ibid., 138.

13. Consider how one might establish a charge of bias against an individual of a particular race. Such a charge might be established against the prejudiced person by pointing out examples of obviously false beliefs which the person expresses in the effort to justify his or her biased attitudes and behaviors. To show that scientists who refused to accept that animals have beliefs and desires are biased, one would have to point out that they were committed to obviously false beliefs in their efforts to justify rejection of this theory. At this time, it seems unlikely that scientists wishing to justify rejecting this theory must appeal to obviously false beliefs.

14. Bacon's ideas on strong arguments are expressed in Francis Bacon, *Novum Organum: True Directions Concerning the Interpretation of Nature*. Descartes' ideas are expressed both in his *Discourse on Method* and also *Rules for the Direction of the Mind*.

15. Stich's views on this matter are expressed in Stich, "Do Animals Have Beliefs?" Frey's position is expressed in Frey, *Interests and Rights*. Stich's argument and part of Frey's argument hinges on difficulties in specifying the content of animal beliefs. Frey also argues that to have desires one must be in command of a human form of language in which one has the concept of a true sentence. These arguments have been criticized in many places in addition to Regan's critique. Another good critique is found in Sapontzis, *Morals, Reason and Animals*.

16. Regan, *The Case for Animal Rights*, 74.

17. See Hugh Lehman, "What is Animal Welfare," along with commentaries on this article and replies to the commentaries in the same source. There are many references to scientific literature on pain in Rollin, *The Unheeded Cry*.

18. Some discussion of anesthetics is found in Daniel C. Dennett, *Brainstorms: Philosophical Essays on Mind and Psychology*. As a member of the animal care committee at the University of Guelph, I regularly participate in discussions with veterinarians and other scientists concerning appropriate anesthetics or analgesics for fish, birds, and mammals.

19. My major evidence for saying this is discussions I have had with animal scientists, including farm animal ethologists, psychologists, etc. One can find discussions bearing on this point in the scientific literature also. For example, V. G. Kite, "Does a Hen Require a Nest?" in *Proceedings of the Second European Symposium on Animal Rights*, 117, which points out that "in the absence of the appropriate stimuli (for building a nest) frustration ensues. Absence of behaviors indicative of seeking or avoidance is taken as indicative of feelings of satisfaction." Other papers in the same volume discuss behavioral and physiological indicators of other emotions or feelings such as fear.

6. Is It Rational to Engage in Moral Reasoning?

SOMETIMES, WHEN I have been involved in discussing, with agricultural scientists, whether some agricultural practice ought to be modified, one of the scientists has remarked, usually near the end of the discussion, that if the practice in question is modified so as to bring it into conformity with valid ethical norms, it will not be for ethical reasons. The scientist alleges that the practice will be modified, if at all, only because the modifications will also serve to increase profits.

On hearing the remark I have been surprised. What, in the context of a discussion of a question concerning a possible moral obligation, is the relevance of a remark such as this concerning motivation? It appears that the reasoning underlying the remark is a conclusion, drawn by the scientist, that discussion of moral obligations is pointless since regardless of what beliefs we may agree to on the basis of our discussion of moral obligations, agricultural producers will not be motivated by any beliefs concerning obligations. Agricultural producers, it appears, will be motivated to act only in ways which will increase their net profits.

The scientist could be construed as saying that agricultural producers are a particularly selfish group of people since, as he seems to be saying, they will not change their behavior for moral reasons. Now, I suspect that it was not the scientist's intention to so characterize agricultural producers. In my experience, agricultural scientists tend to have a high regard for producers, at least for some producers. Perhaps a better interpretation of the scientist's remark is that no one ever acts or modifies her or his behavior except for selfish reasons.

I shall assume, at first, that this interpretation of the scientist's remarks, namely, that no one ever does anything except to benefit him or herself, is the correct one. I shall call this view "moral cynicism." In the philosophical literature this view is often called "psychological egoism."[1] Subsequently, I shall suggest that the scientist's remark should be interpreted as expressing a more restricted theory. The contrast between the restricted theory and moral cynicism will serve to show that even if moral cynicism were correct, there is little reason to think that the scientist's more restricted assumption is so. We shall start this chapter by trying to raise some doubts about moral cynicism.

Perhaps agricultural scientists and others may be assuming that if our behavior is completely determined by selfish motives, then there is no point to engaging in moral reasoning. The point of moral reasoning, they may assume, is to determine what we ought to do, so that we may act in accordance with our moral obligations. But if our actions are completely determined by selfishness, then knowledge of our moral obligations will not modify our conduct. We might then ask, under these conditions could it be rational to engage in moral reasoning? The answer is that in some limited circumstances, it could be rational. Some people might desire to have knowledge of their moral obligations for itself. Given what we have said in a prior chapter about rational desires, for such people it could be rational to try to determine their moral obligations. Some people might simply take pleasure in the labor of moral reasoning. For those people also, it could be rational to engage in moral reasoning. Since, for most people, taking great care in undertaking lengthy reasoning processes is not something they desire for itself or for the purely theoretical knowledge it may produce, if moral cynicism were true, there is reason to think that it would not be rational for them to engage in moral reasoning. Shall we assume that this is true?

Let us tentatively accept this assumption. That will enable us to proceed in the following way I shall try to show that it may well be rational for them to engage in moral reasoning, and to take great pains to do so carefully, since there is very little reason to think that moral cynicism is true. In the end, I shall argue that when we consider the fact that we are social creatures, that is, that we live with other people in societies, then, even if moral cynicism is true, it is still rational for them to engage in moral reasoning. Nonetheless, I want to challenge this thought. I shall do so by arguing first that there is reason to think that moral cynism is not true and thus that there may be good reason to engage in moral reasoning to determine what we ought to do. Further, I shall argue that even if moral cynicism is true, since we are social creatures it is still rational for many people to engage in moral reasoning.

DOUBTS ABOUT MORAL CYNICISM

To call moral cynicism into question we don't have to establish that people never act for selfish motives. It will be sufficient if we can show that, so far as anyone knows, people may sometimes act for moral reasons; that is, that people may sometimes do what they do because they believe they are morally obligated to do that or because they believe that by so acting they will be doing something that will benefit the greatest number of people even though doing so may involve some sacrifice on their own part.

One cannot conclusively refute moral cynicism by pointing at examples of apparently non-selfish behavior, for example, cases of behavior in which a person sacrifices his or her life for the benefit of others. The problem with arguing in this way is that particular cases are subject to alternative interpretations. If one points at such cases to the moral cynic, he or she is likely to respond by pointing out that in the circumstances the sacrificial action may well have had some non-altruistic motive. Perhaps the behavior wasn't freely chosen at all but was simply an automatic response of some sort, or perhaps the doer of the act was in a psychological state which led him or her to perceive the sacrificial act as beneficial to him or herself.

In my judgment, examples of behavior which apparently involve self-sacrifice, while not refuting moral cynicism, do at least raise a question about it. Indeed, in regard to the scientific testing of hypotheses in general, observations of apparent counter-instances to the hypothesis being tested never conclusively refute it. There are always questions of interpretation. One may ask whether the observations were correct, whether the observations were conducted carefully enough, etc. Even if the observed counter-instance is accepted as such, one may ask whether the equipment used in the experiment worked properly or whether there wasn't some unusual parameter which affected the results. Thus, while we cannot refute moral cynicism conclusively, it is not unreasonable to appeal to evidence to suggest that moral cynicism may be mistaken.[2]

There are other reasons for being skeptical about moral cynicism anyway. It is not a scientific theory; it has not been carefully formulated with clear scientific concepts and subjected to rigorous observational testing.

Further, the theory, that no one ever does anything except to benefit him or herself, is unclear because the concept of a self is unclear. The concept of self is a theoretical concept of some sort. We don't observe our selves.[3] Further, there are numerous phenomena, described by neurologists, which suggest that the idea of a unified self, which governs our conscious behavior, is a fiction.[4] Given the lack of clarity of the concept of self, it is not surprising to discover that there is no rigorous confirmation or disconfirmation of moral cynicism.

While I shall not rely exclusively on examples of behavior which apparently is intended to benefit others, I shall call attention to certain widespread cases of apparently other-regarding behavior which have had significant effects in agricultural marketing systems. On the basis of these and other reasons, I argue that moral cynicism is mistaken.

MOTIVES FOR ACTIONS AND PEOPLE'S ROLES

Let us start by dividing people's voluntary behavior into two categories. In the first category are actions in which the person has a significant economic interest. Examples of such actions are purchases of food or other products. In the second category are actions in which the person has no significant economic interest. I often reflect about and make decisions leading to actions on my part on many issues in which I have no economic interest. For example, I may decide that I am in favor of some social policy, e.g., free access to abortions for women, and take steps to support that policy by writing to members of parliament, making contributions to organizations supporting the policy I favor, etc. I envisage no gain or loss to myself as a result of the nation's abortion practices. Nonetheless I act so as to have some influence on the form those practices take. Further, I am sure that I am not unusual in this regard. There are many people who do many things in which they have no economic interest. There are many people, for example, who support environmental causes even though they have essentially no economic interest in the outcome. That people will support such social objectives is a reason for calling moral cynicism into question.

Purchases of food are actions in which a person has an economic interest. Nonetheless, many people have indicated that they are willing to pay more for food in order to accomplish some further objectives. Sometimes these objectives are, or at least appear to be, ethical. For example, many people are willing to pay more for eggs where the hens are not kept in battery cages. Further, many people supported unionization of farm workers in the United States by boycotting certain agricultural products even though those people, no doubt, expected that the outcome of union organization of farm workers would mean higher prices for those food products. That people, through their actions, appear willing to sacrifice their own economic interests to achieve ethical objectives is a reason for doubting the truth of moral cynicism.

Mark Sagoff has argued that people are concerned about the good of society. He says, "Not all of us think of ourselves primarily as consumers. Many of us regard ourselves as citizens as well. As consumers, we act to acquire what we want for ourselves individually; . . . As citizens, . . . we may deliberate over and then seek to achieve together a conception of the good society."[5] Sagoff's remark can be generalized in two respects. First, we tend to think of ourselves not only as citizens of a nation but as morally good people. As such we try to achieve what is, in our judgment, morally good. Often our conception of what is morally good is not identical with our conception of what is good for ourselves. Again we have reason for doubting moral cynicism. Second, on reflection, we think of ourselves as fulfilling more than one social role. We may think of ourselves as agricultural producers, but we also think of ourselves as consumers, as parents, as children, as members of various clubs, etc. This point is of some importance, as we shall now try to show.

Recall that we started this chapter by noting a remark, made several times by various agricultural scientists, that producers won't modify crop production practices except to increase profits. We have taken the scientists who made that remark to be expressing moral cynicism, and we have been trying to present reasons for doubting such cynicism. The realization, however, that the people who are producers also have other roles, that is, are parents, consumers, members of rural communities, etc., suggests a reason for thinking that those scientists were mistaken even if moral cynicism is true.

As a producer, one's objective may well be to maximize net profits. However, as a parent, one's primary objective is the welfare of one's children. While the welfare of one's children will probably suffer if one's income falls too low, the overzealous pursuit of higher income can have seriously detrimental effects on family life and consequently on one's children's welfare also. As a member of a rural community, one may well be strongly motivated to preserve the viability of that community as a means of preserving a way of life that one values highly. While the individuals and families of that community must have sufficient income in order to preserve the community, practices aimed at maximizing the profits of producers can undermine the well-being of the community also. Pollution of wells through use of fertilizers or herbicides can undermine the community. Purchasing practices of a producer trying to maximize his or her own income can undermine the capacity of a community to survive, as happens when producers do not make their purchases locally. Compromising on productivity, and consequently profitability, can sometimes be essential for preserving the quality of life one would like to preserve.

Now consider a person who considers him or herself in a number of distinct roles such as we have been considering. If she or he is wise, she or he will try to achieve ways of satisfying all her primary objectives. To do so will probably require focussing on profitability in her or his production business to a limited extent. However, it will also require some sacrifice of profits in cases where her objectives are to preserve her community or to assure the welfare of her family, etc. The scientist who predicts that improvements to production systems won't occur except to maximize profits is assuming either that producers are nothing but producers, that is, that they have no other primary objectives, or that producers are not wise since they will compromise other primary objectives merely to increase profits. There is, I believe, very little evidence or reason to think that either of these assumptions is true. Most producers also have other objectives which they value highly. Indeed, many people desire to act in accord with their moral obligations. For such people, that is an objective which they value highly. Further, most people are sufficiently wise that they will perceive that to preserve family or community welfare they cannot act solely to maximize profits. It is possible that agricultural production systems will be modified for these other reasons.

Of course, these criticisms of the agricultural scientists are based on guesses, guesses that people have primary objectives other than that of increasing profits and that people will be wise enough to determine ways of achieving a range of primary objectives. Perhaps the agricultural scientist is making the opposite guesses. The experience of the past fifty years or so in agriculture lends some support for his view. Rural—that is farm—populations have suffered large declines in numbers, and consequently rural communities have been uprooted also.[6] This decline is due in large part to technological changes which have dramatically increased productivity per farm worker (at least during the period in question), with consequent decreases in the number of workers necessary to produce food. During this period, people in many industrialized countries permitted this disruption to communities to occur. It may be asked why it is reasonable now to expect that people will strive to achieve satisfaction of objectives other than merely increasing profits, given that they did not do so in the recent past.

There are a number of plausible answers to this question which tell against the agricultural scientist's guesses. First, it is not clear that the decline in farm workers is a result of many people being driven to sacrifice all other objectives to increase profits. I suspect that many people were impressed with what could be accomplished with the power that modern technology yielded. Second, perhaps many of the same people who were so impressed with technological achievements neglected to consider the down side until very recently. Due to criticisms of environmentalists, agrarians such as Wendell Berry, animal welfare advocates such as Ruth Harrison and others, applications of technology will be much more carefully scrutinized. People have learned now that objectives other than merely increasing production are important to them.[7] Third, people in western societies now have, on average, a high enough standard of living that it is not necessary for most people to struggle merely to survive. Such people will not be forced to focus exclusively on increasing meager profits.

Let us return briefly to consideration of moral cynicism. The cynic can argue that his view allows that persons can act so as to achieve all of their primary objectives, and not just maximization of profits. In other words, even if cynicism is true, it is very likely that the agricultural scientists, whose remarks prompted this essay, are mistaken. Even if people do always act so as to benefit themselves, it does not follow that they will act only to maximize profits. People have other objectives as well and, consistently with cynicism, will act to achieve these other objectives. The truth of cynicism, if it is true, does not support the truth of the scientists' remark.

Of course, I am not prepared to agree that moral cynicism is true. As I argued above, it is not at all clear to me that people who are acting to preserve a rural community, or the welfare of some larger political entity, or of people in other nations, or of animals, etc., are necessarily acting to benefit themselves.

MORAL REASONS VERSUS SELFISH REASONS?

At the start of this essay I suggested that the scientists, to whom I have referred several times, were suggesting that reasoning about moral issues was pointless. The suggestion they are making is that since everyone acts to maximize profits (or to benefit him or herself only) there is no point in trying to discover what morally ought to be done. Even if one discovers the morally right thing to do, one won't do it unless it happens to coincide with behavior that will yield maximum profits (or maximum benefit for oneself). We have challenged this argument by challenging the claim that no one ever does anything except to increase profits and even the claim that no one ever does anything except to benefit him or herself. However, the argument that moral reasoning is pointless may be challenged on other grounds.

This argument presupposes that there is an exclusive dichotomy between acting for moral reasons and acting to benefit oneself. That is, this argument presupposes that if a person acts to benefit himself then he is not acting for moral reasons and vice versa. However, this assumption is subject to serious doubt and combines psychological and ethical elements. That this is so may be seen by considering theories about human motivation particularly motivation to be moral or to act morally. There is an old psychological theory which implies that normal people are endowed with a conscience, that is, a faculty for distinguishing right from wrong, and with motivations to act in accordance with the dictates of conscience.[8] In such a theory one's motivation to perform some action could spring both from the desire to benefit oneself (one's self-love) and from the desire to act in accordance with the dictates of one's conscience.

The assumption that we have a conscience, that is, a faculty which enables us to distinguish moral good and evil, has largely, I believe, been abandoned. We are more likely to think in terms of a Freudian super-ego, that is, a faculty for internalizing rules of behavior to which we are originally subjected by our care-givers.[9] The rules which we internalize are not necessarily moral truths, and so our recognition of these rules is not knowledge of moral truths.

Nonetheless, the assumption that our motivation is either moral motivation or selfish motivation and not both is questionable. According to one moral theory, known as rational egoism, our moral obligations are a function of what benefits ourselves. On such a theory moral motivation is simply rational and well-informed selfish motivation. Moral reasoning should serve, in such a view, to determine what is really of benefit to ourselves.[10]

Even if one subscribes to the view that our fundamental moral obligation is to produce the greatest amount of good and the least amount of evil, a moral theory which may be called consequentialism, moral reasons and selfish reasons are not mutually exclusive categories. In aiming to produce the greatest amount of good, one must consider what is good for oneself as well as what is good for others. Indeed, consideration of what is good for oneself could, in a great many cases, be of the greatest importance in such a view since many people in many circumstances are not in a position to do much good for others, but they are in a position to do more good for themselves. There are even deeper reasons for objecting to the view that moral reasoning is pointless because no one ever does anything except to benefit him or herself. This theory presupposes that people have a self, that this self is perhaps (once one is mature) fully fixed or determined, and further, that moral ideals are not part of this self. These presuppositions are questionable psychological assumptions. The self, as we have observed above, is an entity which is postulated on theoretical grounds. Psychological theories concerning the nature of human selves abound. To my knowledge, no one theory is strongly supported by scientific evidence. So far as we know, the self, if there is such an entity, may evolve throughout most of one's life. Further, in the formation of one's self, moral ideals may play a significant role. Indeed, I would guess that this is the case. Virtually all of us have a strong desire to be good people, at least in our own eyes. The psychological or motivational function of much moral reasoning may be to determine one's obligations in accord with ideals that are incorporated into one's idea of him or herself. We may engage in moral reasoning in order to discover what we are morally obligated to do in order to live up to our own ideals. Further, the moral reasoning that we do may contribute to the evolution of ourselves, that is, to the formation of our future selves.

Let us elaborate on the above point. Let us envisage a person in a set of circumstances trying to decide whether to perform act A or act B. Suppose that the person's doing act A will yield the greatest profits, and suppose further that the person believes that such action is morally wrong but that he or she will automatically do act A anyway. However, such a person may regret that he always acts selfishly. In such a case the person might decide to try to change his or her character so that, in future circumstances, when presented with comparable alternatives, he or she will not automatically choose to act selfishly but will act in accord with what he or she determines to be his or her duty. Moral reasoning could play a role in this process, both in the determination of what we ought to do and in the determination of what to do to change our character.

We have been stressing the function of moral reasoning from an individual perspective. However, from a social point of view, it is clear that moral reasoning could be of great value even if we all act only to benefit ourselves. A society of beings motivated solely by self-interest or self-love would need to have some mechanism of achieving sufficient mutual acceptance among the potentially conflicting objectives of the members of that society to enable them to live in relative peace and stability. That would be an objective held in common by virtually all members of any society. For such mutual acceptance to be achieved, it appears that there must be considerable sharing of beliefs regarding acceptable norms of behavior. Clearly, moral reasoning would be of great value as a means of achieving and maintaining such agreement. Let us briefly consider why this is so.

In a society, it is reasonable to expect that there will be divergence of opinion concerning what behavior to tolerate. We need only to think about all the controversies in our societies to see that this is true. Should we tolerate abortion? Should we tolerate capital punishment of any criminals? Should we tolerate pornographic films or literature? Many controversies exist concerning what forms of commercial activities should be tolerated. Should we tolerate drug dealers, prostitutes, etc.? Should we allow corporate executives to profit by trading in stocks on the basis of their insider knowledge? Should we tolerate unregulated monopolies? Clearly, many other comparable questions could be raised. Some of these questions concern agricultural practices. Should we tolerate use of DDT in food production? Should we tolerate elimination of wetlands around farms or windbreaks around farms?

Given that such divergence of opinion exists, how can it be resolved? One method would be to settle such disagreements by force. Clearly, for the most part resort to force is irrational, given that there are alternative methods of resolving disagreements which permit greater realization of individual objectives or lower costs. Such an alternative is to engage in reasoning to try to discover practices which we can all accept without resorting to force. That is a role that moral reasoning can play. Thus, even if moral cynicism is true, moral reasoning should not be dismissed as pointless.

SUMMARY

In this chapter we have been considering whether it is rational to engage in moral reasoning. We have noted that some people may desire to undertake this activity itself, while others may desire the knowledge it yields. Very likely most people do not fall into either of these categories. We have tried to challenge the hypothesis that if moral cynicism were true, it would not be rational for them to engage in moral reasoning. We have argued that it could be rational to engage in moral reasoning since there are good reasons to think that moral cynicism is not true. It presupposes a psychological theory which may well be mistaken. Further, when we think about our many objectives and roles in life, we see that we often have reason not to act selfishly. Besides being producers and consumers, we are also members of a community, parents, etc. We desire to achieve a number of objectives in addition to that of benefiting ourselves. Finally, we noted that when one considers the fact that we live in societies, even if we are merely selfish, moral reasoning will probably be of great value in developing a network of beliefs and patterns of behavior within which we can all live and pursue our individual objectives.

NOTES

1. For a discussion of psychological egoism, see C. D. Broad, "Egoism as a Theory of Human Motives," 111–18.

2. In some people's minds, moral cynicism or psychological egoism appear so obviously true as to be virtually certain. However, this was not always the case. Socrates apparently believed that no one would ever deliberately act immorally since doing so would cause harm to him or herself. See the discussion in *Gorgias*, 468–70. In Joseph Butler, *Sermons on Human Nature*, Butler also argued that the theory that everyone always acts to benefit himself is mistaken. For example, a person who desires to harm someone else may even harm him or herself because the desire to harm the other is greater than the desire to benefit oneself. Butler's views are analyzed in C. D. Broad, *Five Types of Ethical Theory*, 62.

3. This point was made by David Hume. See Hume, *A Treatise of Human Nature*, 251.

4. Much of this material is explained in Patricia S. Churchland, *Neurophilosophy: Toward a Unified Science of the Mind/Brain*, chap. 5.

5. Mark Sagoff, *The Economy of the Earth*, 27.

6. There are many references which report such a decline. Wendell Berry claims that from 1946 to 1976 the farm population in the United States declined from thirty million to nine million. Wendell Berry, *The Gift of Good Land*, 105.

7. Jorge Nef et al., *Ethics and Technology*, is a collection of papers delivered at the University of Guelph, Guelph, Ontario, in which various aspects of modern technology, including agricultural technology, were evaluated on ethical grounds.

8. Butler held such a theory. See reference in note 2, above. The concept of conscience is also discussed in A. Campbell Garnett, "Conscience and Conscientiousness."

9. One account of Freud's views on the super-ego can be found in Sigmund Freud, "Group Psychology and the Analysis of the Ego."

10. For a consideration of the idea that morality is a function of rational self-interest, see David P. Gauthier, ed., *Morality and Rational Self-Interest*, part 3. This book contains a bibliographical essay which contains further references. A sustained effort to defend such a perspective is found in Jan Nerveson, *The Libertarian Idea*.

7. Views of Rationality in Ethics

AGRICULTURAL SCIENTISTS, LIKE many other people, accept many ethical principles. As examples, consider principles such as, that it is morally acceptable to do scientific research in a university context which is supported by profit-making corporations, that it is morally acceptable at the present time to do research aimed at developing pesticide tolerant cultivars, that it is morally acceptable at the present time to do research aimed at increasing efficiency in production of dairy or other products, that it is morally acceptable for virtually all graduate training of scientists to focus on empirical as opposed to ethical issues, etc.

In saying that agricultural scientists accept these and other ethical principles I do not mean to assert that they think that these principles are true, or that they have been proven. I suspect that most scientists are doubtful about the possibility of proving any moral principles. Further, I believe that most agricultural scientists would be reluctant to commit themselves on what they would regard as a non-scientific or philosophical issue, that is, on whether moral principles are either true or false. However, many scientists who do research on increasing productivity of dairy cattle, or on developing pesticide tolerant cultivars, etc., regard such behavior as being morally acceptable. I have no doubt that many scientists would support moral principles such as the above if their activities in accordance with these principles were challenged on ethical grounds.

Since, as noted in prior chapters, scientists are prone to regard their critics as irrational, must they (the scientists) not regard the moral principles that they accept as, somehow, rational or rationally grounded? Indeed, in suggesting that the critic's ethical principles should be rejected since they (either the critics or the principles) are not rational, the scientists are suggesting that ethical principles should be accepted only if the principles are rational. This poses the question which I wish to consider in this chapter, namely, are some ethical principles rational or established on the basis of reason? Since this question poses deep theoretical issues of philosophy, we shall not attempt to establish an answer to it or even to make a significant contribution to contemporary philosophical investigations which have such an objective. Rather, we shall review several theories which imply that some ethical principles can be established on the basis of reason. Since this material may well be regarded as an introductory essay in moral philosophy, I want to say briefly why I regard it as useful to include it in this volume.

First, some scientists take it as obviously true that ethical principles are grounded on emotion or that they are essentially or ultimately merely expressions of feeling. Let us call a theory about ethical principles which has such implications an "emotivist theory." Scientists who subscribe to emotivist theories are unwilling to devote much effort to attempts at finding rational solutions to ethical disagreements concerning agricultural policies or practices. This unwillingness is expressed in many ways. The scientists devote little or none of their own efforts toward thinking about such matters. Further, they tend to discourage other scientists or agricultural students from devoting serious effort to these matters. An agricultural student studying for a master's or doctor's degree in an agriculture department at a university will be allowed to devote very little, if any, of his or her course work or research to an ethical investigation. Editors and referees for almost all scientific journals will not consider manuscripts devoted to ethical issues. Even when scientists have made some efforts to contribute to solving an ethical issue, for example, by writing a paper devoted to ethical issues concerning use of animals in scientific research, little effort has been devoted to study of prior serious philosophical work on the issue or to systematically developing a well-reasoned position on the issue. Often, in such cases, the scientist is contented with attempted refutations of overly simplified statements of contentious issues. Indeed, I have sometimes heard scientists employ fallacious arguments to try to refute ethical claims with which they disagree. For example, I have heard scientists try to refute the theory that animals have moral rights by claiming that the advocates of this theory are getting wealthy by writing books, giving lectures, etc.[1]

However, the theory that ethical principles are grounded on, or merely expressions of, emotion is not obviously true. This is a philosophical assumption. While I will not try to show that this assumption is false, I hope, by a brief introduction to alternative views on this matter, to induce readers who subscribe to such a belief to question their belief. After all, the belief may be false, and further may not be compatible with other assumptions which they make. For example, let us consider a scientist who objects to the tactics employed by some critics of agriculture, for example, to an appeal by a popular singer in support of vegetarianism, on the grounds that resort to such a tactic does not involve appeals to evidence or reason. If the scientist argues that it is morally unacceptable to resort to such a tactic, does that scientist not at least tacitly appeal to some moral principle? But, if the scientist accepts an emotivist theory about ethics, is not the scientist who argues against the tactic appealing to what is in his own view a non-rational principle, a principle which is not grounded on reason or evidence? In other words, by accepting an emotivist view of ethics, such a scientist may be taking a position which implies that his or her objection to the critic's tactics is an unsound objection. By taking an emotivist view of ethics, such a scientist may be cutting off one of the branches which supports his or her own position.

I have indicated above that some scientists with whom I have discussed ethical issues have indicated that they think that all ethical judgments are essentially expressions of emotion and not supported by reason. However, it is by no means true that all agricultural scientists hold such a view. Many scientists appear to subscribe to some version of a consequentialist or utilitarian ethical principle.[2] They express such a view when they argue that some agricultural practice, for example, use of genetically engineered bovine growth hormone to increase dairy production, is morally justified because the benefits outweigh any harms or costs. Apparently they assume that this principle is rationally justified, while appeals to other ethical principles are not rationally justified. But, we may ask, how can the utilitarian principle (or the scientific modification of it) be justified by reason or evidence? The scientist who holds that this or some other ethical principle is rationally justified holds a view which is incompatible with the emotivist views of some of his or her colleagues. This being the case, he or she should be interested in considering how rational justification of ethical principles might be possible. Further, the scientist who holds to a consequentialist ethical principle is open to criticism from thinkers who reject such principles. Again, the scientist should be interested in how rational justification of ethical principles may be possible.

Let us move to my second reason for introducing this material in this work. In my occasional discussions of ethical issues with agricultural scientists, I have often gotten the impression that the scientist with whom I am conversing holds the view that a practice is morally acceptable if and only if adherence to the practice is rational, for example, that it is morally acceptable to use pesticides if and only if it is rational to use pesticides. Let us call this view "principle R."

Principle R: A practice is morally acceptable if and only if adherence to the practice is rational.

Now, we may ask, what is the status of this principle? Is it an expression of emotion, or can it be established by the use of reasoning? If principle R can be established by the use of reasoning, and if principle R is an ethical assumption, then the emotivist theory of ethics must be mistaken, since it would be an ethical principle that can be established by reason, contrary to what the emotivist theory implies. The scientist who is committed to an emotivist theory of ethics and to principle R must also hold that principle R is not an ethical principle or else her or his acceptance of principle R will involve her in self-contradictory beliefs. However, it appears that principle R is an ethical principle, since it is a principle about what is morally acceptable. It appears that principle R is itself an ethical assumption concerning the relations between reason and morality. Further, it is not an assumption with which there is universal agreement. Some thinkers have maintained that our fundamental obligations must be accepted on faith as they cannot be established by the use of our reason.[3] In such views, individual actions or social practices which are performed in order to fulfill such obligations may be ethical even if they are not rational. For example, abstaining from work on a Sabbath day may be ethical even if it is not rational. In any case, if principle R is an ethical assumption, then scientists cannot consistently subscribe both to principle R and to an emotivist theory of ethics. Scientists who find themselves inclined to accept principle R should be willing to consider the ways in which ethical principles might justifiably be said to be rational.

FIRST VIEW OF RATIONALITY IN ETHICS

Plato suggests that all knowledge is true opinion which is established on the basis of reason. Reason, as Plato understood it, excluded reports derived from the use of the senses. Any such reports were, in Plato's view, inherently obscure and so incapable of proof.[4] To contemporary scientists, Plato's view may seem perverse since, in contemporary views, the only evidence capable of establishing the truth of claims is sensory evidence and Plato clearly denies that sensory evidence can play that role. Even skeptics who maintain that we can establish no truths accord sensory evidence a role as a basis for refuting allegedly false scientific claims; however, in Plato's view sensory observation cannot play this role either.[5]

While many thinkers have abandoned Plato's idea of the capacity of reason, they have accepted a modified version of it. This is the view that human knowledge is divisible into two categories. One category consists of almost all scientific knowledge. Such knowledge, for example, knowledge of physics, chemistry, biology, etc., consists of principles established on the basis of sensory evidence. The second category consists of principles established by reason alone. In such views, principles of pure mathematics and logic fall into the second category of knowledge, for example, the principle that no proposition and its denial can both be true. Other examples could be drawn from the simple truths of arithmetic. Until the development of non-Euclidian geometries in the nineteenth century, views of this sort usually cited geometry as an example of a kind of knowledge which rested solely on the basis of pure reason.[6]

Immanuel Kant maintained that some principles of ethics can be established on the basis of pure reason.[7] A contemporary philosopher, Alan Gewirth, has argued that a principle, which he calls the "principle of generic consistency," can be established in this way. According to this principle, we are required to act in accord with the generic rights of our recipients as well as of ourselves. Gewirth's view, like Kant's, starts on the assumption that we can do things, i.e., act. In light of this capacity we are agents rather than merely passive beings, beings who merely endure the effects of causes which modify us. There are certain features which are essential to all actions. Gewirth calls these features "generic features." The generic features of actions are conditions that are necessary for any action to be performed. In arguing for the principle of generic consistency, he maintains that in light of the generic features of actions all agents have certain moral rights, namely rights to liberty and well-being, which must be respected.[8]

I am not going enter into a critical discussion of Gewirth's or Kant's views concerning basic moral principles. I make reference to them here only to call attention to the idea that if a person says that we are obligated only by moral principles based on reason, that person may be interpreted as expressing commitment to a view such as that of Gewirth or Kant. Agricultural scientists who appear to be committed to the idea that we ought to accept only rational moral principles could reasonably be called upon to express some such principle as well as to show how it is applicable to the agricultural context (and perhaps also to defend their thought on this matter against reasonable criticism).

Given the disposition of many scientists to think that the only evidence which could justify our beliefs is sensory observations, it might be of interest to consider some examples which, according to some ways of thinking, indicate that some of our knowledge is justified by pure reason. Prior to moving to consideration of a second view of rationality in ethics, let us briefly discuss the question of how we could know the principles of logic or pure reasoning to which arguments such as that of Kant and Gewirth appeal. To understand this question, it is useful to illustrate it by reference to some philosophical questions regarding very fundamental principles of reasoning.

In our efforts to understand the universe in which we find ourselves, we regularly make use of such basic principles. For example, we distinguish between fallacious reasonings and logically valid reasonings by reference to such principles. Let us give two examples to illustrate. First, it is common in non-scientific contexts to find people arguing that some general principle must be true because it has been found to be true in a great many instances. For example, someone may say that in a great many cases people exposed to drafts have gotten colds and consequently that exposure to drafts causes colds. Clearly, any competent scientist will argue that drawing this general conclusion about colds is not warranted by the evidence cited. The inference in this case to the general conclusion concerning the cause of colds is fallacious. Reasoning to a causal claim is warranted, according to scientific standards, only if the claim has been tested in accord with rigorously developed statistical protocols. Only such protocols are thought to reliably distinguish accidental correlations from valid causal principles. Now, a question which may be raised at this point is whether a sufficient reason can be given for the assumption that scientific reasoning should be restricted in this way. A scientist who holds that this restriction on scientific methods is justified may think it possible to prove that such a restriction is the true method of getting knowledge about the world.

This question, whether it is possible to prove that only the scientific method yields knowledge about the world, is a version of the philosophical problem of induction. It is also sometimes referred to as Hume's problem, since the philosopher David Hume presented strong arguments which may be interpreted as showing that we cannot establish this assumption by any form of human reasoning.9 In a key part of his argument, Hume stressed that we cannot prove that the principle restricting scientific reasoning is correct by a scientific argument, that is, by an argument which appeals to this very principle. To appeal to the correctness of scientific reasoning to prove that standards of scientific reasoning are correct is to beg the very question at issue. If Hume was correct on this matter, and I think he was, and if there is no non-scientific way to establish that the scientific method and only the scientific method yields knowledge of the universe, then there can be no rational or scientific demonstration which would prove the correctness of the scientific assumption.

Second, let us consider an even older example. It is not unusual in reviewing reasonings to observe that at least one assertion which a person has made must be mistaken because some assertion that the person has made contradicts another assertion that the person has made. This argument appeals to a principle of logic known as the "principle of contradiction" and, clearly, is a very fundamental principle of scientific reasoning. However, as with the above example, we can ask whether any demonstration can be given which shows that the principle of contradiction is correct; as might be expected, it has been recognized, at least since the work of Aristotle in ancient times, that this principle cannot be proved. Any alleged proof of the principle of contradiction would appeal to the principle of contradiction itself and so beg the question at issue.

Given that we cannot give a non-circular proof of such basic methodological or logical principles, one may ask what reason we can have for accepting them as correct. One answer is a theory of knowledge known as "intuitionism." We shall next briefly explain this theory. Consideration of this theory will also provide a motivation for looking at a second view of rationality in ethics.

Intuitionist theories of knowledge may be divided into two categories. In the first category are theories which affirm that some principles are known to be true without proof. Such principles are said to be "self-evident." These principles were referred to traditionally as axioms. According to such theories, whatever knowledge we possess is either an axiom or deducible from such axioms by rules of inference which are themselves axiomatic, i.e., known to be true without proof. With regard to the principle of contradiction and to the methodological principle regarding inference to general causal principles, the intuitionist could claim that such principles are known by intuition, that is, by our capacity to recognize the truth of self-evident truths. Further, the intuitionist would claim that the assumptions on which Kant and Gewirth based their proofs of fundamental moral principles were also known by intuition.

Intuition, as a basis for knowledge, has fallen into disrepute during much of the nineteenth and twentieth centuries. This consequence appears largely to be a result of doubts arising concerning principles formerly thought to be known by intuition. In the nineteenth century doubts were cast on geometrical assumptions. Later, doubts were cast on a principle of logic (though not on the principle of contradiction) thought to be known by intuition through the discovery that the principle (in conjunction with other intuitively warranted principles) had paradoxical implications. Given that intuition led to results which were either doubtful, as in the geometrical case, or false, as in the case of the logical principle, the assumption that through intuition we had a type of knowledge of basic principles of reasoning was called into question.[10]

In a more moderate form, the intuitionist rejects the assumption that intuition is itself a source of knowledge of basic truths of logic or of ethics, and holds only that intuition is a type of evidence for such principles which must then be rigorously evaluated largely through the attempt to develop a complete and internally consistent system of beliefs. Some principles, which are apparently acceptable on intuitive grounds, are ultimately rejected, as they do not readily yield such a system of beliefs.[11]

Many scientists will no doubt be skeptical even of the moderate form of intuitionism. The basic scientific objection to intuitionism was expressed by the philosopher C. S. Peirce at the end of the nineteenth century when he said of such a view that "It makes of inquiry something similar to the development of taste; but taste, unfortunately, is always more or less a matter of fashion."[12] That something is widely felt or thought to be true is not regarded as evidence that it is true.

While this notion of rationality is a reasonable interpretation of the claim that we should accept only rational principles as our basic ethical norms, I am going to assume that this is not a correct interpretation of the views of agricultural scientists. Even if such scientists were willing to accept intuition as a basis for some knowledge, I suspect the scientists' faith in rationality does not involve a belief that we can establish ethical principles on the basis of pure reason, that is, on the basis of reasons which exclude all claims based on sensory evidence. Let us then move on to consideration of other notions concerning rationality.

SECOND VIEW OF RATIONALITY IN ETHICS

People's beliefs or opinions are rational, in one sense of the term, if they are established scientifically. In our discussion of the rationality of attributing beliefs or desires to animals, we discussed two views concerning the scientific justification of beliefs, extreme empiricism and pragmatism. A possible view concerning the rationality of ethical principles is to hold that people's ethical beliefs are rational providing that they are scientifically justified. Possibly, then, this is what scientists have in mind when they suggest that ethical principles are acceptable if they are rational.

The suggestion that ethical principles can be scientifically warranted may appear questionable. How is it possible to establish a moral principle scientifically? For example, let us ask, how is it possible to establish, on scientific grounds, that it is morally acceptable at the present time to develop herbicide resistant cultivars for various vegetable crops? For a statement to be established on scientific grounds, either the statement must be a report of careful observations or else the statement must play an essential role in explanations of sensory observations. Could a claim such as that about herbicide tolerant cultivars be established in either of these ways?

Let us assume that a statement, such as that it is morally acceptable to develop herbicide resistant cultivars, is not a report of an observation and so cannot be established in the way that such reports are established. Few people will challenge this assumption; further, it seems clear that moral acceptability is not literally seen, or heard, or smelled, or touched, and so, in general, is not observed. Statements of moral principle, if they are to be scientifically warranted at all, must be warranted through entering into explanatory contexts. How is this possible?

Some philosophers have attempted to show that moral statements can be confirmed through treating such statements as a sub-category of value statements, and treating value statements in turn as a sub-category of biological or psychological statements. For example, Herbert Spencer suggested that when we describe conduct as morally good, what we mean is that such conduct is "conducive to life." In general, he thought, "good" and "bad" are terms which refer respectively to pleasurable and disagreeable sensations, or to conditions which tend to produce such sensations. Given the assumption that conditions which are "conducive to life" are conditions which produce a "surplus of pleasurable feelings," moral goodness consists then in actions which are conducive to life.[13] Given that conditions which are conducive to extending individual lives or to development of further varieties of life forms can be determined by scientific methods, in Spencer's view, ethical principles could be determined in such a manner also.[14]

I suspect that some scientists may find themselves disposed to agree with a view such as Spencer's. Often, when scientists are engaged in controversies regarding what ought to be done, they assume, often without question, that the controversy should be settled by appeal to scientific reasoning. Such scientists may be assuming that a view such as Spencer's is correct. They may feel that through scientific reasoning one can determine which action, among the available alternatives, will yield a surplus of pleasure over pain.

However, other philosophers and scientists would be inclined to reject Spencer's views for any of a number of different reasons. Some thinkers would object to the idea that whatever is conducive to life is, ipso facto, morally good. Conditions which lead to an increase in the numbers of microorganisms are conducive to life of a certain sort, but many of us would be inclined to think that they are not always morally good. Even if "life" is restricted to "human life," we might not agree with Spencer. It might not be good, or morally good, to increase the quantity of human lives. Further, some people will object to the value assumption which underlies Spencer's view, that is, the assumption that value consists in pleasurable feelings.

Other thinkers might challenge Spencer's assumption that observational evidence can serve to establish (or to disconfirm) ethical judgments. Consider the example which we have mentioned above, namely that it is morally acceptable (or morally required) for scientists to develop herbicide tolerant cultivars. But does this judgment play a role in any such explanations: that is, are there any observational data such that the best explanation of these data includes the above moral judgment? Conceivably someone might argue for an affirmative answer to this question as follows: Some scientists have been observed doing research aimed at developing herbicide tolerant cultivars. Someone might argue that this observation is best explained by the claim that those scientists, because of their background and knowledge, and because of societies' need for such cultivars, are morally obligated to do such research. Here, there is a claim that the best explanation for the observed behavior of the scientists includes a claim about moral obligations. The person who made this claim could argue that the statement about the moral obligation enters into the explanation of the behavior and, in consequence, the moral judgment receives some degree of confirmation.

However, other thinkers, including scientists disposed to accept an emotivist analysis of moral judgments, would deny that the above argument shows that moral judgments can receive observational confirmation. They will argue that the scientist's observed behavior is best explained by reference to his (or her) *beliefs* about his (or her) moral obligations; they will say that what this example illustrates is how judgments about beliefs in moral obligations can be confirmed and not how moral judgments can be confirmed. Those who take this position will not agree with Spencer's view that moral judgments are established by scientific evidence, and thus may not accept the conclusion that moral judgments are rational.[15]

THIRD VIEW OF RATIONALITY IN ETHICS

Thus far we have considered two views of rationality. According to the first view, judgments are rational providing they are established by reason itself, where reason is understood as excluding any dependence on sensory observations. According to the second view of rationality, judgments are rational providing that they are established in accordance with canons of good scientific reasoning. Possibly some scientists, who both reject the idea that we have a faculty of intuition capable of recognizing fundamental moral truths and accept the idea that moral judgments cannot be established by scientific methods, would be prepared to conclude at this point that moral principles cannot be rational since they cannot be established by human reason. However, drawing this conclusion at this point would be premature.

A still broader notion of rationality is possible. According to the second notion of rationality, the ultimate evidence for all rational beliefs is sensory evidence. However, it is possible to maintain that in addition to sensory evidence, certain of our feelings count as evidence. Theorists who subscribe to this notion of rationality may speak of moral feelings or feelings of moral obligation. Such feelings play roles in moral reasoning comparable to the roles played by sensory observation in scientific reasoning. Whereas scientific generalizations can be disconfirmed by observed counter-instances, moral generalizations can be disconfirmed by moral judgments based on feelings of moral obligation which are counter-instances to those moral generalizations. For example, consider the generalization G(1):

G(1): It is always morally acceptable to use herbicides that are effective, providing the herbicides have not been proven dangerous to human health. Suppose that in particular circumstances some people have a feeling that they are morally obligated not to use an effective herbicide even though the herbicide has not been proven unsafe. In light of such a feeling, they might reject G(1). According to this third view of rationality, rejection of G(1) because it conflicts with the moral feeling in question is perfectly rational.[16] Just as some thinkers hold that scientific generalizations can be confirmed by observed instances, one could hold that general moral principles are confirmed by the appropriate moral feelings.

Some people might object to this theory concerning moral reasoning by claiming that feelings are too subjective to be taken as evidence that can serve to confirm or disconfirm ethical generalizations. In support of this it might be argued that feelings are psychological states, and vary from one individual to another. However, this objection, at least as it is stated here, should not be accorded any weight. To see this, it is sufficient to note that sensory observations are also psychological states of individuals and vary from one person to another. It is part of the human predicament that any judgments we make about the nature of the external physical world are a result of psychological states (observations) which are due, in part, to interactions between various forms of energy and our sense organs. Similarly, our moral judgments might also be a result of psychological states (feelings) which are due, in part, to various forms of energy and (perhaps other) parts of our nervous systems; since we accept one sort of psychological state as evidence for scientific judgments, why should we not take another sort of psychological state as evidence for moral judgments?[17] Of course, we have not presented enough argument here to settle the issue posed by the objection under consideration. Pursuing this objection further would raise complex metaphysical or epistemological matters. Let us rather move on to a fourth view of rationality.

A FOURTH VIEW OF RATIONALITY

Up to now we have been considering whether ethical judgments could be rational by considering whether such judgments could be proved or shown to be warranted by reason. Our three views of rationality are three views concerning the nature of the evidence or reasons which conceivably might be the rational support for ethical principles or judgments. Now let us describe another view of the way that ethical judgments might be said to be rational. According to this view of rationality, a person is said to be rational if he or she acts (perfectly) prudently. Moral principles might be said to be rational if they are the principles that such prudent people would adopt. Let us discuss this idea in more detail.

By definition, a perfectly prudent person will never be motivated to sacrifice his or her own desires or objectives to achieve the objectives of other people. This is not to say that such a person must not be concerned about the welfare of others. A prudent person could be concerned about the welfare of others as a means of furthering her or his own welfare. Further, a prudent person might have desires to benefit some other people, for example, his or her loved ones, and could be motivated to sacrifice some of her or his desires to achieve this desire. This is simply an instance of a prudent person having to sacrifice some desires when his or her desires are incompatible with each other.

It is generally accepted that acting in accordance with moral principles sometimes, perhaps often, involves sacrifice of some of one's desires. Thus, it is reasonable to ask, would a prudent person deliberately act in accord with moral principles? From what we have said about prudent people we can say that sometimes they will. Sometimes acting in accord with moral principles will have the same implications for action as acting prudently. This could occur, for example, if both moral principle and prudence enjoined a person to help someone, e.g., a neighbor. If you help your neighbor when she or he needs help and you are likely to need help at some point in the future then the neighbor is more likely to help you, at least if he or she thinks that you would be likely to help him again should the need arise. In other ways, also, moral principle could require the same behavior that the prudent person desires to do anyway.

However, it appears that not all moral behavior will coincide with behavior dictated by individual desires, and thus that sometimes, acting morally is imprudent and so irrational. Is this true? Will a person who always tries to act morally necessarily act irrationally on some occasions? Some philosophers have developed theories, and arguments based on those theories, which imply a negative answer to these questions. These theories are referred to sometimes as "rational egoism" and sometimes as "contractarianism." Basically, what these theories assert is that if a person is not only prudent but also rationally evaluates his desires or interests fully, so as to determine the way to maximize the satisfaction of his desires, he will discover that, by being generally honest, faithfully keeping contracts, respecting property of others and, in general, acting in recognizably moral ways, he achieves the greatest overall satisfaction of his desires.

It would be inappropriate here to discuss contractarian views in great detail. Let us indicate sketchily their basic approach. People are assumed to be essentially prudent, as indicated above, that is, in general, people are not interested in benefiting others. However, if a person seeks to benefit himself through harming others, e.g., injuring them or taking what the others have produced, he will suffer retaliation. Further, if a person refuses to cooperate in the achievement of joint projects, e.g., mutual defense, then he will be subject to attack by others who realize that he can be overpowered.

In some contractarian views it is assumed that people are sufficiently rational to realize that they will be better off, on the whole, if they abstain from injuring others, providing that the others abstain from injuring them, and if they participate cooperatively in the achievement of certain objectives which they have in common with others. People enter into agreements with each other, under conditions which require that the agreements be kept in order to achieve the mutually beneficial consequences of such arrangements.[18] In other contractarian views it is suggested that moral principles are the principles which prudent people would adopt if they were perfectly rational.[19]

Contractarianism is a highly controversial ethical perspective. Questions have been raised concerning the concept of a rational being, a concept which is clearly central to this perspective.[20] Serious problems have been raised concerning the rationality of keeping contracts. Further, since presumably one has obligations, in such a view, only to beings who are capable of understanding contracts and of retaliating if they are violated, it appears that in contractarian views we have no obligations to animals or to people who are too feeble to defend themselves.[21]

At this point, we cannot say that contractarianism is the correct moral perspective. Nonetheless, it is appropriate to include the idea of contractarianism in this essay in which we are considering whether ethical principles are rational. Agricultural scientists who take the position that ethical principles are not rational are, in effect, assuming that each of the four perspectives on rationality which we have described is mistaken. This is a major assumption—one which should not be accepted without careful thought. Agricultural scientists inclined to accept principle R (or some similar principle) should clarify their thought by trying to determine to which view of rationality they subscribe.

SUMMARY

In this chapter we have tried to indicate that the question, whether ethical principles can be rationally justified, should be of some interest to agricultural scientists. Some scientists hold emotivist views which imply that ethical principles cannot be justified. Such scientists hold views which may undermine the rational basis for some of their objections to positions taken or tactics used by agricultural critics. Other scientists apparently hold that certain ethical principles are justified by reason. They need to think about the nature of rational justification of ethics in order to engage in discussion with critics who appeal to alternative ethical principles.

To prompt some attention to this important matter, we have briefly reviewed four views as to the possibility of rational justification of ethical principles. According to one view, ethical principles are justified by appeal to principles known to reason, such as the principle of contradiction in logic, because such principles are self-evident or evident to us through our faculty of intuition. According to a second view, ethical principles are justifiable by reference to observations in a manner essentially the same as that used in science to establish the truth of non-ethical principles. According to a third view, the evidence which supports ethical principles or ethical judgements consists of moral feelings (and perhaps sensory observations as well). This third view is closely tied to a view we discussed earlier in our discussion of reason and emotion. In that chapter we suggested that feeling and emotion might themselves be a kind of evidence or reason. The fourth view is that ethical principles which would be accepted by a perfectly rational prudent being (or such a being who was required to compromise with other beings in order to obtain his or her objectives) are rationally justified.

NOTES

1. The fallacy that the scientist is committing in this case is called "ad hominem." Clearly, ad hominem argments do not establish the correctness of claims about causes and effects. Such arguments are equally unsatisfactory where the issue is an ethical claim. I should, no doubt, give some reference to written examples of such statements. I have seen much superficial discussion concerning the use of animals in scientific research both by scientists, who tend to support such uses of animals, and by those people opposed to such uses.

2. Utilitarianism is the view that an action is morally acceptable if overall it produces the greatest balance of pleasure over pain.

3. For one discussion of the relations of faith and reason, see John Locke, *An Essay Concerning Human Understanding*, vol. 4, chap. 18.

4. Plato's views on knowledge are discussed in a number of his dialogues. Of particular importance are the Republic, Theaetetus, Sophist and Meno.

5. A contemporary thinker who holds such a skeptical view is Karl R. Popper. See Karl R. Popper, *The Logic of Scientific Discovery*.

6. An example of a thinker who held such a view is Immanuel Kant. See Immanuel Kant, *Critique of Pure Reason*.

7. Immanuel Kant defended such a position in Immanuel Kant, *Critique of Practical Reason*. Kant referred to the basic principle of morality as the categorical imperative. In one formulation this principle is: Act so that the maxim of your will could always hold at the same time as a principle establishing universal law. In formulating the categorical imperative in this way, Kant was assuming that when we do something, i.e., act, we have in mind a guiding rule or maxim. According to the categorical imperative, we are obligated to act in accordance with maxims that could be the basis for legislation that would be acceptable to all rational beings.

8. Gewirth's views are explained in his book Alan Gewirth, *Reason and Morality*.

9. Hume discussed this issue in both of his major works, namely David Hume, *A Treatise of Human Nature*, vol. 1, part 3, and David Hume, *An Enquiry Concerning Human Understanding*, section 7. There are many discussions concerning efforts to circumvent Hume's reasoning concerning the problem of induction in modern works on philosophy of science.

10. The logical principle called into question is called the "axiom of comprehension." According to this axiom, for each meaningful descriptive expression there is a class of entities, namely the class of entities of which that expression is true. The paradoxical implication derived from this principle is known as "Russell's paradox" after its discoverer, Bertrand Russell. Russell's paradox is described, along with a number of other paradoxes, in Bertrand Russell, "Mathematical Logic as Based on the Theory of Types," 59.

11. A view such as this was expressed in John Rawls, *A Theory of Justice*. The theory has been widely discussed and is known as the "theory of wide reflective equilibrium." Tom Regan adopted this theory as the epistemological basis for the moral theory he developed in Regan, *The Case for Animal Rights*, 133.

12. C. S. Peirce, "The Fixation of Belief," 16.

13. Spencer's thought is contained in Herbert Spencer, *The Data of Ethics*. A brief excerpt is contained in Sontag et al., *Approaches to Ethics: Representative Selections from Classical Times to the Present*, 329.

14. A more recent expression of the idea that ethical statements may be established on the basis of scientific evidence is found in Ralph Barton Perry, *Realms of Value: A Critique of Human Civilization*. Perry's view, like that of Spencer, hinges on defining value as a psychological characteristic. Perry's view is open to objections similar to those directed against that of Spencer. In addition, attempts to define ethical concepts by reference to non-ethical concepts are open to a range of other criticisms. These are reviewed in William K. Frankena, *Ethics*, 2d ed., chap. 6. Further criticisms of such views are found in Morton White, *What Is and What Ought to Be Done, An Essay on Ethics and Epistemology*.

15. A contemporary philosopher who rejects the idea that moral principles can be confirmed by observational evidence is Gilbert Harman. See Gilbert

Harman, *The Nature of Morality: An Introduction to Ethics*, 9.

16. A theory of moral reasoning based on moral feelings is developed in White, *What is and What Ought to be Done*. Actually, White would maintain that his theory is a theory of reasoning and not just of moral reasoning. Professor White does research at the Institute for Advanced Study in Princeton.

17. I have suggested that emotions might be taken as evidence concerning the nature of the external world in part three of my discussion of reason and emotion. The suggestion here is related to that one, but different. In the discussion of reason and emotions I was not suggesting that feeling or emotion was evidence relevant to the acceptance or rejection of moral judgments.

18. Such a view is expressed in Thomas Hobbes *Leviathan: Or the Matter, Form and Power of a Commonwealth Ecclesiastical and Civil*.

19. A contemporary contractarian position is developed in D. Gauthier, *Morals by Agreement*. Gauthier's views are critically discussed in P. Vallentyne, *Contractarianism and Rational Choice: Essays on David Gauthier's Morals by Agreement*.

20. Some of these problems are discussed in R. Campbell and L. Sowden, eds., *Paradoxes of Rationality and Cooperation: Prisoner's Dilemma and Newcomb's Problem*.

21. Jan Narveson, "Animal Rights Revisited."

8. Does Rationality Require Holistic Thinking in Agriculture?

RECENTLY, A NUMBER of people have criticized agricultural research on the grounds that such research has adhered to a reductionist, rather than a holistic, approach.[1] The distinction between a holistic and reductionist approach to research is often not explained. Further, critics do not always explain exactly what they think is wrong with reductionist approaches. As the sense of the distinction may not be immediately obvious, it should be useful to attempt some explanation of the distinction and, as well, to explore some thoughts concerning the ramifications of the recommendation, that agricultural research should be holistic. What is wrong with reductionism? What modifications in the thought and practice of agricultural science should one expect to emerge as a result of including a holistic approach as part of one's research program?

THE REDUCTIONIST APPROACH

The reductionist approach should perhaps be called "methodological reductionism" to signify that it should not be confused with metaphysical views that may be called reductionist.[2] Metaphysical reductionism is committed to the claim that ultimately whatever exists is composed of particles that cannot be further reduced. Greek thinkers called the particles atoms, though in modern times the particles called atoms have themselves been shown to be complex structures. Methodological reductionism consists of views about the proper method to use for resolving the problems with which one is confronted. Someone could be a methodological reductionist without being committed to metaphysical reductionism. Methodological reductionism may be traced to ideas concerning the nature of science expressed by Descartes. According to Descartes, if we follow a proper methodology we will be able to free our minds of false opinions and replace them with knowledge. The proper method, as Descartes saw it, is reductionist. To advance one's knowledge, Descartes recommended that we divide each of the difficulties which we encounter into as many parts as possible. Further, he recommended that we always proceed by attempting to solve the simplest of our remaining problems before moving on to more complex matters.[3]

To illustrate a reductionist approach, let us consider a hypothetical production problem on a farm. Suppose that a reduction in yield has occurred. The farmer wants to discover the cause of the reduction, or at least, to take steps to reverse the reduction in the future. The reductionist approach to the problem consists in analyzing the steps of the production processes into distinct stages. If these stages are complex, the reductionist would reduce them still further. For example, the complex production process may be analyzed into stages consisting of preparing the soil, sowing the seeds, weeding, destroying insects, and harvesting. Each of these stages can be further analyzed. For example, the chemical processes resulting from the application of fertilizers can be studied, or chemical and biological processes in soil can be studied.

A reductionist approach to agricultural problems consists of reducing the process in which the problem occurs to a set of constituent processes and investigating the constituent processes as well as the relationships between the constituent processes within the set in order to determine the way that each constituent process contributes to the entire process. The rationale for taking a reductionist approach is suggested by Descartes' view of knowledge. Applied to our hypothetical agricultural example, Descartes might suggest the following. The claim that such and such is a way of increasing the yield of some crop is a complex claim. To determine whether this complex claim is correct, one must analyze it so as to reduce it to a number of simple claims. Using correct scientific methods, the truths of these simple claims can be established and those truths, in turn, would contain information from which the truth of the complex claim can be determined.

As an example of reductionist thinking, consider a suggestion that the cause of the decline in yield of a crop is the activities of some insect pest. Following a reductionist approach to this suggestion would require analyzing the activities of the insect into a sequence of stages, and at the same time analyzing the development and growth of the crop in order to see at what stage the activities of the insect reduce the rate of growth or the production of seed. A reductionist solution to the farmer's problem would consist of finding a way to modify either a stage of development of the plant or of the insect so that the insect will be prevented from interfering with the development of the plants in question.

Now, the advice that when confronted with a complex problem one should try to analyze the problem into simpler problems which may be thought of as elements of the complex problem, and that one should try to solve the simpler problems first and then use the solutions to the simpler problems as a basis for solving the original complex problem, is reasonable. The suggestion that we should adopt holistic approaches to dealing with the problems that confront us should not be thought of as a recommendation that we not analyze problems or try to discover solutions to simpler constituent problems. A producer confronted with a production problem, say a reduction in yield, would be well-advised to analyze the production process and focus on its elements in his or her efforts to discover the cause of the reduced yield.

Nonetheless, solutions of agricultural problems obtained by taking reductionist approaches may not be panaceas. Consider how a reductionist approach to agricultural problems can go wrong through failing to consider the context in which the problem arises. Suppose the problem is perceived solely as finding a way to increase income for a farmer so that his or her standard of living may be raised. A natural suggestion to a reductionist might be to increase production of the crop through use of an insecticide which will reduce the extent of damage from the insect pest. This might yield a satisfactory solution. Alternatively, this might not be a good solution. The suggestion might lead to contamination of the drinking water supply for the person in question and so would not lead to a higher standard of living. Alternatively, the suggestion, if implemented, might cause the food production of the farmer to become dependent on inputs from off the farm, inputs which fluctuate in price or in supply, thus rendering the farmer vulnerable to problems from which, prior to implementing the suggestion, he or she had been insulated. By focusing on a problem in isolation from the context in which the problem arises, a person who takes a reductionist approach is more likely to fail to note important ways in which agricultural practices contribute to the well-being of individuals or communities, and thereby to arrive at suggested solutions which are inappropriate or which aggravate the condition that gave rise to the initial narrow perception of the problem.

What this suggests is that one problem with reductionist analyses of problem situations is that they are incomplete. They point at one stage in the process of problem solving, the stage consisting of reducing a problem to simpler constituent problems, but they ignore another stage, the stage in which the suggested solution is studied in relation to the context which would result if the suggested solution were implemented. To discover whether the suggested solution is a good solution, one must consider whether it really works to solve the original problem. However, one must also consider what effects it will have on other aspects of the production system and on the communities of which the production system is itself a part. Given that the problem with reductionist solutions is that they are incomplete, a rational approach would be to undertake more complete analyses than those envisioned under reductionist ideals.

THE HOLIST APPROACH

As was the case with reductionism, we may distinguish methodological holism from metaphysical or ontological holism. Ontological holism is committed to the idea that the alleged elements or constituents of the processes, such as growth and reproduction, are unreal. Talk abut such elements is fiction; the only reality is the whole system. Many scientist and others will probably find metaphysical holism implausible. As was the case with reductionism, we can accept the validity of methodological holism without being committed to the metaphysical theory.

The holistic approach to an agricultural problem may be understood as correlative to the reductionist approach. Rather than considering a production system as a complex process which can be reduced to elements (which can be studied in isolation, modified and recombined to obtain some improvement in production), if one takes a holistic approach she or he will consider the production system as an element (or set of elements) of larger biological and social systems. Instead of thinking of the growing crop as a sequence of stages of development, a holist will think of the growth of the crop as a part of a system which includes soil, climate, many other types and communities of organisms, people, economies, etc. Instead of trying to prevent insect damage by interfering with the stages of development of the insect, the holist might try to modify other aspects of the system to reduce or eliminate the impact of the insect on the plants. For example, a holist might consider changing the time at which the crop is planted or introducing an insect predator.

Any modification of a production system, suggested as a result of reductionist analyses, would, if put into practice, modify the working of those larger systems. To determine whether a solution to an agricultural problem, suggested on the basis of reductionist analyses, is a good solution, one must consider whether those modifications of the larger systems are, on the whole, beneficial. A solution to an agricultural problem which increases productivity for a few years but involves agricultural practices which are dependent on non-renewable energy supplies could eventually lead to a calamity when the energy supply is exhausted.

Considering production systems in agriculture from a holistic perspective calls attention to an assumption often taken for granted by reductionists. The reductionist often assumes that her or his perception of a set of elements as constituting some complex process will not be affected by consideration of larger contexts within which the complex process is embedded. One can readily see this assumption in Descartes' thought. Descartes assumed that the elements of a complex proposition were not determined or modified by the network of concepts or propositions of which that initial complex proposition was itself a part. In other words, in Descartes' view, if one were trying to determine whether some complex proposition is true, one could focus attention on that proposition itself, analyze it to discover the simple elements, and then show how the complex proposition was correctly obtained by combining those elements. The idea that the elements at which one arrived as a result of the analysis might vary given alternative conceptual networks did not occur to Descartes.

The reductionist assumption is very doubtful. At the very least, if one considers an agricultural problem in relation to larger contexts, one is likely to take into account additional elements that are not seen as part of the initial problem. Further, if one considers the problem holistically, the elements of the problem will probably be conceived in different terms. Instead of simply seeing an insect as an insect pest, one will see the development of the insect as a stage in a larger cycle. Perhaps the insect, in its destructive phase, will be seen as a consequence of the destruction of creatures that had preyed on the insect through the introduction of insecticides at a prior phase of the process. What was originally seen as an inexpensive way of increasing output of the crop, e.g., applying a pesticide, may come to be seen as a process which over time endangers the entire production process through destruction of natural enemies of some insect. To reiterate, consideration of the larger context may lead to considerations of elements, for example natural enemies of a pest, that would have been ignored if the process was conceived reductionistically. Further, consideration of the larger context may lead to modifications of the concepts through which elements of the process were identified, e.g., a pesticide comes to be thought of as a threat to a useful part of an ecosystem, or soil comes to be considered as a unified entity (perhaps even as a living entity), rather than merely as a collection of items useful for supporting and nourishing plants.

The Cartesian reductionist assumption, that a complex process can be correctly analyzed in isolation from other, more inclusive processes, is called into question by evidence drawn from the history of scientific thought. Contrast, for example, the analysis that might be assigned to Copernicus' hypothesis in the context of Aristotelian physics in which it was first introduced with the analysis that would be assigned to this proposition in the context determined by Galilean-Newtonian physics shortly thereafter. Analyzed in Aristotelian terms, the Earth is an elemental substance, the natural place of which is below other substances such as water or fire.[4] In such a view, if the Earth is in motion around a heavenly body then there must have been some non-natural cause of this motion which displaced the Earth from its natural place. The way that an Aristotelian would analyze the question What causes the Earth to move? is clearly quite different from the way that modern scientist would analyze this question. In the Aristotelian view the set of simple elements is Earth, air, fire, and water. In the Galilean-Newtonian view those things are seen as complexes subject to reductive explanations. Adoption of the new context gives rise to viewing as complex what had been regarded as simple. Ultimately new elements must be considered. Clearly, the advances in astronomy and physics that we have witnessed in the last few hundred years make it clear that advances in knowledge require both holistic and reductionistic approaches.

Consider an agricultural example in this light. Suppose the problem is how to increase productivity of grains. Analyzed as it was, in the period following World War II this was reduced to a number of other problems, e.g., how to supply pesticides, what chemical nutrients to add with fertilizer, how to supply water to grains where the water supply is inadequate, how to bring more land into cultivation, how to increase the amount of grain that a person could harvest. At the present time, if the same question is raised, additional elements enter into the analysis, e.g., whether the grain can be genetically modified to use sunlight more efficiently, or to divert more of its resources to producing seeds and less to producing stalks, or to genetically manufacture its own nutrients. If a holistic perspective is taken, other questions may be raised, such as whether the amounts of seed can be increased by methods that don't add to loss of topsoil or don't involve contaminating ground water with excess nitrates or other substances. Such questions reflect awareness of the fact that the farming system is part of more inclusive biological systems. Other questions would indicate that the farming system is part of more inclusive social systems. The analysis of any particular problem will vary depending on other beliefs and problems posed in the context in which the particular problem is raised. Further, what is deemed acceptable as a solution to the problem will likewise vary.

While we shall not attempt a systematic review of holistic perspectives, it should be of interest to discuss some other descriptions of holism. First I want to point out that some descriptions of holism are so abstract as to be quite useless. For example, to say that a perspective is holistic because it focuses on the pattern of relations among parts and the whole says essentially nothing.[5] Any description of a farming system, no matter how reductionistic, which mentioned the elements and some of the temporal or causal relations among those elements would qualify as focusing on the pattern of relations among parts and the whole. Holistic approaches are sometimes said to be distinctive because they construe systems as forming coherent wholes. This, too, is not a particularly useful description to offer. Reductionist scientists will simply be confused by being told that they would do better to construe agricultural systems as coherent wholes; they will think that that is what they have been doing all along.

Sometimes holists claim that in a reductionist approach wholes are understood or explained by reference to the properties or relations of the parts, whereas in holistic approaches the parts are understood or explained by reference to the whole of which they are parts. This way of describing the difference has some validity, though it tends to exaggerate the difference between the two approaches. Saying this sort of thing, namely that in a holistic approach the parts are explained by reference to other elements can only be explained by saying that the nitrogen is part of a whole rather than by appeal to chemical theories concerning chemical compounds, valence of atoms, etc. This is misleading: a holist need not reject the explanatory relevance of chemistry or molecular biology.

However, there are a number of ways in which it is correct to say that understanding of the behavior of the parts is better achieved through consideration of the whole. For one thing, as we have noted above, some of the parts of agricultural systems are complex entities. The identification of these entities as parts of the system may well be a consequence of consideration of the part of larger biological or social wholes. Further, the behavior of some of the elements of the system may well be determined by spatial, temporal, or other relations among the parts. The whole system may determine the boundary conditions for the chemical or molecular processes, and thus reference to the whole system may indeed be essential for explaining those processes. Finally, the very presence of certain elements as parts of agricultural systems may well be a function of the activity of the whole system. Living things tend to modify themselves in the course of carrying out their behavior. There may be elemental nitrogen or other substances in a system because the activity of the system reduces other substances to these elements.

I suspect that many scientists would respond to the above remarks by saying that the advice to consider whole systems, of which the production processes under consideration are a part, is nothing new. Agricultural scientists have long known that they must consider soil, climate, ground water, etc. to discover successful production systems. Thus, they may say that the advice to take holistic approaches is nothing new. While it is true that agricultural scientists have long known that they must consider the context in which production will occur, the criticism of reductionism has been significant anyway. The claim that agricultural research has been flawed as a result of its reductionist approach indicates that we need to be reminded to consider certain wholes. We were ignoring these wholes. Even though agricultural scientists may have long studied some whole systems of which agricultural production is a part, they may not have studied certain systems or wholes, for example, the human communities or the ecological communities.

J. Baird Callicott contrasts a holistic perspective not with what he called reductionism but rather with a mechanistic perspective.[6] Mechanism, as he conceived it, is characterized by reference to Newtonian physics. In such a view the world is conceived as consisting of individual entities (atoms or parts of atoms) moving through absolute space and time in accordance with Newton's laws of motion. According to this view, everything is explainable ultimately by reference to the mass and motion of the individual atoms.

In modern physics this mechanistic view has been drastically modified. The behavior of entities cannot be explained by reduction to descriptions of the mass and motion of the individual components. Perhaps, for this reason, Callicott characterizes modern physics as holistic.

It may well be that if one takes a holistic perspective to understanding agriculture, one will be led to reject mechanism. However, as mechanism has been rejected in physics except as a useful approximation in some contexts, agricultural scientists would eventually reject mechanism anyway, even though they continued to ignore holistic approaches. Given the nature of agricultural research, consideration of biological processes has been rare at levels of analysis at which the corrections introduced to physics by quantum theory have significant effects. Very likely it will increase as modern analyses proceed to investigate processes at sub-atomic levels. We should expect modern agricultural research to be increasingly concerned about the effects of events at the quantum level on the phenomena they study. However, they could reject mechanism without rejecting methodological reductionism in their studies of agricultural processes.

There are reasons for taking holistic approaches even without consideration of quantum theory. As we have noted, agricultural systems are parts of social systems, of systems of human beings in societies. Many thinkers have urged that human behavior cannot be understood by reduction to the behavior of non-living components. Now, to some degree this is mistaken. Aspects of human behavior can be explained, at least in part, by reference to chemistry. For example, understanding the behavior of human intestines or kidneys can (in part) be so understood. Further, there continues to be progress in understanding the effects of chemicals on moods or emotions. We can expect some new insights into the effects of genotypes on behavior. However, even if ultimately such a view is mistaken, it is certainly true at the present time (and for the foreseeable future) that we cannot explain much of human behavior by reference to chemistry or molecular biology. In studies of human culture, economics, politics, history, etc. we explain behavior by appeal to human purposes and choices. Whether such explanations can be reduced to physical or chemical explanations continues to be controversial. It appears that there is ample reason to favor some scientific investigations of agricultural issues from a holistic perspective. This can be expected to remedy some of the incompleteness that arises from patterns of investigation which are too strongly influenced by reductionist assumptions.

HOLISM AND THE ADMINISTRATION OF SCIENTIFIC RESEARCH

The influence of reductionism in research institutions has led to the formation of groups of scholars who focus on very narrow areas of scientific research. Here, at the University of Guelph, there is a department of animal and poultry science. As one would expect, the scientists who work in such a department study problems of beef and dairy production as well as of egg and poultry production. However, one can see the influence of reductionism. Thus, one finds some people who specialize in physiology, some who specialize in reproduction, some who specialize in animal behavior. Scientists who study animal nutrition are in a separate department. Scientists who study animal diseases are not even members of the same college. They are members of the Ontario Veterinary College rather than the Ontario College of Agriculture. Some scientists who study animal behavior are not part of the agricultural college either. They may be rather members of the department of zoology which, in turn, are parts of the College of Biological Sciences. Alternatively, they may be members of the department of psychology which is contained in the College of Social Sciences. Further, until recently there have been few collaborations between scientists studying specific aspects of crop production and scientists studying the human communities which consist of farmers, farm workers, etc.

Suppose that one wants to investigate a new method of producing eggs. Under the influence of reductionist perspectives in the past, such a proposal would have been considered in a department of animal or poultry science by people who specialize in egg production. Conceivably, those people who develop the new method might not be very familiar with poultry behavior and, in consequence, the first efforts to implement the new method might be attended with serious problems. Perhaps many of the hens will be injured or become ill due to the activities of other hens, or to parts of the production system on which the hen injures herself. Since the illness or injury affects production, the scientist will begin to reflect on ways to modify the system to reduce the incidence of such events. For example, a new system introduced for egg production involved keeping hens in relatively small cages commonly known as battery cages. Hens in such cages engaged in pecking each other, sometimes causing death. Further, the hens injured themselves due to the design of the floor or other aspects of the cage. This led to modifications in cage design as well as to the practices of beak trimming or debeaking. Similarly, since the scientists who introduced the new methods were probably not specialists in rural sociology, they did not investigate the impact on rural communities which would result from the modifications in poultry production. Again, since the scientists were not ecologists they did not consider ecological consequences of such modification.

Of course, it is not reasonable to expect one person to master many areas of scientific knowledge, such as rural sociology, agricultural economics, animal behavior, and poultry reproduction. So, one might ask, is not specialization of studies inevitable? How, in general, could holistic investigations be undertaken?

Suppose that at the time this new system was introduced, someone wanted to undertake a more holistic study. Such a study might have raised questions about the effects of the new system on the welfare of the hens, on the welfare of the farmers if the new system were introduced, on the effects of the new system in regard to rural communities, and on the effects of the new system on the biological systems within which egg production units are a part. It would have been difficult to undertake such a scientific study. For one thing, at the time, there were few if any scientists who specialized in the study of poultry welfare. Further, carrying out such studies would have required establishing ties between departments of rural sociology, agricultural economics, poultry science, biomedical sciences, and perhaps others. Devising means to obtain and allocate funding, faculty time, research space, equipment, and perhaps other matters would have posed serious problems. While these problems could have been overcome, it is very likely that the studies would not be undertaken because of the additional problems involved.

However, we should expect that introduction of new technologies into agricultural production systems based only on limited scientific investigations (as one would expect from universities or research institutes organized under the influence of reductionist perspectives) would lead to serious problems. After all, the new methods often involve large-scale modifications of biological or social systems. Often, the only investigations undertaken prior to introduction of the new technology concerned the question of whether the new method led to increased production. More recently, there have been investigations relating to the safety of new technologies for human health, for example, in cases in which use of chemical pesticides is involved. It is still the case, however, that new technologies can often be introduced without investigations of environmental impacts or effects on rural or urban communities.

A shift to a holistic perspectives will involve creating administrative structures that facilitate undertaking investigations which tend to cross boundaries of distinct groups of specialists. This does not mean that departments which specialize in narrow investigations need to be dismantled. Efficient acquisition of knowledge may require such specialization. There are limits to the breadth of knowledge that any individual can master. However, such specialized units need to be supplemented by additional administrative structures. Such structures are necessary to encourage and facilitate participation of specialists from a range of disciplines in discussions concerning social, environmental, and ethical issues arising from the development and potential implementation of new technologies. Such administrative structures could, in addition, facilitate wise decision making regarding funding, allocation of space, use of researcher time, and other resources, in order to combine specialists from various areas to address questions provoked by taking holistic perspectives.

It is reasonable to expect that undertaking holistic investigations of agricultural matters in addition to the kinds of investigations which have been undertaken in the recent past would add to the cost of developing new technologies. This addition would be a consequence of the cost of the additional studies and perhaps also a result of the greater investment of time required to undertake such studies. Thus, were society to require such holistic studies to be undertaken, it is reasonable to expect that the pace of technological change in western society would be reduced. More time would be required to undertake studies of technological investigations; perhaps more time would be required to amass the capital necessary to finance such studies.

Some people might appeal to this factor as a reason for not requiring such holistic studies to be undertaken prior to making major technological innovations. They might allege that making such a requirement would be impractical because it would make innovation too expensive. However, this objection to requiring holistic studies does not appear very strong. Slowing down the pace of technological innovation in societies would have some advantages. For one thing, we would expect it to reduce negative impacts of rapid social change on the welfare of individual human beings or other creatures. In this way, such holistic studies might ultimately serve to reduce costs of new technologies. Such studies might reduce the incidence of cases in which costs of new technologies are not distributed fairly. Further, we would expect that such holistic studies might reduce the likelihood of some serious harms which have resulted from the precipitous introduction of new technologies in the past, harms such as the ozone hole, the nearly silent spring to which Rachel Carson called our attention, unnecessary suffering of animals in agricultural production systems, etc.

SUMMARY

In this chapter we have explained reductionism as the view that holds that problems are to be solved, and knowledge advanced, by reducing the processes in which the problems occur to their elements and modifying the elements to eliminate the problem. We called this methodological reductionism as opposed to metaphysical reductionism. Methodological reductionism may be contrasted with methodological holism, in which the approach to the problem is to look at the system in question as a part of one or more larger systems to determine how relations with elements of the larger systems may effect the behavior of the system in question. The reductionist approach to advancing knowledge was explained and advocated in the early 17th century by Descartes and is characteristic of much scientific work. On the basis of this approach, scientific workers tend to become narrow specialists, and research institutions have developed which do not facilitate cooperative work among scientists from all the specialties in which there are pieces of knowledge relevant to dealing with our problems. Recently this has been changing under the influence of criticisms from people advocating holistic approaches.

NOTES

1. One such criticism is expressed in F. L. McEwen and L. P. Milligan, "An Analysis of the Canadian Research and Development System for Agriculture/Food," 21.

2. For further discussion on this see J. Baird Callicott, "Agroecology in Context," 3–10.

3. See Rene Descartes, *Discourse on Method*, part two. See also Rene Descartes, *Rules for the Direction of the Mind*, particularly Rule 5.

4. In Book 2 of the *Physics* Aristotle says that some things exist "by nature." Among such things are the simple, i.e., non-complex, bodies: earth, fire, air, and water. Such things have within themselves a cause of motion or stationariness in respect to place. Earth, for example, by nature moves toward its place and then remains stationary unless caused by something else to be displaced.

5. I have seen such descriptions of holism frequently. One place is in a work which describes holistic economic perspectives. See Charles K. Wilber and Kenneth P. Jameson, *Beyond Reaganomics: A Further Inquiry into the Poverty of Economics*, 188.

6. Callicott, "Agroecology in Context."

9. Rationality and Family Farming

IN A RECENTLY published work, Michael Boehlje claimed that "proponents of family farming continue to espouse emotional arguments that are not well substantiated except by selective references to history."[1] However, this claim is not born out even by Boehlje's own discussion. There are theoretical arguments which have been offered in support of the advantages of family farms. It is misleading to call such arguments purely emotional. It appears that Boehlje is using the term "emotional" as a pejorative term. He appeals to the idea that emotional arguments are opposed to arguments based on reason, while providing no explanation of the distinction. In earlier chapters I discussed this distinction. I shall assume that to provide a rational defense for a social policy of supporting family farms, Boehlje would want to see arguments that purported to show that the benefits of family farms outweigh the harms or costs. Further, he would want to see the claims about benefits and harms supported by statistically significant results obtained in empirical scientific studies.[2] In this chapter I shall try to show that some of Wendell Berry's arguments may be regarded as a stage in the development of a rational defense of family farms. To defend this claim, I shall have to engage in some discussion of scientific method. I shall do that in the second part of this chapter. In part one, I shall discuss the criteria by reference to which the benefits or harms of family farms are to be evaluated.

Some people might suggest that to proceed with this discussion we need to have a definition of "family farm." Presumably such a definition would capture the essence of family farms, that is, would correctly report the features by reference to which family farms are distinguished from non-family farms. However, it is not possible to give such a definition. To see this, consider efforts to try to express the essence or nature of family farms. Is a family farm simply a farm that is owned by a family? Is a family farm one that produces nearly all of the food and fiber which is necessary for a family to survive? Must a family farm be operated by the family that owns it? Is a family farm a business? Does (or can) a family farm combine all of these features? I believe that to try to resolve these questions at the start would be to put the cart before the horse. In part, debates over the value of family farming are debates over the nature of the family farm.

Berry maintains that a family farm is a farm that is owned, lived on and worked by a family over a long period of time, and which is preserved by the family, i.e., its resources are not depleted.[3] Boehlje distinguishes two dimensions which may overlap to yield various definitions of "family farm." Must the owner of the farm also be the farm operator? Must the farm be owned by a family as opposed to a non-family corporation? Suppose a farm is owned by a corporation but operated by a traditional family. Is that a family farm? Suppose a family owns some land and leases other land on which the family members farm. Should that be described as a family farm? Boehlje allows for a number of alternatives here as to what counts as a family farm. Given the problems we have indicated above in trying to arrive at a definition, Boehlje's approach to this matter is not unreasonable.[4]

DOES BERRY FOCUS ATTENTION ON ATTRIBUTES OF FAMILY FARMS?

Boehlje urges defenders of family farming to focus attention on a set of attributes by reference to which, he believes, the overall value of family farming may be assessed. It appears that Boehlje is complaining that Berry did not do so.[5] I shall argue here that Berry does indeed focus attention on attributes of family farming. However, there is disagreement between them as to what set of attributes should be considered.

Contrary to what Boehlje claims, reading some of Berry's written work should convince the reader that Boehlje's complaint is unwarranted. Berry has attempted to enumerate valuable consequences of family farming. These include both attributes of family farms individually and attributes of social systems which include family farms. Berry has claimed, for example, that the benefits of family farms may be divided into two categories: agricultural benefits and non-agricultural benefits. In the latter category he locates both cultural and political benefits.[6] What are the agricultural benefits of family farms? Berry has suggested that these include preservation of the quality of the soil, as opposed to either loss of topsoil through erosion or degrading of soil through compactification or pollution, preservation of the ecological diversity on which a high quality of human life depends, production of crops of a high quality, etc. Among the cultural benefits which he attributes to family farms are preservation of democracy, preservation of rural populations, and, perhaps correlatively, preservation of a high quality of civilization in our cities.[7]

Boehlje enumerated nine qualities of farms in his analysis. We are to presume that it is better, in Boehlje's judgment, for a farm to possess these qualities than to lack them. Further, many of these qualities can vary in degree, and apparently, Boehlje believes that it is better for a farm to have these qualities in higher rather than lower degree. For example, it is better for a farm to be more rather than less efficient. The qualities that Boehlje considered are economic efficiency, financial stability and risk bearing, standard of living, resource conservation, employment, entrepreneurial prerogatives, ability to adopt new technology, community contributions, and independence.[8]

Interestingly, among the benefits which Berry attributes to family farming, it is arguable that there are several which Boehlje included in his study. Among these are standard of living, resource conservation, community contributions, and independence. Still, Boehlje has asserted that the claims that family farms are better in these regards have not been substantiated by scientific or logical argument. He alleges that all that has been offered by way of argument are emotional or dubious historical claims. However, it is worth asking whether Boehlje's claims about Berry's arguments are correct.

Boehlje's claims that family farms are stronger in regard to the attribute he calls "independence." His argument that family farms are stronger in this regard is not supported by reports of observational studies and statistical analysis. Rather, this claim is supported by further claims. Presumably these claims are based on reason rather than on emotion. Boehlje allows that owner-operators have greater control over their resource bases than do tenants, and, consequently, greater capacity to make decisions independently. These are claims with which Berry would probably agree. He has maintained that a family farm had great independence, both in regard to its sources of energy and in regard to is need for money.[9] Boehlje suggests that the greater independence of owner-operators is determined by the laws regarding property rights. Similarly, he allows that family owners, as opposed to corporate owners, given constraints operating on corporate business, have greater freedom to control the decision-making processes for the farm. Apparently he regards this claim as reasonable even in the absence of empirical evidence. The absence of empirical data and statistical analysis is not taken as evidence that the argument is purely "emotional."

Let us now look at some of Berry's arguments with regard to what he regards as advantages of family farms. In particular, let us consider the alleged advantages which overlap with attributes in Boehlje's list. Consider the attribute "standard of living." While Boehlje labels the attribute under consideration as "standard of living," he argues that the "economic standard of living" is not necessarily greater on family farms. The measure of economic standard of living, according to Boehlje, is financial compensation. The financial compensation of family farmers may be less than that of tenants or of corporate employees.[10] In part, Berry might reply to Boehlje by noting that the claim that standard of living of family farmers is higher than of non-farmers is intended as a generalization. The fact that in some cases the financial compensation of corporate employees is greater than that of family farmers does not show that in general tenant farmers or corporate employees are better off. When Berry discusses matters related to standard of living he clearly is not concerned primarily with financial compensation. Rather, he suggests that farm laborers or corporate employees are often required to work in ways that involve little or no thought or skill. The worker, he suggests, can take no pride in such work; the worker's life is devalued. In other words, his or her standard of living is reduced.[11]

Berry's claim about the relative advantage in this regard of family farming may not be correct. However, he has offered a reason for his claim; further, it is a reason which is based on plausible psychological grounds. The claim that Berry makes in regard to farm workers has been made many times before about workers in industrial society. That the claim has some basis in fact is supported by the fact that many corporations have tried to modify corporate practices so as to give employees greater opportunity to contribute to decision making and, in general, to have more meaningful work. (The possibility of modifying corporate working conditions to make worker's working lives more meaningful is, however, a possibility that Berry needs to take seriously. If this could be arranged it would undermine a major part of his argument.) Berry's claims about the quality of life of farm workers in family farms as opposed to either workers on tenant farms or those on corporate farms is based on some plausible reasons, and it could be tested by further empirical research. It is not merely an expression of emotion. It could be argued that some agricultural economists should devise rigorous observational methods of testing it.

Berry does call attention to what he regards as attributes of good farming as well as to features which inhibit good farming. However, part of his disagreement with Boehlje (and no doubt others) concerns whether some attributes of farms are beneficial or not. Berry's writings suggest that he thinks that some of the features, which Boehlje regards as features of good farming, are not features of good farming. Let us review some of these controversial attributes.

One of the criteria which Boehlje considers an attribute of good farming is "ability to adopt new technology." He alleges (though without a reference) that defenders of family farming have claimed that family farms are superior in this regard. Presumably, what Boehlje was thinking was that where a new technology or management practice could lead to greater efficiency in production, adopting it would improve the farm. A farm with a greater ability to adopt new technology would thus have an advantage over other farms. What is particularly interesting about this particular criterion is that one suspects that, everything considered, Berry might regard the ability to adopt new technology as a defect rather than as a virtue. Consider what he said specifically about mechanization of farming: "The coming of the tractor made it possible for a farmer to do more work, but not better. And there comes a point, as we know, when *more* begins to imply *worse*. The mechanization of farming passed that point long ago."[12]

What specifically has gone wrong with farming because of mechanization? Berry suggests that the increased mechanization of farming has led to the decline in farm populations. He suggests that the movement of these people to the cities has aggravated urban problems, and that withdrawal of human populations from rural areas has led to neglect of farmland and, consequently, to deterioration of the land. There is a great deal of plausibility to these claims. Many people have noted the loss of rural population to the cities. Increased population in the cities has contributed to urban problems in many ways. Transplanted rural people could not transplant the rural culture and lifestyle. The need to adopt to new cultural practices is often demoralizing. Of course, Berry's reasoning is open to challenge. Conceivably, Berry is mistaken about the cause of the above problems. Mechanization may itself be an effect of other causes which also led to declines in farm populations, etc.

There are, of course, other consequences to which the mechanization of farming contributed. Many people would regard the physical labor associated with pre-mechanized farming as drudgery. They would suggest that the lives of many people have been improved because the number of people required to engage in such drudgery is greatly reduced. Berry argues movingly in favor of the value of work.[13] However, while challenging work may be essential for meaningful lives, hard physical labor such as hoeing under dusty, hot, insect-infested circumstances may wear a person down. It is doubtful that spending many summer hours at such work improves the quality of one's life. Determining whether the mechanization of farming is, overall, a benefit or a harm would require extensive consideration and evaluation of its consequences. Berry is to be commended for challenging our facile assumption that new technology is necessarily an improvement.

Another criterion which Boehlje adopts and which Berry would clearly challenge is "economic efficiency": a ratio of income or profits to costs. If one farm is more economically efficient than a second farm, then, given the same costs the former farm will have greater income. However, economic efficiency is not the only type of efficiency. A farm can be economically efficient but be inefficient in regard to its use of land or in regard to its use of other resources, such as oil or topsoil.[14]

Often, economic efficiency has been achieved through the use of very large farm machinery. For such machinery to be used efficiently, farm fields, and indeed farms themselves, have tended to get larger and larger. Berry, however, has claimed that "fields can be too big to permit effective rotation of grazing".[15] This conclusion is echoed in the work of E. Ann Clark, wherein she argues in favor of using (some) fields for pastures at least some of the time. She argues that cash cropping on large fields has not been ecologically sound. Economic efficiency which leads to destruction of the ecosystems on which agriculture depends does not appear wise or rational as a long-term policy.[16]

Conversations with many agricultural scientists have suggested to me that they regard a commitment to economic efficiency as a criterion of good farming as equivalent to a commitment to logic in matters of reasoning. Of course, not all agrologists have taken this position. Indeed, some have recognized that a commitment to efficiency is what I would call an ideological commitment rather than a dictate of reason itself. Where increased economic efficiency is achieved through increasing the efficiency with which resources, e.g., fuel, fertilizer, etc., are converted into products, e.g., food, fiber, etc., then, given limits to the demand for those products, the ideal of increasing efficiency eventually comes into conflict with other ideals. Where increased efficiency in production leads to oversupply, prices of farm products fall; consequently, the farmer does not get an adequate or fair return for his or her products. Politicians concerned with agriculture have been trying to reconcile this conflict of ideals—efficiency in production versus a decent or fair return on investment—for many years.[17]

Berry also argues that large farms have led to a situation in which a relatively small number of people own and control relatively large proportions of farmland. He suggests, echoing agrarian thinkers of earlier times, that this state of affairs is not conducive to the preservation of democracy.[18] The existence of non-democratic regimes in countries such as those in Central America is evidence, if not proof, in support of his view in this regard. One is reminded of the arguments in Plato's *Republic* in which Plato's suggestion that society be efficiently organized appeared to lead to the conclusion that politically the society should be ruled by philosopher-scientist kings. Earlier in this century, many people praised fascist governments, as opposed to democratic ones, on the grounds that they are more efficient. Again, economic efficiency achieved in a way which leads to the replacement of democratic political structures by totalitarian or plutocratic regimes is not a rational policy.

We could go on at greater length challenging the claim that the arguments of Berry and other agrarians are purely emotional rather than rational; however, I believe we have argued sufficiently to make this point. Of course, this does not mean that we have shown that it would be rational for our society to reverse long-standing trends in agriculture by adopting policies that effectively re-created family farms. It might be rational. However, such policies would first have to be formulated and then subjected to critical scrutiny. At present, I do not know whether it is even possible to re-create an agricultural system based primarily on family farming in something approaching Berry's sense of the term.

Perhaps we should turn to scientific studies to resolve controversies over the advantages of family farms. However, doing so would be both difficult and expensive. Let us turn to consideration of this matter.

DIFFICULTIES IN EVALUATING CLAIMS ABOUT ADVANTAGES OF FAMILY FARMS BY USE OF SCIENTIFIC PROCEDURES

Empirical testing of claims relating to the standard of living of farm workers, either on family or on other sorts of farms, would not be a straightforward matter. For Boehlje, whether a farm is a family farm is not a simple question. Overlapping the two parameters that he distinguishes yields four categories. Presumably he would regard a farm owned and operated by a family as a family farm. Presumably he would allow that a farm owned by a corporation and operated by employees is a non-family farm. However, what of the intermediate categories? Consider a farm owned by a corporation but lived on and operated over a long period of time by a family. Is that a family farm? While Berry's concept of a family farm overlaps that of Boehlje, the two are not identical.

WHAT IS A FAMILY FARM?

	OPERATED BY FAMILY	OPERATED BY NON-FAMILY
Owned by family	family farm	?
Owned by non-family	?	non-family farm

Clearly, farms that may be considered family farms according to Boehlje's definition are not family farms according to Berry's. Berry's concept of a family farm is a narrower concept. The difference in definitions will affect not only the gathering of data but also the analysis or interpretation of such data. Consider, for example, a remark of Boehlje's concerning whether family farms make a better contribution to the community than do farms owned by corporations or farmed by tenants. He says, "Concerns about whether large-scale farming operations will bypass local input supply and product purchasing firms for regional and wholesale outlets are legitimate. But size, not ownership structure, is most likely to be the determining factor here."[19] Boehlje is suggesting that a large family-owned farming operation might make less of a contribution to the local community. However, in Berry's account, such a large farm would not count as a family farm. The fact that such a farm did not make a significant contribution to the local community would not tend, according to Berry, to undermine the claim that family farms made a stronger community contribution than other farms.

The differences in the two concepts of family farms may be perceived by considering farms excluded from the concepts. According to Berry's concept, a farm is not a family farm if it is farmed by a tenant farmer or if it is owned by a corporation. In Berry's account of the nature of a family farm, a farm need not be a family farm even if it is small and is owned and used by the family that owns it. If the family has bought it solely for speculative purposes, it is not a family farm. A small farm, owned and operated by a family to produce a crop without regard for the loss of topsoil or the decline in soil fertility, is not a family farm, according to Berry. Indeed, he suggests, to produce crops in such a way is not even farming.

Among the alleged benefits of family farming is resource conservation. Boehlje disputes the claim that family farms are better in this regard. He cites empirical studies which indicate that family-owned and operated farms do not have less soil loss due to erosion than do farms operated by tenants, that corporations do not lose more soil to erosion than farms owned in other ways, and also that owner-operators with small farms tend to adopt minimum tillage methods (a conservation practice) more slowly than other groups do.[20] Boehlje grants that there are theoretical reasons for expecting family farms to be better in regard to conservation, e.g., there would appear to be little reason for tenant farmers to be concerned about conserving topsoil if they can abandon the farmland when it is exhausted. While Berry does have some theoretical grounds for affirming that family farms have an advantage in regard to conservation, the empirical studies challenge this a priori judgment.

Of course, Berry need not regard such evidence as a strong challenge to his view, since he could deny that many small family-owned farms are family farms in his sense of the term. Farms, even small family-owned farms, operate in a system of agricultural production which is highly oriented toward commerce. Farm owners, to survive in such a system, must be primarily concerned with profit and loss, rather than with preservation of farmland or topsoil. Berry could say that such farmers, operating in such a system, are not family farmers. When one looks at Berry's position in this way, it is clear that it would be very difficult and expensive to test the accuracy of his views according to scientific criteria. All we can say at this point is that, given that he has theoretical reasons for expecting family farms to be better in regard to conservation, the basis for his position is not purely emotional. Similar remarks apply to claims that family farms are superior in regard to standard of living or to contribution to the community.

That Boehlje and Berry are operating with different concepts of family farming is indicated by the fact that the criteria by reference to which they would evaluate farming are distinct. Interestingly, while Boehlje considers nine criteria for evaluating farms, he does not compare farms with respect to quality of farm products. Berry clearly suggests that it is reasonable to expect quality of farm products to be higher on family farms.[21]

While producers have long suggested that food products are of high quality as a consequence of competition for consumers, there are theoretical and empirical grounds for supposing that product quality in large-scale farming might be sacrificed. Products have to be harvested and packaged easily and must survive shipping over long distances and varying climactic conditions. One might expect such characteristics as flavor to be sacrificed. Advertising by local producers often stresses arguments based on this theme. Further, I have often heard people say that certain products don't taste as good as they formerly did, for example, chicken or tomatoes; it has also been argued that food producers recognize, in many instances, that the quality of the food products they produce has declined. They allegedly recognize this by producing a bit for themselves without the full benefits of modern technology.[22] The recent development of genetically engineered food products, such as tomatoes which allegedly taste better, is also evidence that product quality in regard to flavor had been sacrificed.

Whether such conflicting views about product quality could be tested scientifically would depend on agreement as to what features count as good quality. Here, serious questions have to be faced. For example, consider which apple has better quality, one that looks nicely colored and free of blemishes or one that has significantly lower quantities of pesticide residues? How does the quality of broiler chickens produced today on a large scale compare with the quality of broilers produced in earlier times? Testing Berry's claims about product quality would be especially difficult not only because of the problem of determining which farms are family farms but also because of problems associated with competing ideals of quality. Similar problems confront comparative evaluation of family and non-family farms with reference to other criteria suggested by Boehlje.

Given the conceptual differences between Berry's and Boehlje's concepts of family farms, Boehlje's project of making straightforward comparisons of family and non-family farms with respect to the criteria he considered indicates that he did not perceive the extent of the differences between his view and that of Berry. Family farms as conceived by Berry are defined with reference to a network of assumptions, including assumptions about what is the case and assumptions about what is valuable, which are different from some of the assumptions which underlie Boehlje's conception. This is reflected in the results noted above, namely that the results which Boehlje takes as refuting Berry's claim that the family farm is superior are irrelevant to Berry's view, as he (Berry) conceives it.

We might use the term "paradigm disagreement" to characterize the debate concerning the merits of family farms. The difficulties involved in using scientific methods to evaluate the merits of family versus non-family farms might be expressed by saying that the conflict between Berry and his critics is not simply a conflict over scientific details amongst a group of thinkers all of whom are working under the influence of the same farming paradigm.[23] A paradigm involves an entire network of assumptions. Straightforward comparison between items, even items referred to by the same term, across boundaries of paradigms is often not possible. In this context, as we have noted, even though Boehlje and Berry both speak of family farms, they are not referring to the same entities.

Boehlje laments the paucity of empirical data available to him as a basis for challenging Berry's arguments. We have explained why we should not expect to find straightforward empirical assessment of this disagreement. This does not mean that we should regard Berry's arguments, or Boehlje's either, for that matter, as merely emotional. Perhaps it would be useful to appeal to a distinction here between two stages of scientific procedures. Berry may be regarded as arguing in support of the hypothesis that family farming is better farming. His arguments are intended to show that the hypothesis is plausible. However, those arguments, even if they succeed, will not show that the hypothesis is true. If they succeed, they can show that it would be useful to try to develop or frame empirically testable scientific hypotheses.[24] Proof or disproof can only be obtained at that subsequent stage. Developing testable hypotheses in ways that are sensitive to the problems created by the debate over family farming involves a conflict amongst farming paradigms is a very difficult matter.

Rational evaluation of Berry's claims must consider them in the theoretical context in which they are expressed, that is, with respect to the assumptions that Berry makes concerning what is a family farm and what is good in a farm and in a human life. Boehlje did not undertake such an analysis. This is not, of course, to say that to evaluate Berry's views concerning family farming we must agree with his assumptions either of facts or of values. Such assumptions may be subjected to critical scrutiny also, and should be accepted or rejected only for adequate reasons. Nor is this to say that observational or scientific studies aimed at evaluating Berry's claims cannot be undertaken. No doubt, such studies could be undertaken—with due regard for Berry's theoretical assumptions. Very likely, the results of such studies would be very interesting. Indeed, under the pressure of critics of agriculture, especially of critics who have concerns about the state of our environment based on ecology, research institutions are now beginning to support research on finding environmentally sounder ways to farm. Indirectly, this research may ultimately tend to challenge some of Berry's contentions.

SUMMARY

In this chapter we have been concerned with the alleged irrationality of Wendell Berry's arguments in support of preserving family farms. Contrary to what Michael Boehlje implies, Berry does try to enumerate what he takes to be valuable aspects of family farms. However, even when that is done, direct comparison of the merits of family versus corporate (or industrial) farms is not easy to achieve. There is disagreement concerning whether some features of farms, e.g., readiness to use new technology, is necessarily advantageous. More basically, there is disagreement over what counts as a family farm. In light of conflict concerning the nature of family farms and concerning the value of particular attributes, we have suggested that the conflict between Berry and others, such as Boehlje, should be regarded as a conflict between advocates of different paradigms. The arguments that Berry advances can be regarded as arguments in support of the plausibility of the hypothesis he favors, rather than as scientific proofs of that hypothesis.

NOTES

1. "Responses of Berry and Boehlje," in Gary Comstock, ed., *Is There a Moral Obligation to Save the Family Farm?* 377.

2. See Michael Boehlje, "A Response to Wendell Berry," in ibid., 377.

3. Wendell Berry, "A Defense of the Family Farm," in ibid., 347.

4. The question of defining "family farm" is considered in Comstock, Introduction to ibid., xxiv. It is also considered in Hugh Lehman and Frank Hurnik, "The Disappearance of the Family Farm," 237–40.

5. See Boehlje, "A Response to Wendell Berry," 377.

6. Berry, "A Defense of the Family Farm," 349.

7. I have inferred that Berry attributes these benefits to family farms from the discussion in Wendell Berry, "Agricultural Solutions for Agricultural Problems," in *The Gift of Good Land: Further Essays Cultural and Agricultural*, 113–24.

8. Michael Boehlje, "Costs and Benefits of Family Farming," in Comstock, ed., *Save the Family Farm?*, 361–74.

9. See, for example, his remarks in Wendell Berry, "Energy in Agriculture," in *The Gift of Good Land*, 126. There he is discussing a small farm, and he stresses, among other qualities, its high degree of independence in regard to energy and cash.

10. Boehlje, "Costs and Benefits of Family Farming," 367–68.

11. Berry, "A Defense of the Family Farm," 350.

12. Wendell Berry, "Horse-Drawn Tools and the Doctrine of Labor Saving," in *The Gift of Good Land*, 105.

13. Wendell Berry, *The Unsettling of America*, 12.

14. According to Berry, the efficiency of agribusiness is "an efficiency calculated in the productivity of workers, not of acres." See Berry, "Agricultural Solutions for Agricultural Problems," 115. According to Lester Brown, at the beginning of the twentieth century farmers "were largely self-sufficient in energy." This is no longer true, due to the great use of fossil fuels to produce fertilizer as well as to run power machinery. Further, energy is used in pumps for irrigation. The increase in efficiency of labor is matched by a decrease in efficiency with regard to use of fuel. See Lester R. Brown, "Sustaining World Agriculture," in *State of the World—1987*, 130.

15. Berry, "Agricultural Solutions for Agricultural Problems," 122.

16. E. Ann Clark, "Resolving Conflicting Priorities in Ontario Agriculture," 275–89.

17. For one discussion of conflicts of ideals or values by an agricultural economist, see Willard W. Cochrane, "Beliefs and Values Underlying Agricultural Policies and Programs," 50–63.

18. Berry, "Agricultural Solutions for Agricultural Problems," 121. See also James A. Montmarquet, *The Idea of Agrarianism: From Hunter-Gatherer to Agrarian Radical in Western Culture*, chap. 4, 5.

19. Boehlje, "Costs and Benefits of Family Farming," 370.

20. Linda K. Lee, "The Impact of Landownership Factors on Soil Conservation." Linda K. Lee and William H. Stewart, "Landownership and the Adoption of Minimum Tillage."

21. Berry, "A Defense of the Family Farm," 350.

22. One sees this argument in many places. One place is in Rachel Carson's preface to *Animal Machines*, by Ruth Harrison.

23. Those familiar with recent work in philosophy of science will recognize the reference here to the thought of Thomas Kuhn. See Thomas Kuhn, *The*

Structure of Scientific Revolutions. Kuhn's thought on paradigms is discussed in many places. See especially Margaret Masterman, "The Nature of a Paradigm."

24. A distinction between scientific arguments aimed at establishing the plausibility of a hypothesis and arguments which might serve to prove or refute it is found in Wesley Salmon, "The Foundations of Scientific Inference," 245.

Part Two
Ethics

10. Ethical Grounds for Sustainable Agriculture

Awareness that agricultural practices in much of the world are exhausting the resources on which agriculture depends, combined with the belief that the life and well-being of most human beings depends on agricultural production, has led to efforts to develop sustainable agriculture. As a recent report notes, "the principle of sustainable agriculture" is widely accepted.[1] However, as is documented in the above report and in other sources, there is a range of mutually incompatible definitions of "sustainable agriculture."[2] Given the range of alternative and incompatible definitions of "sustainable agriculture," we cannot simply say that *the* principle of sustainable agriculture should be accepted. It is necessary first to decide what sustainable agriculture is. I undertake to do this in the first part of this chapter. In the second part, we consider problems which arise in trying to develop an ethical justification for having sustainable agriculture, and I argue that we have an obligation to make agriculture sustainable.

Prior to starting, let us note one unsatisfactory definition of "sustainable agriculture." According to this definition, "A sustainable food and agriculture system is one which is environmentally sound, economically viable, socially responsible, non-exploitative, and which serves as the foundation for future generations."[3] For a definition to be satisfactory, it should not rest on obscure terms. This definition contains a number of such terms, such as "environmentally sound," "economically viable," "socially responsible," "exploitative," and "foundation" are all very obscure. In light of these obscurities, it would not be possible to get general agreement in applying this definition to food and agriculture systems in a way that will yield consistent judgments as to what food or agriculture systems are sustainable. Perhaps, at this stage of our inquiries concerning sustainable agriculture, it is not possible to achieve perfect clarity—clarity is a matter of degree anyway. We shall consider some definitions in the first part of the chapter which are clearer than this definition, though they are unsatisfactory in other ways. In the end we shall try to formulate a definition of "sustainable agriculture" which is clear as to the objectives of sustainable agriculture, which does not conflate sustainability with other objectives, and which gives a (hopefully) reasonably clear indication of some conditions that must be satisfied to achieve sustainable agricultural production, that is, of methods for achieving sustainable agriculture.

WHAT IS SUSTAINABLE AGRICULTURE?

In this section I shall critically review a number of definitions of "sustainable agriculture" and then shall propose a definition. We start with a definition which apparently is favored by many agricultural scientists in Canada and the United States. In one place this definition is expressed as follows: "Sustainable agri-food systems are those that are economically viable, and meet society's need for safe and nutritious food, while conserving or enhancing. . . natural resources and the quality of the environment for future generations.[4] I shall call this definition 1. A very similar definition is expressed as follows: Sustainable agriculture is "food or fiber production which employs ecological production strategies to reduce inputs and environmental damage while promoting profitable, efficient, long-term production."[5] I shall call this definition 2.

I shall proceed by commenting on a number of elements of these two definitions. They both identify sustainable agriculture by reference to certain objectives. According to definition 1, the objectives of sustainable agriculture are to be economically viable, to meet society's need for safe and nutritious food, to conserve or enhance natural resources, and to conserve or enhance the quality of the environment. Definition 2 also specifies food production as an objective (I shall assume that it means safe and nutritious food) but it adds production of fibers. In place of "economic viability" it refers to profitable production. It adds that the production be efficient and long-term. Definition 2 refers to reduction of environmental damage as an objective. I shall assume that this is the same as conserving or enhancing natural resources. One further difference between definitions 1 and 2 is that definition 2 specifies a method or strategy for achieving the objectives of sustainable agriculture, namely, that sustainable agriculture employs ecological production strategies.

These definitions are open to a number of criticisms. I shall consider a number of these. First, definition 2 stipulates that sustainable agriculture should be profitable. Presumably what this means is that if a producer is engaging in sustainable agricultural production, then the income from production exceeds production costs. Indeed one of the principles of the program for low input sustainable agriculture (often called LISA) is that a method of farming is sustainable only if it is profitable.[6] This claim is open to serious question. Consider an agricultural production system which conserved resources, achieved relatively high energy outputs given its energy inputs, provided for needs for food, etc. for a community of people in a safe way, but did not yield income in excess of its costs. Would we really agree that such a system is not sustainable? Such a system could be carried on indefinitely unless there were a catastrophe which eliminated sunlight or some other element essential for biological processes.

A defender of the idea that sustainable agriculture must be profitable might urge that unless the production system is profitable then it will not sustain the life or well-being of the human beings who operate the system. Such people would be forced to seek support elsewhere and so the production system would not be sustained. However, this reply to our criticism is mistaken. The well-being of the people of the production system could be maintained through the provision of subsidies to the system, as is often the case with contemporary agricultural production. Alternatively, we could think of a production system as a self-sufficient community, that is, a community of people who work to produce everything they need. Agricultural production in such a community need not be profitable to endure.

Definition 1 did not stipulate that sustainable agriculture is profitable. However, it did refer to economic viability. Perhaps by the use of this term the advocates of definition 1 meant profitability. In that case, definition 1 is open to the same objection. However, it is not clear that economic viability is the same as profitability. Perhaps all that the advocates of definition 1 meant by "economically viable" is that the production system, or the community of which it is a part, must provide for satisfaction of the needs of the human beings engaged in agricultural production. People will not work in a production system if they are not enabled through their work to obtain what they must have to satisfy their needs.[7] A system which was not economically viable, in this sense of the term, could not endure for long (and so would not be correctly described as sustainable) unless it were supplied with laborers to replace those laborers who were lost to the system as a result of failure to satisfy their needs. Such a supply of laborers could be maintained only by force. We would object on moral grounds to a system of agricultural production which could endure only by use of forced labor.

Given that we object, on moral grounds, to forced labor, we should require that our production systems (agricultural or otherwise) should be economically viable in the second of the above senses of the term. However, economic viability, in this sense, appears entirely distinct from the capacity to endure indefinitely. Given the right circumstances, it is possible to have a sustainable agricultural system, i.e., one which can endure indefinitely, which is not economically viable. Thus, I suggest that we should not require that economic viability be included as an essential component of sustainable agriculture. To make this requirement is to lump together elements that should be distinguished.[8]

Definition 2 also stipulates that a sustainable production system must be efficient. Efficiency is a matter of degree. A system can be more or less efficient. Further, to speak of efficiency is virtually meaningless unless we are told the respects in which the system should be efficient. Should the system be efficient in the use of land or other natural resources? Should the system be efficient in the use of human labor? Should the system be efficient in the use of energy? Perhaps, the stipulation that the production system be efficient reflects the assumption that resources essential for production are in limited supply. Eventually they will be used up, and at that point in time production would have to be discontinued. Given this assumption, we can agree that a production system would be sustainable for the longest possible time if it were efficient in its use of essential resources. For this reason, we would agree that a sustainable production system would be efficient in this respect.

However, in contexts of discussions of modern agriculture, the term "efficiency" normally has other connotations. In my discussions with agricultural scientists who use this term, I get the impression that they regard one system as more efficient than another if the former system yields relatively more income for every unit of costs. In other words, the term "efficiency" when used in discussions of agricultural matters, normally connotes economic efficiency. Further, the time frame over which the system is economically efficient is usually not specified. Now, as has often been pointed out, a production system can be economically efficient for a period of time while it is rapidly consuming or dissipating resources which are essential for long-term functioning of the system. Thus, an agricultural production system can be both economically efficient and relatively non-sustainable. If the term "efficiency" is understood to mean economic efficiency then, I do not agree that efficiency is essential to sustainability. A sustainable production system could operate in ways that are not economically efficient given prevailing economic circumstances.

Definition 2 also implies that reduced inputs are essential to sustainable agricultural production. We may understand the term "input" to refer to substances introduced to a production system from sources which are external to the system. Thus, the use of the term presupposes a distinction between what is internal to the system and what is external to it. With regard to farms, this distinction is perhaps clear enough. Inputs are material originating off the farm which are brought onto the farm to facilitate production. If we think of the supply of inputs as finite, then clearly, for production to endure for an indefinitely long period of time, sustainable agriculture requires that there must be no inputs. However, not all inputs need be in finite supply. Some inputs to a farm might consist of material that was exported from the farm and is being returned to the farm. For example, suppose that some element, such as phosphorous, is contained in agricultural products that are exported from a farm or production system. If, after this element is used, it is collected and recycled, then we need not envisage the agricultural production as terminating, that is, as being non-sustainable. Thus, rather than saying that for sustainable production we need low inputs, we should perhaps say that for sustainable production we need to recycle materials back into the production system which are essential for that production.

Definition 1 speaks of conserving natural resources and preserving the quality of the environment as essential for sustainable agriculture, and definition 2 speaks of avoiding damage to the environment. What do these expressions mean? "Damage to the environment" can refer to the loss of resources, such as topsoil or water, which are essential for production. "Damage to the environment" can also refer to contamination of water or air which undermines the health of human beings exposed to that contamination. "Damage to the environment" can also refer to changes to fields, forests, streams, etc., which render the environment less aesthetically pleasing. Clearly, some of these factors are essential elements of sustainable agriculture. Given that production systems require topsoil and fresh water, agricultural production systems which cause loss of topsoil or of supplies of fresh water are not sustainable.

Definitions of sustainable agriculture may be compared with respect to what it is that is envisaged, in those definitions, as being sustained. Both of the above definitions agree in that they envisage the capacity to produce food and other crops as being sustained (in sustainable production systems). Some other definitions of sustainable agriculture are similar to both of the above definitions in focussing attention on the capacity to produce crops. They may differ in that they do not regard profitability or economic viability as essential to sustainable agriculture.[9] Such definitions are open to criticisms similar to those above in that they may conflate ideas which should be kept distinct from the idea of sustainability with that idea. Further, they may be criticized in that they fail to make explicit the assumptions that they have taken for granted.

Still other views of sustainable agriculture apparently focus on agriculture as consisting of certain modes of production. Modes of production that did not involve the growth or reproduction of living organisms would not count as agriculture. Further, agriculture consists of intentional or deliberate manipulation of biological processes beyond merely collecting the products of such processes. Sustaining agriculture does not include sustaining communities of humans which thrive exclusively by hunting or gathering. Some views concerning the nature of sustainable agriculture may go further in restricting the modes of production that count as agricultural production. If production of crops became too much like industrial production in not requiring sunlight, soil, or seeds, some people might not regard it as agricultural production.[10] In such a view, sustainable agriculture would require sustaining a particular mode of production. Again, some views concerning sustainable agriculture may be concerned primarily with the preservation of certain forms of social organization, forms such as may be found in traditional rural agricultural communities.

In this book I shall restrict my concern by considering sustainable agriculture as a sustainable capacity to produce food, fiber, and other crops and shall not try to distinguish agricultural production of such crops from other possible modes of production. Further, I shall not be concerned with modes of social organizations either, except, of course, as some modes of organization may not be conducive to sustaining the capacity to sustain production of food or other crops. This narrowing of the definition of "sustainable agriculture" cannot be justified by a proof. I choose this definition because it enables me to formulate a ethical claim which I believe to be correct, namely that we are morally obligated to sustain our capacity to produce food, fiber, and other crops which are essential to sustain the life and well-being of most human beings who are alive or will be alive. Those who are concerned with other ethical claims may choose to define "sustainable agriculture" differently.

We have challenged other definitions of "sustainable agriculture" on the grounds that they stipulated conditions which are not essential for preserving or sustaining the capacity to produce food, fiber, and other crops which can satisfy human needs for an indefinitely long temporal period. I now wish to comment briefly on this reference to a temporal period. It is reasonable to believe that the resources available to human beings for sustaining human existence are finite. Conceivably some essential resources can be recycled. However, in light of the basic principle of physics, the law of entropy, there is reason to think that eventually our capacity to sustain future human existence will be exhausted. The law of entropy may be understood as saying that the energy available to us for growing crops, etc. is finite and is continually decreasing. Ultimately, none will be left. However, I do not believe that it is possible, at this point, to make a rational prediction as to the point in time when, due to entropy, we will no longer be able to grow crops. Further, very likely there are other considerations which will restrict the span of human existence even more narrowly than the limits that one might deduce from considerations of entropy. There may well be other limitations on our power to convert the material of the universe to forms in which it can serve our needs. These limitations are also, in my view, unpredictable. Consequently, I speak of sustaining our capacity to produce what we need "indefinitely." I think we should try to extend it as long as it is possible for humans to live well. I suspect that this is a very long time, relative to the 10,000 or so years that agriculture has existed, providing we use resources wisely; that is, so long as we don't render our habitat uninhabitable by virtue of activities which we could avoid.

Other interesting issues arise from considering further questions regarding definitions 1 or 2 above. For example, definition 1 says that for agriculture to be sustainable it must supply crops in sufficient quantity to satisfy the needs of the human population. However, one may ask what human population. Conceivably, given the limitations imposed by the environments that exist on Earth and by human technology, the human population is already so large, or will inevitably become so large, that no system of agricultural production could be sufficiently productive to satisfy even the nutritional needs of all human beings. In the horrible event that we were to get ourselves into a situation in which our food production systems will not yield enough to satisfy our nutritional needs, we would have some nasty ethical problems to resolve. Such a situation would constitute a lifeboat situation on a very large scale.[11] Consideration of this point indicates that our definition of "sustainable agriculture" must take account of the size of the human population. If the human population continues to grow indefinitely, then ultimately no agricultural practices will be sustainable. In advocating that we havesustainable agricultural production, we are ipso facto advocating that the world's human population be sufficiently restricted in size.

Reflection on the idea of sustaining the capacity to produce sufficient food and other crops to meet nutritional and other needs of a limited human population suggests that the term "sustainable agriculture" may be misleading. Use of this term may suggest that the achievement of sustainable agriculture may leave all non-agricultural human activities or practices out of account, so that, for example, humans in urban environments who are not engaged in crop production need not be concerned about conditions necessary for sustainable agriculture. But this suggestion is mistaken. Given assumptions to which we have called attention, such as that human population must be limited and that some resources essential for crop production are finite and so must be recycled, it is clear that aspects of human activities not normally conceived as agricultural activities will have to be modified in order to achieve sustainable agriculture. Human reproduction may have to be limited. Elements such as phosphorous will have to be recycled.[12]

Given that sustainable agriculture consists of sustaining the capacity to produce food or other crops there may, as I have indicated above, be restrictions on political and economic relationships which may obtain in human communities. While I have argued that profitability or economic viability (in some sense of that term) are not essential to sustaining our capacity to produce sufficient quantities of crops, this is not to say that the objective of achieving sustainable agriculture has no implications concerning economic or political relationships. For example, given that achieving sustainable agriculture will require extensive knowledge of environments in which agriculture occurs, it appears likely that to have sustainable agriculture, people with such knowledge will have to be trained, and further, that such people will have to have sufficient political power to influence methods of agricultural production. While it is conceivable that dictatorial political systems, such as existed in the former Soviet Union, could have hit on sustainable agricultural production systems, it appears most unlikely that they will do so. In such systems the people who have the political power normally lack sufficient knowledge of agricultural processes. Even in democratic political systems, too much power may rest in the hands of those who lack knowledge or incentive to make agricultural production sustainable. For example, because of the influence of wealthy individuals or corporations, agricultural development in many countries has often been non-sustainable.

Before concluding the first part of this chapter, I believe it will be of interest to comment briefly on a third definition of "sustainable agriculture." According to this definition, "sustainable agriculture" restricts inputs of non-renewable resources and preserves "ecosystem integrity."[13] Interesting questions might be raised about the notion of "non-renewable resources." For example, it could be argued, contrary to what many people would say, that oil is a renewable resource. However, I want to raise a question here concerning the notion of ecosystem integrity. In my view this notion is unacceptably obscure.

To see this, consider the question of what an ecosystem is. An ecosystem is a collection of causally interrelated elements within a geographical area. However, we may ask, what unites such a collection into an ecosystem? It appears that the ecosystems to which ecologists or others refer are determined in part by reference to the ecologists' choice of geographical areas. Different choices would yield different ecosystems, albeit systems which could overlap and which would have elements and systematic relations in common. Thus, it is a mistake to speak simply, as in the above definition, of preserving the integrity of *the* ecosystem of which some agricultural production units are a part. One must at least relativize this claim, that is, must refer to the ecosystem relative to some particular region. However, there is an even more serious difficulty.

While ecosystems change, I have not been able to find any clear explanation of the principles by reference to which one could distinguish changes consistent with ecosystem integrity from changes not consistent with ecosystem integrity. Suppose, for example, that a forest changes over time. The proportion of trees of particular types changes. Perhaps the proportions of various species of animals in the forest changes. How should we describe this? Shall we say that an older ecosystem lost its integrity and was replaced with a newer ecosystem? Or shall we say that the forest which undergoes these changes has preserved its integrity? Again, consider an agricultural ecosystem, that is, a set of objects in a region which are causally interrelated but which includes a human crop-production system. If the farmer eliminates shrubs around stream beds or eliminates some patches of woods between his or her fields, shall we say that the farmer has replaced one ecosystem with another, or that he or she has undermined the integrity of the first ecosystem. To my knowledge, no clear principles which can serve to make such a distinction in a consistent fashion have been formulated.[14]

Let us summarize our discussion of the nature of sustainable agriculture in the following terms. A definition of sustainable agriculture can specify the purpose or goal of sustainability. Further, a definition can specify the methods for achieving sustainability. The goal of sustainable agriculture, in our view, is to sustain the capacity to produce food, fiber, and other crops which are required for satisfying conditions essential for preserving the lives and well-being of human populations for an indefinitely long time. The methods of achieving sustainable agriculture involve devising technologies which conserve essential resources, such as topsoil, fresh water, and various minerals; devising modes of social organization which facilitate deployment of those technologies; and restricting the size of human populations. At this point, given the limitations of human knowledge, it would be premature to try to specify the methods of achieving sustainable agriculture in detail.[15]

OUR OBLIGATION TO ACHIEVE SUSTAINABLE AGRICULTURE

It is widely accepted today that we ought to have sustainable agriculture. Sometimes this is explicitly stated; sometimes it is simply taken for granted. However, it is also widely recognized that achieving sustainable agriculture will involve conflict with other objectives. Agriculture has long been recognized as an industry to which people in countries such as the United States and Canada look for generation of wealth. Generation of wealth in the recent past has rested on deploying modern technologies and use of mineral and energy resources in ways that are apparently non-sustainable. Production of vast quantities of grain coincides with rapid losses of agricultural land and with dependence on relatively inexpensive supplies of petroleum.[16]

Those engaged in the development of agricultural and food production industries in the recent decades have, I believe, operated under the moral assumption that they were entitled to do so. I am not aware of any explicit efforts to justify this assumption in agricultural matters. However, many discussions with agrologists and agricultural scientists have indicated underlying moral assumptions to which one might appeal in trying to formulate such a justification. In particular it is widely assumed

1. that activities which tend on the whole to produce more good than harm are morally acceptable, and
2. that economically efficient production of agricultural products does, on the whole, produce more good than harm.

Of these two assumptions, assumption 1 is a moral assumption. It is a version of a moral theory which philosophers call 'utilitarianism'. We may refer to it here as the "principle of utility."[17] By referring to the principle of utility as a moral assumption, I mean that it makes a claim as to what activities are morally permissible or obligatory. Assumption 2 is a claim about the balance of values which results from certain forms of agricultural activity. Clearly, this assumption rests in turn on assumptions about values, that is, assumptions about what is good and what is bad or harmful. In my judgment, it is widely assumed that what satisfies preferences or desires is good and that what causes pleasure is good. Further, it is widely assumed that what frustrates preferences or desires is harmful or bad and that what causes pain or discomfort is bad.[18] Frequently people make additional value assumptions in conjunction with these assumptions.

Often, I believe, agrologists, agricultural scientists, etc. do not think long and hard about their value or ethical assumptions. Perhaps, as long as they are not confronted with conflicts as to what activities or practices are morally acceptable, it is not necessary for them to do so. However, as I have indicated, the belief that we ought to have sustainable agriculture does apparently conflict with the belief that we are entitled to develop agriculture in ways that are economically efficient for agricultural producers. To determine the nature and limits of this conflict, and to resolve it in accord with the results of reasoning, requires that we engage in reasoning about values and ethics, in addition to engaging in scientific reasoning, to determine, as far as we are able, what courses of action produce the greatest value. I would urge agrologists, agricultural scientists, and others to engage in careful reflection about their value assumptions so that they can contribute in constructive ways to developing reasoned resolutions to conflicts concerning agricultural policy and practice.[19]

Given the assumption of the principle of utility and of value assumptions such as those indicated above, we may ask whether it follows that we have an obligation to convert agricultural practices to make agriculture sustainable. Some agricultural scientists appear to believe that this consequence indeed obtains, and since they are basically committed to these value and moral assumptions, they think that we have an obligation to make agriculture sustainable.[20] However, it is not clear that this is the case. Some philosophers have argued that we cannot justify the claim that we are obligated to make agriculture sustainable on utilitarian grounds.[21]

One problem with trying to show that sustainable agriculture will produce more good than harm on the whole is that much of the good that would obtain from having sustainable agriculture will not occur until a relatively long time into (what is still) the future, whereas some of the harm that will occur from transforming currently used agricultural practices will occur sooner, in the form of higher costs for production of agricultural products. Further, many of the people who will reap the benefits (or avoid harms) from our changing to sustainable agriculture are not born yet. One may wonder whether we have moral obligations to change our behavior to provide benefits for or to avoid harms to people who are not yet born.

In my view, we do have moral obligations to people yet unborn. We are morally obligated not to act in ways which cause harm, so far as we can determine, to such people.[22] I regard this as a straightforward application of the principle of utility. That principle does not imply that the time at which a person exists is morally relevant in regard to the determination of our obligations to that person. The time at which a person exists is as irrelevant as the place at which a person exists.[23]

Further, in my view, there are strong utilitarian reasons to think that we have moral obligations to bring about sustainable agriculture even if one sets aside obligations to unborn people. Perhaps the development of agricultural practices in the industrialized world since World War II has caused great benefits for many people, largely through the provision of relatively cheap food. However, this same development has also caused great harms to many people. Many people have lost their farms. Many people have been harmed by the various practices, such as the use of pesticides. Environmental costs have been extensive.[24] Some people may argue that on the whole, the benefits have outweighed the harms—this may indeed be true. However, it is reasonable to think that now we can obtain greater benefits or reduce harms for many of the people now alive, without great increase in costs or other harms, by making a gradual transition to sustainable agricultural practices.

To corroborate this last point, consider the sorts of practices which are characteristic of much contemporary agriculture and which are alleged to contribute to making agriculture non-sustainable (in the sense of the term we have specified in part one of this chapter). Input costs of agricultural, production through use of fertilizers and pesticides, are relatively high. By reducing dependence on such inputs, there is reason to think that costs could be reduced at the same time that we increase the probability that we will be able to continue such agricultural practices for a longer time in the future. Similarly, loss of topsoil through erosion both reduces productivity and increases the probability that we will not be able to engage in such agricultural practices in the future. Reversing this tendency should make agriculture more sustainable and not contribute to great increases in costs. Indeed, reversing this tendency may ultimately lead to significant reductions in the cost of agricultural production at a future time. In some regions, current agricultural production is draining aquifers at a significant rate. Such production is non-sustainable. Further, such production puts agricultural practices in direct conflict with other uses for that water. Eliminating the practices which use aquifers should thereby yield both extended life-expectancy for agriculture, i.e., more sustainable agriculture, and other benefits—which will accrue within the lifetimes of many of the people now alive.

The same conclusion can be supported by other considerations. We have not yet considered all of the harms associated with agricultural practices which are thought to be non-sustainable. To some degree, contemporary agricultural practices have contributed toward reducing the diversity of existing life forms. This has occurred through the loss of habitats of wild creatures due to agricultural practices, e.g., to draining swamps and eliminating forests and windbreaks between fields. This in turn has contributed to wind erosion and thereby to non-sustainability. Similarly, the destruction of insects, such as bees and insect predators, has harmed agricultural production. The reduction in biodiversity may make our agricultural practices more vulnerable to pests and, in general, is believed by some people to weaken the networks of elements on which the good quality of our life depends. Reversing this tendency may be expected to increase sustainability of agriculture and to provide other benefits, such as aesthetic benefits, that may well compensate for any increased costs of production. Given these conclusions, it is reasonable to believe that by making such a transition we will produce more good and less harm than by not making such a transition. Thus, given only the ethical principle of utility, and setting aside possible obligations to people yet unborn, there is strong reason to believe that we have an obligation to make agriculture sustainable.

The recognition that we have an obligation to make agriculture sustainable is not the end of ethical issues confronting agriculture. Determining the procedures which will obtain both maximum good in the present time and maximum good in the future will not be easy. In addition to conflicts concerning the rate and path to sustainability, there are other conflicts to be confronted also, for example, questions about our obligations to animals. Thus, we may expect that there will continue to be many controversies concerning our obligations concerning agricultural practices.

SUMMARY

In this chapter we have investigated an ethical issue, namely, whether we have an obligation to make our agricultural practices sustainable. To pursue this issue it was necessary first to formulate a reasonably clear definition of "sustainable agriculture." We undertook to do this in the first part of this chapter. In part two we presented two arguments in support of the conclusion that we have an obligation to make agriculture sustainable. The first argument is that not making agriculture sustainable causes harm to people not yet born and that making the change will bring benefits to them. We have argued that we have obligations, in accord with the principle of utility, to such people. The second argument is that even if obligations to such people are set aside, we are obligated to make agriculture sustainable in light of the increase in benefits and decrease in harms to people who already exist.

NOTES

1. *It's Everybody's Business: Submissions to the Science Council's Committee on Sustainable Agriculture: A Discussion Paper*, 5.

2. See Patricia Allen and Carolyn Sachs, *What Do We Want to Sustain? Developing a Comprehensive Vision of Sustainable Agriculture*.

3. Patricia Allen et al., *Expanding the Definition of Sustainable Agriculture*. A similar appeal to obscure concepts appears in a statement of "principles of sustainable agriculture and food production." According to some of these principles, sustainable agriculture requires "thorough integration of the farming system with natural processes," "efficient production, with an emphasis on . . . conservation of soil, water, energy, and biological resources," and "development of food processing, packaging, distribution, and consumption practices consistent with sound environmental management." These principles are stated (along with some other principles that are slightly less vague) in *Sustainable Agriculture: The Research Challenge*, 15–16. Another vague statement is found in Terry Gips, "What is Sustainable Agriculture." Gips said that "sustainable agriculture should be conceived as agriculture which is economically viable, ecologically sound, socially just and humane."

4. *It's Everybody's Business*, 7.

5. This definition is attributed to the National Research Council of the United States. It is quoted in Patricia Allen et al., *Expanding the Definition of Sustainable Agriculture*, 2.

6. Ibid., 5.

7. In discussing "sustainable agriculture" we refer at times to the needs of human beings and to the well-being of people. Clearly these are controversial notions. There may well be disagreement as to what conditions are needs, that is, are necessary for life or well-being. Further, such disagreements will involve disagreements about what is of value and not just disagreements which can be settled by biologists or other scientists through application of scientific methods.

8. For further discussion of "economic viability," see Hugh Lehman, Ann Clark, and Stephan Weise, "Clarifying the Definition of Sustainable Agriculture."

9. See, for example, Timothy Crews et al., "Energetics and Ecosystem Integrity: The Defining Principles of Sustainable Agriculture."

10. This idea is suggested in James Montmarquet, *The Idea of Agrarianism: From Hunter-Gatherer to Agrarian Radical in Western Culture*, 18. For more discussion of the meaning of "sustainability," see Gordon K. Douglass, "The Meanings of Agricultural Sustainability," 4.

11. A lifeboat situation is a situation in which there are more people in the lifeboat than can be sustained by the provisions or capacity of the lifeboat.

12. I am indebted to E. Ann Clark for forcefully calling my attention to this point.

13. Crews et al., "Energetics and Ecosystem Integrity," 147.

14. One scientist suggested that changes to an ecosystem which tend to preserve the ecosystem are changes which count as preserving ecosystem integrity. This definition is clearly circular, that is, one must already understand "ecosystem integrity" to understand "changes which preserve the ecosystem."

15. One explicit statement is "Canadians must chart a new path toward an agricultural system that is sustainable, safe, and responsive to market needs." *Sustainable Agriculture: The Research Challenge*, 13. Notice that in this statement, sustainability is distinguished from market needs. This is in accord with the definition of sustainability that we have advocated here.

16. In Canada "some 20 million hectares of food-producing land are abandoned each year because of waterlogging, salinization, or alkalization of soils." *Sustainable Agriculture: The Research Challenge*, 17.

17. The classic statement of the theory of utilitarianism is John Stuart Mill, *Utilitarianism*.

18. I have discussed the nature of value and moral assumptions more thoroughly in my essay: Hugh Lehman, "Values, Ethics and the Use of Synthetic Pesticides in Agriculture," in *The Pesticide Question*, ed. David Pimentel and Hugh Lehman.

19. There are many philosophical works which (in addition to this book) can serve to initiate agrologists to careful thought about ethical matters. One is Peter Singer, *Practical Ethics*, 2d ed. For further work by this author see Peter Singer, *Animal Liberation*.

20. This appears to be the attitude expressed in the documents of the Science Council of Canada to which I have referred.

21. See "The Morality Behind Sustainability," 118.

22. This remark should not be taken as implying that we have moral obligations to create future people. Nor should it be taken as implying that a person who becomes pregnant is morally obligated not to have an abortion. The formation of a person is a part of a continuous process. Where one makes a cut in this process to demarcate the initial stages in the existence of a new person is a matter to be decided on the basis of moral considerations. Many so-called "pro-lifers" assume that the existence of this cut is a scientific fact and that the cut clearly occurs at the moment of conception. This assumption is subject to serious doubts.

23. The question of whether we have moral obligations to members of future generations has been much discussed. One source is E. Partridge, ed., *Responsibilities to Future Generations*. Also see J. Woodward, "The Non-Identity Problem," 804–31.

24. Some harms are discussed in a number of papers in Pimentel and Lehman, *The Pesticide Question*.

II. Marginal Cases and Killing Animals

MOST ANIMAL SCIENTISTS believe that use of domestic (or wild) animals for human purposes, including provision of flesh for foods, is morally acceptable. In consequence, they confidently go about their research concerned with understanding behavior and physiology, improving the efficiency of processes involving use of animals, etc., without giving serious consideration to the profound reasonings which underlie the objections of moral vegetarians to killing animals for food. These reasonings also support comparable objections to killing animals for clothing, entertainment, scientific research, and possibly even for scientific research devoted to solving problems of human medicine.[1] Failure to give these profound reasonings serious consideration exposes animal scientists to a second criticism on ethical grounds.[2] Being morally responsible requires making serious efforts to determine whether one's behavior is morally acceptable. Failure to give serious consideration to well-publicized arguments which express deep criticisms of one's behavior is at least an indication that one is not acting responsibly. On the assumption that taking these profound criticisms seriously requires engaging in philosophical thought, there is a strong argument for saying that animal scientists ought to study philosophy as well as animal science. The material of this chapter should facilitate their entry into philosophical discussions of the morality of killing animals for food or other purposes.

In this chapter I formulate and critically assess one argument which purports to show that killing farm animals for food is morally unacceptable.

The argument is called the "marginal cases argument." I shall criticize this argument by calling attention to the controversial assumptions on which it rests. In part one of this chapter I state one formulation of this argument and defend it against one criticism. In the second part we explain the moral theory called "utilitarianism," and show that on utilitarian grounds, the marginal cases argument is unsound. In the third part I explore some other criticisms of the marginal cases argument.

THE MARGINAL CASES ARGUMENT

Among the deep arguments that call uses of animals for food into question is an argument called the "argument from marginal cases."[3] The argument proceeds on the assumption that if beings (human or otherwise) have a moral right to life (which is equal to the right to life of human beings), there is some explanation of why this is so. By reference to that explanation, one should be able to discern both why human beings have this moral right and why other things such as dandelions (*Taraxacum officinale*) do not (assuming that dandelions do not have such a right to life). Further, the argument assumes that if one is able to explain why human beings have a moral right to life (and dandelions do not), then there will be some criterion by reference to which possessors of this right are distinguished from beings that lack this right. All and only the beings that satisfy this criterion would have the right to life.

It may be argued that animal scientists, since they assume that it is morally acceptable to kill animals to eat animal flesh, as well as for other purposes, assume that animals do not have a moral right to life which is equal to a human right to life.[4] To proceed with the discussion in terms of rights it is necessary to assume that the animal scientists accept the idea that human beings have a moral right to life. However, in discussions many scientists have expressed skepticism concerning the validity of the concept of moral rights. Rather than entering into consideration of tangential issues regarding the validity of this concept, let us reformulate the issues by reference to what is morally acceptable, and so avoid use of the concept of moral rights. In general, animal scientists, I assume, agree that it is morally acceptable to kill animals to eat them but that it is not morally acceptable to kill human beings, even marginal human beings, to eat them. ("Marginal human beings" are all humans, except those who are permanently comatose, who lack some of the mental [including sensory and emotional] capacities exhibited by normal adult or paradigmatic humans.) At this point it is natural to ask whether there is some fact of the matter by reference to which this social behavior can be morally justified. Tom Regan appealed to the marginal cases argument in the effort to call into question the possibility of there being any such fact of the matter, as well as to challenge the belief that the practice of killing animals for food is morally acceptable.

The marginal cases argument may be stated as follows:

Part 1:

Premise:

1. Certain criteria concerning what it is morally acceptable for humans to kill for food imply that it is morally acceptable to kill and eat some marginal human beings.

Conclusion:

If it is not morally acceptable to kill and eat marginal human beings, then each of the criteria referred to in premise 1 is mistaken.

Part 2:

Premise:

2. Any justifiable criterion concerning what is morally acceptable for humans to kill for food which implies that it is always unacceptable to kill and eat marginal human beings also implies that it is unacceptable to kill and eat farm (and certain other) animals.

Premise:

3. It is morally acceptable to kill animals for food if and only if there is a justifiable criterion which implies that such activity is morally acceptable.

Conclusion:

If it is morally unacceptable to kill and eat marginal human beings then it is unacceptable to kill and eat farm (and certain other) animals.[5]

Let us briefly explain the argument. Premise 1 refers to certain criteria concerning what it is morally acceptable for humans to kill for food. Regan is thinking of criteria such as rationality. Someone who takes rationality as a criterion would say that it is morally acceptable for humans to kill irrational creatures for food. The first premise of this argument points out that if this were correct, then, since some human beings are irrational, it would be morally acceptable to kill and eat such human beings. However, if it is not morally acceptable to kill and eat such human beings, then it is not the case that it is acceptable to kill and eat irrational beings. The criterion of rationality is mistaken.

For another illustration of the intent of this argument, one might consider the capacity to understand moral concepts or to govern one's life in accordance with moral rules. If someone maintains that it is morally acceptable to kill beings for food if they lack this capacity, but not acceptable to kill beings that possess this capacity for food, then that person's view implies that it is morally acceptable to kill human infants for food, since they lack the capacity in question. If we grant that it is not morally acceptable to kill human infants for food, then this criterion must be rejected. (This also is one of the criteria referred to in premise 1.) According to the marginal cases argument, the same fate attends any other plausible suggestion regarding the criterion in question.

The marginal cases argument, by itself, does not imply that it is morally wrong to kill and eat animals for food. To derive this conclusion one must add an additional premise, namely, that it is morally wrong to kill and eat marginal human beings for food. We shall assume that readers of this book accept this premise. Assuming that animal scientists accept this premise, then, unless they find fault with the marginal cases argument, if they are rational they will have to conclude that it is morally wrong to kill cows, pigs, chickens, or certain other animals for food. In my view, for them to find fault with the argument, they must find fault either with premise 2 or with premise 3.

Some animal scientists might try to circumvent the marginal cases argument by claiming that on the basis of Biblical authority, the belief that it is morally acceptable to kill domestic (or wild) animals for food but not morally acceptable to kill human beings for food is rationally justified. However, this approach will not work unless it is possible to show both that the Bible clearly and consistently implies this injunction, and that acceptance of injunctions which are clearly and consistently implied by the Bible is justifiable by reference to justified ethical grounds. Even if the Bible does contain the injunction in question, mere appeal to Biblical authority does not yield rationally defensible explanations as to why our moral beliefs regarding killing humans or animals for food are correct beliefs.[6] The fact that something is commanded by God may give one a reason for doing that thing; it does not yield an explanation as to why that is the morally right thing to do unless we can explain why God would command only what is right. To have such an explanation would require an understanding of God's reasons for what he or she (allegedly) does. To discover such reasons one has to engage in philosophical thought. In other words, in order to determine whether there is a satisfactory rebuttal to the marginal cases argument and, if so, what that rebuttal is, it is necessary to engage in philosophical study of ethics. Again, there is a reason why animal scientists ought to pursue such philosophical studies.

A UTILITARIAN APPROACH

Utilitarianism is an ethical theory according to which one's actions are morally acceptable if and only if there are no alternative actions which would yield greater satisfaction of desires or pleasure.[7] The question of finding an explanatory criterion for the view under consideration, namely that it is morally acceptable to kill animals for food but not to kill humans for food, could be avoided, on utilitarian grounds, providing that there was no alternative to action in accord with this view which would yield greater satisfaction or pleasure.

I suspect that utilitarian arguments can be given which provide a rational moral justification for killing animals for food under certain circumstances. There are many circumstances under which it is readily conceivable that killing animals for food will lead to greater satisfaction of desires or pleasure than not doing so. Consider a group of human beings who will die of malnutrition unless they kill a deer or a cow to eat. It is arguable that any action other than killing the cow or deer would yield less pleasure or satisfaction. Again, consider a situation in which a population of animals has grown too large to survive within their environmental circumstances. Some of the animals will die from disease and some from starvation. Their deaths will be prolonged and painful. Conceivably, not killing some animals and eating them will yield less pleasure or satisfaction than the alternative.

Of course, such arguments do not show that raising and then slaughtering domestic animals to eat them is morally acceptable as a regular social practice such as that in which we engage in the industrialized world. Indeed, various aspects of our common practices regarding the raising and killing of animals to eat can be soundly criticized on utilitarian grounds. Physicians, nutritionists, and others have suggested that people would be healthier, and so presumably happier, if they consumed less animal fat. Assuming that overconsumption of animal fat is not morally justified by reference to the happiness experienced by the animals before they are slaughtered, this is a strong utilitarian argument for reducing the numbers of animals killed and eaten.[8]

Similarly, there have been reports that clearing of forests at the present time, to increase land for grazing of animals to be killed for food, is contributing to serious environmental problems which must be solved for humans to have a high quality of existence.9 While clearing the rain forests may produce some short-term gains in regard to satisfaction, owing largely to reduced costs for animal production, in the longer term it is reasonable to expect this practice will cause declines in quality of life due to environmental deterioration. Often the grazing land acquired by clearing tropical forests deteriorates too quickly due to erosion of soil, and so the gains from any particular piece of cleared land do not last long.

Furthermore, at the present time land is often used to produce grain to feed animals which are ultimately consumed by human beings. It has been argued that it would be more efficient to produce grains for human consumption, as a significant portion of the grain fed to animals does not turn into human food. Given that human food were in short supply or that the price of human food could be reduced for poor people, there could be some gains in utility from reducing or eliminating the practice of using grain for animal feed.

However, all of these arguments, that is, arguments regarding fat intake, eliminating tropical forests, or inefficiencies in using grain to feed animals, show, at most, that some increase in pleasure or satisfaction could be gained from modifying our animal production practices in certain ways. These arguments do not show that there would be increases in pleasure or satisfaction were we all to abandon killing and eating animals. Further, it appears that there are strong arguments in support of the conclusion that, in many circumstances, some killing of animals to eat produces more pleasure or satisfaction than any alternative course of action. People derive pleasure out of eating animal flesh. Within the limits of contemporary technology there is no alternative way to produce certain of those pleasures.

In addition, animals raised properly can have pleasant lives prior to their being killed, and killing methods could be improved so as to significantly reduce fear or pain associated with such practices at present. Further, for many people, eating only vegetarian meals, no matter how well prepared, would not produce equivalent amounts of pleasure. Also, we should not forget that there is pleasure derived by hunters from killing animals. While I am persuaded that there are utilitarian reasons for modifying present-day animal production practices, I am also persuaded that, for the foreseeable future, some production of animals to be killed for food can be justified on utilitarian grounds. This applies to production in highly industrialized countries as well as to killing of animals in other societies.

So far, our argument that some practices involving production and killing of animals for food can be justified on utilitarian grounds does not refute the marginal cases argument. A conclusion of that argument is that any reasonable criterion which implies that it is morally acceptable to kill animals for food will also imply that it is morally acceptable to kill certain human beings for food. The utilitarian arguments support the contention that providing we significantly reduce or eliminate animal suffering in our animal production and slaughter practices, and don't consume too much animal fat, and don't degrade our environmental life-support systems, producing animals to be killed for food is morally justified. Could a similar argument be given to show that killing human beings for food or even producing human beings to be killed for food, under proper circumstances, would be morally justified? To show that we could make a significant challenge to the soundness or validity of the marginal cases argument, on utilitarian grounds, we must show that no such argument can be developed.

There do seem to be strong objections on utilitarian grounds to any practice involving regularly killing human beings for food. Humans, other than infants or very severely mentally defective people, would not have a pleasant life if they knew, as they would, that they shortly were to be killed and eaten. Further, the prospect of restricting the practice so that only young infants or severely retarded people could be eaten does not seem promising either on utilitarian grounds. Human females, and no doubt many males also, would not contentedly produce offspring for such purposes. While there are reports of human cultures in which killing of humans and eating parts of the victims were practiced, such practices would not be approved on utilitarian grounds. One can envisage hypothetical scenarios according to which beings resembling human beings but who have the mental capacities of bovine or other domestic animals are created. With respect to such creatures some of our objections to killing and eating human beings would be overcome. However, it is unclear what such hypothetical speculations show. Even if it were possible to create such beings, it appears that the prospect of doing so would be so repugnant to so many people that the practice could not be justified by appeal to utilitarian considerations.[10] It appears, then, that there is a utilitarian justification of the practice which involves both killing farm animals for food while prohibiting killing of human beings for this purpose.[11]

From a utilitarian perspective, the marginal cases argument fails to establish one of its conclusions. The utilitarian would reject premise 2 of the marginal cases argument as we have formulated it above. There is a criterion concerning the nature of the creatures that it is acceptable to kill for food. Specifically, the creatures must not be human, they must satisfy human tastes, and be nutritious. Further, this criterion, according to the utilitarian, is justifiable on rational grounds.

One may doubt that the utilitarian theory provides a rational justification for the view that it is acceptable to kill animals for food but not acceptable to kill humans. To raise this question calls attention to some complex theoretical issues. Let us discuss these briefly. Clearly, a defender of utilitarianism could argue that her or his view does yield such a rational justification. She or he would say that such a practice leads to goodness equal to the greatest achievable amount of goodness in the circumstances, since there is no alternative social practice which yields greater pleasure or satisfaction of desires. This argument rests on some significant assumptions. Among these are (1) that pleasure and the satisfaction of desires are intrinsically good or valuable, (2) that nothing else is intrinsically good, (3) that producing the greatest amount of good gives a sufficient reason for why a thing should occur or be done.[12] Given these or related assumptions about what is intrinsically valuable, and that something's being valuable is a reason for getting it or doing it, utilitarianism provides moral reasons for the opinion about the acceptability of killing animals or humans for food. In this way utilitarianism differs from the simplified religious view that the practice in question is acceptable because it is implied to be so by statements in the Bible. For the Biblical theory to provide a rational justification for the social practices in question, it would need to be developed so as to include theories about moral reasons for human actions.

The utilitarian theory about moral reasons for actions rests on a theory of values, the theory that pleasure or satisfaction of desires is intrinsically valuable. Further, the appeal of the utilitarian theory rests in part on the assumption that deriving pleasure or satisfaction are in general motivating reasons for human beings. The utilitarian theory assumes that motivating reasons can also yield a moral justification for actions. However, these assumptions, on which utilitarianism rests, can be challenged.

That pleasure or satisfaction are good in themselves has been doubted. That there are no other intrinsically valuable things or states of affairs has been doubted. Plausible reasons can be given for challenging these assumptions; these cannot be conclusively refuted. In light of this, it is not possible to provide rationally compelling proofs that the assumptions underlying the utilitarian theory are correct. For this reason, we cannot say that the appeal to utilitarian moral theory provides a conclusive refutation of the marginal cases argument. Furthermore, many scientists, when called on to justify claims about what is permissible or obligatory, appear to appeal to some form of utilitarian theory. An animal scientist who had determined that he or she was a utilitarian could reject the conclusion of the marginal cases argument with some peace of mind. Such a person could hold that it is morally acceptable to kill and eat cows, etc., for food even though he or she did not think that it is morally acceptable to kill and eat marginal human beings. However, on reflection, some animal scientists may determine that they are not utilitarians. If such scientists wish to maintain that it is morally acceptable to kill and eat pigs, etc., but not marginal human beings, they will have to find other grounds for challenging the marginal cases argument.

OTHER CHALLENGES TO THE MARGINAL CASES ARGUMENT

Is the utilitarian reply to the marginal cases argument satisfactory? Clearly, that depends on whether utilitarianism is satisfactory as a moral theory. While many thinkers have defended utilitarianism, many others have rejected it. We shall not undertake here to further the discussion of the adequacy of utilitarianism.[13] Those who find utilitarianism unsatisfactory as a moral theory may try to challenge the premises of the marginal cases argument on other grounds. In my judgment, premise 1 is acceptable. However, premise 2 may be open to challenge. For convenience let us reiterate premise 2 here: Premise: 2. Any justifiable criterion concerning what is morally acceptable for humans to kill for food which implies that it is always unacceptable to kill and eat marginal human beings also implies that it is unacceptable to kill and eat farm (and certain other) animals.

Could there be reasons for doubting premise 2 other than utilitarian reasons? It appears that there can be such reasons. The utilitarian challenge to premise 2 consisted of an attempt to make a case for saying that the practice of allowing the killing of animals for food but not allowing the killing of human beings for this purpose produces the greatest achievable amount of pleasure or satisfaction of desires. Some other grounds for challenging premise 2 might rest on theories of value other than that contained in the utilitarian theory. Further, still other grounds for challenging premise 2 might rest on theories of moral obligation other than the utilitarian theory, according to which our moral obligations consist in producing the greatest achievable amount of value.[14] Let us briefly indicate how such alternative theories of value or of moral obligation might be formulated.

According to the theory of value of utilitarianism, as described above, intrinsic goodness consists in pleasure or the satisfaction of desires.[15] However, some people have maintained that other things are intrinsically valuable. For example, some people might maintain that love is intrinsically valuable, i.e., that it has value even if it is not desired either for itself or as a means to achieving something else. Similarly, while most people might say that knowledge is only instrumentally valuable, some people might hold that it is intrinsically valuable. Some people have maintained that life is intrinsically valuable. Some have held that beauty is intrinsically valuable. Some people have held that only certain moral virtues or a good moral character are intrinsically valuable.[16]

Will a change in one's theory of intrinsic value yield a defensible moral theory which implies that it is acceptable to kill animals for food but does not imply that it is acceptable to kill human beings for such purposes? We cannot address this question with respect to each value theory. Let us try to sketch a general approach to this issue. In some value theories, intrinsic value is realized only in states of consciousness. In other value theories, value is value is realized in non-conscious entities. If we assume that we are obligated always to try to achieve a maximum of value, then, assuming value theories of the latter sort, we could be obligated to kill human beings to achieve such values. For example, if we think that the beauty of wild ecosystems is intrinsically valuable and if we are obligated to try to achieve maximum value, then we may have to conclude in some circumstances that human beings must be killed to achieve maximum beauty. However, when we reflect that marginal human beings exist, then even if we hold that value exists only in states of consciousness, our moral theory could still imply that it is acceptable to kill some human beings to achieve an increase in total value. Thus, it appears, so long as we are committed to maximum value consequentialism, then regardless of our basic assumptions about what is intrinsically valuable, our moral theory may yield a problematic result, namely that it is acceptable to kill some human beings to achieve maximum value.

Clearly, this problem can be raised as a challenge to utilitarianism also. Defenders of utilitarianism have countered this sort of criticism through arguments which state, in general, that killing human beings does not produce more value than not doing so, although, in some cases, killing human beings to achieve certain purposes does produce maximum value and, in consequence, killing human beings is morally acceptable. For example, if there is a case in which sacrificing an innocent person would prevent the deaths of others, then the sacrifice, however regrettable, would be morally acceptable.

This same result holds even if Tom Regan's theory of inherent value is combined with maximum value consequentialism. According to Regan, beings who are subjects-of-a-life have inherent value. Beings are subjects-of-a-life if they have beliefs and desires, perception, memory, some degree of anticipation of their own existence in the future, emotions, awareness of pleasure and pain, the capacity to take steps to satisfy their own desires, and other related capacities.[17] Regan's argument that mammals of one year of age or more have the requisite capacities to be subjects-of-a-life is open to question, as we have seen in an earlier chapter. However, at this point let us set that criticism aside. Here, let us ask whether all humans, other than permanently comatose humans, are subjects-of-a-life. In particular, are all marginal humans subjects-of-a-life? It is arguable that some marginal humans are not subjects-of-a-life. Some people with Alzheimer's disease or other severe mental dysfunctions may continue to be conscious and even have some feelings of pleasure, pain, satisfaction, or discomfort, and yet retain so little mental capacity that they are no longer subjects-of-a-life. While Regan's view does not imply that it is permissible to kill such human beings, it does not rule out that possibility either. His view does not show that it is always morally unacceptable to kill human beings for food.

The basis of the utilitarian challenge to premise 2 of the marginal cases argument rested on both a value theory and a theory of obligation. We have looked briefly at alternative value theories to see whether there might be a satisfactory alternative which would also yield such a challenge. An alternative basis for challenging premise 2 of the marginal cases argument could rest on the acceptance of some alternative theory concerning our moral obligations. The utilitarian theory of moral obligation may be called "maximal value consequentialism." According to this theory, each person capable of having moral obligations is morally obligated to act so as to produce consequences of maximal value. While many agricultural scientists may be inclined to think that maximal value consequentialism is a correct theory of moral obligations, some philosophers, concerned about questions that they have raised with this theory, have advocated alternative theories concerning moral obligation.

Maximal value consequentialism may be challenged on the grounds that it fails to do adequate justice to some of our moral obligations. For example, it is at least conceivable that a course of action which would produce maximal value by a relatively small amount would also entail major sacrifices by some people, sacrifices which are not shared equally or fairly. Could it not be the case that we have a strong obligation not to require such sacrifices where they will yield only a small increment in maximal value? Alternatively, maximal value consequentialism has been challenged because it allegedly implies that we have some moral obligations which, in the eyes of the objector, we do not have. In some views, for example, we have moral obligations only if a perfectly prudent person would assent to such obligations. Even if recognizing an obligation not to kill animals would yield maximal value, a perfectly prudent person might not assent to such obligations.[18] Still another alternative justification of criteria concerning acceptability of killing might appeal to several fundamental assumptions regarding obligation, rather than to the single assumption that all our moral obligations derive from our obligation to maximize value. On the basis of such assumptions we might believe that, while we have some moral obligations to animals, we are entitled to kill them for food under various circumstances even though we are not entitled to kill humans for food. For example, suppose our basic moral theory rests on a number of independent assumptions concerning the scopes of the moral principles of the theory. Other assumptions of the theory might be that we ought not to kill humans for food, that we ought not to cause sentient creatures to suffer unnecessarily, that distribution of harms and benefits ought to be fair, that we have moral obligations to future generations of human beings, etc.

    A theory of moral justification which appealed to a number of distinct basic assumptions concerning moral obligations would lack the simple unity of a theory which appeals only to a single principle, such as the principle that we ought to maximize satisfaction of desires or that we ought to respect all beings who are subjects-of-a-life. While such unity may be desirable, given the present state of our understanding, it may be impossible to achieve such a unified theory. Perhaps any single-principle theory which we can formulate may have implications regarding our obligations which some reasonable people, who have thought carefully about the matter, judge to be mistaken. Indeed, it may be ultimately impossible to achieve such a highly unified theory. Fundamental theories of mathematical truth have not achieved such a high degree of unity; why then should we expect to achieve such unity in regard to ethical theory?[19]

If in trying to justify criteria regarding killing (or other things) one appealed sometimes to one fundamental assumption and other times to other assumptions, then it need not follow that any justifiable criterion concerning that it is morally acceptable to kill for food, which implies that it is never acceptable to kill humans for food, would also imply that it is never acceptable to kill animals for food.

SUMMARY

In this chapter we have reviewed one of the most persuasive arguments for moral vegetarianism, the view that it is morally unacceptable for human beings to kill animals for food. Indeed, the marginal cases argument has persuaded many people that they ought not to tolerate killing of animals for any purposes other than self-defense. We have reviewed several grounds for criticizing the marginal cases argument, grounds which appealed to utilitarianism and grounds which appeal to alternative theories of value or obligation. We have not discussed the third premise of the marginal cases argument. In the next chapter, in which we discuss speciesism, we will consider reasons for challenging premise 3 also.

NOTES

1. Profound reasonings have been developed by a number of thinkers in books concerned with our moral obligations to animals. Among these are Tom Regan, *The Case for Animal Rights*; Peter Singer, *Animal Liberation*; Bernard Rollin, *Animal Rights and Human Morality*; Mary Midgley, *Animals and Why They Matter*; and S. F. Sapontzis, *Morals, Reason and Animals*. Also of interest is Peter Singer, "Animals and the Value of Life."

2. The first, of course, is the criticism of those such as Regan: that it is morally wrong to kill certain domestic animals for food or other purposes.

3. This argument is discussed in Tom Regan, "An Examination and Defense of One Argument Concerning Animal Rights," in *All That Dwell Therein: Essays on Animal Rights and Environmental Ethics*, 184–205.

4. They may allow that animals have a weaker sort of right to life. To simplify formulation of the discussion that follows: when I speak of a right to life, I mean a right which is equal to a human right to life.

5. This is not the way Regan formulated the argument. For his formulation see Regan, *All That Dwell Therein*, 131.

6. It is, of course, an ancient issue as to whether the ethical and theological doctrines expressed in the Bible can be shown to be true or reasonable on rational grounds. I assume that this cannot be done. In making this assumption I am taking a position which would be accepted by all theologians who hold that theological or moral views expressed in the Bible ought to be accepted on faith since they cannot be justified by human reason. Even if I am wrong in this assumption, to the best of my knowledge, nobody has yet provided a rational explanation based on Biblical theology for the dichotomy in question.

7. This definition of utilitarianism needs, for some purposes, to be made more complex. There are several versions of utilitarianism and conflicts as to which version, if any, is correct. As I understand utilitarianism here, it is a theory which consists of a theory of values combined with a theory of moral

obligations. According to the theory of values, intrinsic goodness consists of pleasure or in being an object which is desired for itself. According to the theory of obligation, a person is morally obligated so as to act in such a way that no alternative course of action will yield greater value, that is, pleasures or other objects or experiences which are desired. I do not need to pursue certain complexities at this point and so I have not introduced them here as part of a more complex explanation of what utilitarianism is. There are many philosophical works or texts in which utilitarianism is explained and discussed.

8. Claims regarding reducing fat intake in diets of people in industrialized nations are legion. One source is *University of California, Berkeley: The Wellness Encyclopedia*, 94.

9. See the discussion of the clearing of rain forests in Central America in Norman Myers, *The Primary Source: Tropical Forests and Our Future*, chap. 7.

10. Human embryos are used for purposes of medical research and transplantation. At present, deliberately producing and then killing embryos for these purposes is not approved. Suppose a society were to adopt the practice of producing such embryos explicitly for such purposes; how would such a practice be evaluated on utilitarian grounds? It is difficult to say. Processes of collecting the eggs for the production of embryos can hardly be pleasant for the women involved. Conceivably, these women could be sufficiently compensated for the trouble involved in producing and supplying the ova; however, there would still be a question about unpleasant consequences arising from the emotional reactions of the women and others involved. Another possibility is that such embryos could be produced without significant inconvenience to anyone by a process of cloning. Further, there is serious question as to whether to count human embryos as human beings. Consequently, even if use of human embryos were approved on utilitarian grounds, it is not clear that this would salvage the conclusion even of a restricted version of the marginal cases argument.

11. Of course, this argument is not a conclusive proof that the social practice in question is justified on utilitarian grounds. The problem is that to apply the utilitarian theory the values obtained through pleasures or satisfac-

tion of desires must be sufficiently comparable to each other that they can be summed. To determine what one is obligated to do, on a utilitarian theory, one must compare the total values accruing from all alternative actions open. However, arriving at such comparisons is often imppossible in practice even if it is possible in principle. Suppose, for example, that to provide sufficient grain for human purposes, several tens of thousands of rodents are denied existence or killed. How could we tell whether the value lost by the non-existence of those rodents is less than the value gained by the humans or other sentient creatures who exist instead?

12. In saying that pleasure, or anything, is intrinsically valuable or good, what is implied is that it is good itself and not merely good because it yields something else which is good. Something which is good because it yields something else which is good is said to be instrumentally good.

13. An introduction to some criticisms of utilitarianism can be found in Paul W. Taylor, ed., *Problems of Moral Philosophy: An Introduction to Ethics*, 2d ed. Many other introductory works on moral philosophy would be appropriate also.

14. The utilitarian theory of moral obligation may be called a "consequentalist theory." Non-consequentialist theories of moral obligation are referred to traditionally as "deontological theories."

15. The term "intrinsic goodness" or "intrinsic value" is perhaps confusing. Something may have intrinsic value, according to the account here, if it is desired for itself. This may cause confusion because intrinsic value so conceived is not a property of the object itself. It arises in an object if that object satisfies desires. A theory of intrinsic value is a theory of what properties or relations are essential to explain how any object comes to have value. Intrinsic value may be contrasted with instrumental value. An object has instrumental value if, while it is not desired for itself, it is desired because it is part of a process which leads to the existence or acquisition of something with intrinsic value.

16. Immanuel Kant said, "Nothing can possibly be conceived in the world, or even out of it, which can be called good without qualification, except a good will." Immanuel Kant, *Fundamental Principles of the Metaphysic of*

Morals, 11. This may be taken as implying that only a good will has intrinsic value. Holmes Rolston III argued that natural objects have intrinsic value in Holmes Rolston III, *Environmental Ethics: Duties to and Values in the Natural World*, chap. 1.

17. Regan's view is elaborated in Regan, *The Case for Animal Rights*, chap. 7, 243.

18. For relevant discussion concerning the obligations of a perfectly prudent person in regard to animals see the discussion of libertarianism in J. Narveson, "Animal Rights Revisited."

19. Of course, it is always possible to reduce the number of basic axioms of a theory to one. One can do this by forming the conjunction of whatever other axioms are assumed. But such trivial manipulation of the fundamental assumptions of a theory does not yield unity.

12. Speciesism and Confinement Rearing

SOME PHILOSOPHERS AND others have suggested that intensive animal production practices, such as battery-cage production of chickens or close confinement of sows, are morally unacceptable because they are speciesist. In this chapter we intend to investigate this claim. Complicating this matter, we find there are two distinct notions of speciesism which have served as a basis for this criticism. To investigate this charge carefully, we shall have to consider both concepts of speciesism. In the first part I shall explain the first version of speciesism, developed by Peter Singer in a number of his works. In part two we shall consider whether any form of confinement rearing is necessarily speciesist by reference to this first concept of speciesism. In part three I shall explain the second version of the concept of speciesism, expressed in the work of James Rachels. In the fourth part we shall consider whether intensive confinement rearing is morally unacceptable because it is speciesist in accordance with this second concept of speciesism.

SPECIESISM AND EQUAL CONSIDERATION OF INTERESTS

Peter Singer defined "speciesism" by reference to a principle which is called the principle of equal consideration of interests. According to this principle, in trying to determine what we ought to do, the interests of every being affected by our action are to be taken into account and given the same weight as the like interests of any other being.[1] This principle is a moderate equality principle. More extreme equality principles would say that every being (or every being of a certain sort) is entitled to exactly the same treatment; for example, that we must treat cows in exactly the same as we treat pigs or people. The principle of equal consideration of interests does not say that. To explain what it says, we must make reference to Singer's basic assumptions regarding our moral obligations.

Singer is a utilitarian. As noted elsewhere, this means that he assumes that we are obligated always to act so that no alternative action which we could perform would lead to a greater sum of values. Further, his being a utilitarian means that he identifies values either with feelings of pleasure or pain or with objects which lead to satisfaction or frustration of desires or preferences. For the sake of brevity, his theory concerning what is valuable is expressed by saying that some beings have interests, for example, interests in avoiding pain, having adequate nutrition and protection from predators, etc. Presumably, pleasure or being an object which satisfies desires counts positively toward the sum of values and is called a "positive interest," while pain or being an object which frustrates desires counts negatively and is called a "negative interest."

Clearly, given his theory of values, Singer does not assume that every creature has interests. He believes that some creatures do not experience pleasure or pain and do not have desires or preferences. Creatures who feel nothing pleasant or painful and who have no desires do not have interests. Thus, in Singer's view, so far as we know, plants do not have interests, and many types of very simple animals do not have interests either. Presumably single-celled animals don't have interests. Determining the boundary between creatures with interests and creatures which lack interests is a difficult matter, and there may well be creatures, such as insects or other invertebrates, about which we have some doubts as to whether they have interests or not.

Singer assumes that interests vary in weight. Satisfaction of some interests may lead to greater pleasure than satisfaction of other interests. Again, some desires may be stronger than other desires, and satisfaction of stronger desires has greater weight than satisfaction of weaker desires. A creature may have a greater interest (or an interest of a greater weight) in having adequate nutrition at some time than it has in being able to explore some object which has attracted its attention. In determining the overall value that our potential actions may yield, these differences in weight of interests must be taken into account.

An important assumption of Singer's value theory is that all values associated with interests are comparable, so that it makes sense to think of summing them all together to arrive at a total value that it is reasonable to consider as the value of an action. Singer's view on this matter is in conflict with other theories of value, such as that of Tom Regan, who holds that individuals of certain sorts have a distinct type of value which is not commensurable with the value associated with satisfaction of interests.[2] To illustrate Singer's view, let us suppose that we have the choice of three actions A, B, or C. We can consider the consequences which would result from our performance of each of these actions. Then we can consider how those consequences would lead to satisfaction or frustration of interests of all the creatures that would be affected by our actions. Finally, we can choose whichever of A, B, or C yields the greatest sum of interests.

Now, the principle of equal consideration of interests means that in determining what a person ought to do (or what social practices or policies are acceptable), all interests ought to be taken into account. No creature's interests should be ignored in arriving at the sum of interests which would accrue from the performance of any possible action. Further, each interest should be accurately weighed in arriving at the sum. A weighty interest of, let us say, a cow, should not be counted only as a small interest just because it is the interest of a cow rather than an interest of a human being.

It should be noted that while the principle of equal consideration of interests implies that we are obligated to consider all interests and assess the weights of interests accurately in trying to determine our moral obligations, it does not imply that we are obligated to give equal satisfaction to the interests of all individuals. Consider two individuals: let us call them A and B. Suppose that A is a human being and B is a chicken. Suppose further that A and B each have only two interests and that all these interests are of equal weight. Suppose further that it is possible to satisfy only two of the four interests. Maximum value can be achieved by satisfying one interest of each individual or by satisfying two interests of either individual and none of the other. The principle of equal consideration of interests does not imply that we are obligated to satisfy one interest of each individual. Indeed, recall that Singer's ethical theory is utilitarian. A person's moral obligations on this view are to act so that no alternative course of action will yield greater value. Since the principle of equal consideration must be understood in the overall context of a utilitarian moral theory, it cannot yield a result that contradicts utilitarianism. Given that we can achieve maximum value in the example in question either by satisfying one interest of the chicken and one of the human or two interests of the chicken (and no interests of the human) or two interests of the human (and no interests of the chicken), we are free, so far as utilitarianism is concerned, to choose any of these three alternatives.

"Speciesism," as Singer conceives it, may now be defined. Singer says, "Speciesism is a prejudice or attitude of bias toward the interests of members of one's own species and against those of members of other species."[3] In other words, if, when a person is trying to determine what he or she ought to do, he or she tends to omit inclusion of interests of members of other species, or, while including such interests, treats weighty interests of members of other species as if they were not weighty, then that person is a speciesist. In Singer's eyes, speciesism is morally unacceptable. He suggests that it is essentially as unacceptable as racism or sexism.

Singer's definition of "speciesism" as an attitude of bias gives rise to a problem given the use that he wishes to make of this concept. Singer is not merely expressing moral criticism of certain attitudes, as his words seem to suggest. Singer wishes to condemn certain practices, such as confinement rearing of animals, as speciesist and therefore as morally wrong. Consequently, we need to explain what it means to say that a certain action or general practice is speciesist. I shall assume that Singer would accept the following definition. An action (or general practice) which is performed by a human being is speciesist if there was an alternative action which could have been performed which would have produced a greater sum of values because of providing more pleasure (or less pain, or greater satisfaction of desires, etc.) to members of some non-human species.[4]

SPECIESISM AND EGG PRODUCTION

Singer maintains that some agricultural practices, such as battery-cage egg production, are "forms of speciesism."[5] I am inclined to believe that Singer is correct in implying that most of us humans were and continue to be speciesist. Most people would not yet recognize or agree that we have a serious moral obligation to take the interests of farm animals into account and to assign them appropriate weight in our efforts to determine what we ought to do. However, now, in consequence of the writings of Singer and others, we have become aware that our treatment of farm animals may be morally unacceptable because it is speciesist. Some of us may agree that we have a moral obligation to guide our actions in accord with the principle of equal consideration of interests. If we now believe that we must take the interests of farm animals into account in determining what agricultural practices are morally acceptable, we have to consider whether we are required to modify current agricultural practices to bring them into accord with the dictates of the principle of equal consideration.

Must we abandon all forms of confinement rearing of farm animals, or are some forms of confinement rearing acceptable? In order to answer this question in accord with the moral principles which Singer professes, it is not sufficient to consider only the ways in which animals suffer under conditions of confinement rearing. We must consider further the pleasures and satisfactions of preferences which domestic animals experience. Further, we must consider the pleasures, suffering, satisfactions, etc., of human beings in so far as they are affected by agricultural practices. We may also have to consider the interests of other creatures, e.g., the wild animals that may be affected by our production practices. Were we good utilitarians, we would try to consider all of those interests, and assess their weights accurately, in order to determine which of the actions open to us would yield the greatest sum of pleasures and satisfactions.

There are a range of actions which are open to us in regard to animal production practices which involve confinement rearing. To speak carefully about these, it is necessary to define the term "confinement rearing." Idyllic conceptions of animal production often picture animals as wandering freely in farmyards or fields. But even such yards or fields were fenced. The animals were subject to some confinement. Presumably, when Singer or others suggest that confinement rearing is to be condemned as speciesist, they do not include such idyllic farms under the category of confinement rearing. Presumably, Singer is talking about intensive confinement rearing. Examples of this include battery-cage egg production, as well as forms of close confinement currently in use in white veal production or production of pigs using crates. "Free range" production would not count as confinement rearing.

Consideration of these examples does not settle the terminological question perfectly. Some types of cages proposed for egg production are much larger than battery cages and include facilities for the chickens to roost and even for dust-bathing. Further, egg production may be done by keeping chickens in large rooms which are called aviaries. Aviaries are more confining than free range, but provide some opportunity for flying, roosting in a nest, getting away from dominant birds, etc.

What actions are open to us? It is useful to consider both the perspectives of producers and of consumers. As producers, we can continue to use battery cages for egg production. Alternatively, we can attempt to modify such cages in various ways. We could move to larger cages or we could move toward aviary production. Further, producers have the option of adopting free-range egg production systems. Of course, they might choose to abandon egg production altogether. Consumers have a number of alternative actions available to them also. They can restrict purchasing habits, for example, by purchasing only eggs from free-range chickens. Further, they can exercise their options as citizens of democratic nations and try either to have or to avoid having restrictions on egg production by enactment of laws.

Let us, for a moment, adopt the perspective of producers. Assuming that we wish to avoid being speciesist, could we choose any form of egg production under which chickens were reared in cages? To simplify our consideration of this question, let us assume that, of the options open to us, any option which would require that most people abandon use of poultry eggs for food or food products is morally unacceptable on utilitarian grounds. To assume this is to assume that there are some options under which we continue to have hens producing eggs which yield greater satisfaction of interests than any alternatives in which egg use is abandoned. This simplifying assumption may well be correct anyway. If we are going to try to avoid speciesist practices, we must then consider which of the alternative modes of egg production produce the greatest overall satisfaction. Would aviary production produce greater overall satisfaction than any form of cage production, once the hen's interests are properly taken into account? This is still a very complex question to try to answer.

To proceed let us consider the specific criticisms directed against the use of cages. Some cages have been criticized because the flooring leads to foot deformities or other injuries. Some cage systems have been criticized on the grounds that too many birds are crowded into a cage. Some cage systems have been criticized because the birds cannot display various species-specific forms of behavior, such as dust-bathing, flapping of wings, etc. Some cage production systems have been criticized because birds raised in such systems injure each other through pecking or because, to avoid such injuries, the birds' beaks are trimmed. Some cage systems have been criticized on the grounds that there is inadequate ventilation or because the design of the system permits contamination of the birds' food or water by waste products. Some egg-production systems have been criticized on the grounds that they impose undue burdens on the surrounding environment within which they exist. Perhaps there are other criticisms as well, but the above constitute a good sample.

Let us assume that agricultural engineers devise methods of meeting a number of these criticisms. Cages may be developed which reduce or eliminate certain types of injuries. Ventilation systems already can provide high-quality fresh air. There has been research on larger cages which allow for a larger degree of normal species-specific behavior for hens. Suppose that the arrangement of cages permits sufficient inspection of hens to discover when hens are injured or have died and suppose that management practices involve regular, careful monitoring of the hens in the cages. We may suppose that, to some degree, the environmental criticisms directed against huge intensive confinement systems are addressed as well. Implementing these or other improvements to a cage egg production system would involve some costs. There are costs involved in developing the improvements. There may be increased costs involved in operating such a system. Reducing the density of birds per cage may lead to higher egg costs. If we are good utilitarians, we must try to consider all of the interests that would be affected by the adoption of such a system—the interests of the hens, of the producers, and of the consumers. Somehow we must arrive at the total value of this alternative. We must do the same calculations with respect to the other alternatives under consideration, that is, larger cages, aviaries, and free-range systems. Implementing the improvements to cage production systems will increase costs to humans. There presumably would be benefits to the hens. The hens would have a better quality of life; within the total value assessment, that value would offset, to some degree at least, the increases in production costs.

In considering whether cage production systems are speciesist, other costs and benefits must be considered also. Many humans satisfy some of their nutritional needs by eating eggs. But it may be that some people eat too many eggs and thereby consume too much cholesterol. Reduction in egg production below levels required to meet human nutritional requirements would be a significant negative consequence. How can we combine all of these cost and benefit considerations to arrive at an overall assessment of various forms of egg production? Some people have argued that there is no meaningful way to combine all these values, and consequently that the utilitarian approach is flawed.[6]

At any rate, given the difficulty in arriving at such total sums of values, we can say that, so far as we know, some cage-production system of egg production could be the system which yields the greatest overall value. If that were the case then cage egg production would not be speciesist. We are not entitled to infer, on the basis of what we currently know, that a system of egg production is speciesist (given the concept of speciesism advocated by Singer) merely because it is a cage production system.

Some people might object to what we have said here by advancing the following argument. Singer has suggested in his discussion of the use of animals in scientific research that the practice of using animals in research is speciesist, since it involves using animals in circumstances in which we would not tolerate use of severely retarded human infants who are orphans. Such people might apply this consideration to egg production and argue that since we would not keep such human infants in cages, keeping chickens in cages is speciesist. However, I do not believe that this is a serious objection. Severely retarded children (or adults) often are and probably should be kept under close confinement for their own well-being. The confinement of such humans may be regarded as comparable to confinement of hens in improved cages. Consequently, this objection does not show that keeping hens in improved cages is speciesist.

AN ALTERNATIVE CONCEPT OF SPECIESISM

Actually, James Rachels introduced two concepts which he regarded as concepts of speciesism. One he called "unqualified speciesism," and the other he called "qualified speciesism." To explain these concepts we must explain the notion of "moral relevance." The concept of moral relevance is introduced by Rachels and Regan in the context of a theory which I call "explanatory rationalism." Let us turn to explaining these ideas.

Let us say that an action is morally acceptable providing only that it is not morally wrong to do it. However, let us say that an action is morally justified providing both that it is morally acceptable and that we can provide a rationale or theory of some sort which explains why the action is morally acceptable. Some writers, Rachels and Regan included, appear to assume that actions are morally acceptable if and only if those actions are morally justified. In other words, they assume that our actions or social practices are not morally acceptable unless we can explain why they are acceptable. Let us call this assumption the "assumption of explanatory rationalism."

We cannot be certain that Regan and others make the assumption in question since they have not, in general, noted the distinction between an action's being morally acceptable and its being morally justifiable. However, in his discussion of the moral obligations of non-vegetarians, Regan appears to make this assumption in statements which imply that non-vegetarians act immorally in killing and eating animals unless they can present rationally compelling reasons why this practice is morally acceptable.[7] Rachels, I believe, is even clearer in regard to making this assumption. He maintains that the following is a fundamental rule of moral reasoning, namely, "When individuals are treated differently, we need to be able to point to a difference between them that justifies the difference in treatment."[8] This implies that killing cows for food, or keeping hens crowded in cages, given that we don't kill humans for food or keep them crowded in cages, is morally unacceptable unless we can point at differences by reference to which we can explain why it is morally wrong to kill humans for food (or keep them overcrowded in cages) but not morally wrong to kill cows for food or keep hens overcrowded in cages.

We can now explain "moral relevance." Consider some action that we might perform that would affect some individuals. Some quality of individuals, or relation among individuals, or some state of affairs in which individuals are involved, is morally relevant with respect to that action if reference to an occurrence of that quality, relation, etc., can serve as the basis for an explanation of why that action is or is not morally acceptable. For example, consider an action which consists of your hitting another person who has not threatened or hit you. Reference to the pain that hitting the person would cause is morally relevant because reference to the occurrence of such pain would explain why hitting the person is morally unacceptable.

To see how the notion of moral relevance has been used in moral arguments, consider a type of argument which Rachels and Regan have used. Rachels argued that animals, such as rabbits or cows, have certain natural moral rights, such as the right to liberty. He argued for this conclusion by claiming that humans have a natural moral right to liberty and that there is no morally relevant difference between humans and animals. Given that humans have this moral right and that there is no difference between humans and other animals which would explain why those animals do not have this right, that is, no morally relevant difference, it would follow that those other animals have this right also.[9] Of course, it would have been fairly easy to specify some characteristic by reference to which humans and other animals (for example cows) are different. The characteristic might be being a featherless biped with broad nails. Alternatively, it might be having a certain sequence of genes as part of its DNA. However, Rachels would argue that such differences as this are not morally relevant. Reference to strands of DNA will not explain, in his view, why it is morally acceptable to keep hens in cages given that it is not morally acceptable to keep humans in cages.

We can now explain "unqualified speciesism" and "qualified speciesism." "Unqualified speciesism" is a view which logically implies that some species differences are morally relevant for explaining any difference in regard to what it is acceptable to do to a creature. To illustrate this idea, let us suppose that someone says that while it is wrong to keep humans in crates which are so small that they cannot turn around, it is morally acceptable to keep veal calves in such cages because they are cows. Here the reference to being a member of a distinct species allegedly explains why it is acceptable to treat cows in a way in which it is not acceptable to treat human beings. If someone believes that any difference between what it is acceptable to do to humans and what it is acceptable to do to cows (or other animals) can be explained merely by reference to the difference in species, that person accepts unqualified speciesism.[10]

"Qualified speciesism," if I understand Rachels correctly, is a more restricted theory. The qualified speciesist picks out some specific feature which differentiates humans from animals which correlates positively with a morally relevant feature, but applies it in the effort to justify differences in treatment to which the morally relevant feature is not relevant. For example, it might be appropriate to explain why mature humans are entitled to certain rights, such as a right to a fair trial or a right to vote, while farms animals lack these rights, because humans have certain biological or psychological features which the animals lack and which are morally relevant, that is, would serve as a basis for explaining why humans have these entitlements. However, the qualified speciesist tries to justify other differences in treatment by reference to these features, differences in treatment with respect to which the features are not relevant. For example, the qualified speciesist might appeal to the fact that humans are free to choose and can understand political issues, which is a feature that is relevant with respect to the right to vote, to explain why keeping animals in close confinement is (allegedly) morally acceptable, even though these psychological capacities are allegedly not relevant to justify this difference in the way that the farm animals are treated.

Now, I wish to agree with Rachels that unqualified speciesism is a fallacious moral theory. I suppose, as is generally the case in regard to ethical theory, that this cannot be conclusively proved. It does not appear that unqualified speciesism is logically inconsistent. However, I cannot think of any reason which would support this theory. If one appeals to utilitarianism, or to principles such as the golden rule, or to theories based on the concept of moral rights, it does not appear plausible to maintain that the biological differences by reference to which biologists differentiate members of distinct species have any moral relevance. Further, Rachels' view of unqualified speciesism coincides with my view of racism or sexism. These are views which imply that purely biological differences, the sort of differences by reference to which races or sexes are distinguished, are morally relevant. Such merely biological differences, by reference to which we make distinctions among races or sexes, have no moral relevance in themselves. Since racism and sexism are mistaken theories, so also is unqualified speciesism. Similarly, I have no wish to defend qualified speciesism. Given the way that the theory is explained by Rachels, it is clearly a false ethical theory.

SPECIESISM AND CONFINEMENT REARING REVISITED

Is confinement rearing speciesist? Rachels' definitions of speciesism do not imply that confinement rearing is speciesist since, as he defines these terms, only certain ethical theories are speciesist. Suppose that someone wanted to say that confinement rearing is speciesist in Rachels' sense of the term. I think that the fairest way to interpret this remark is to construe it as meaning that the only reasons that can be offered in support of the claim that confinement rearing is morally acceptable are theories which are forms of speciesism, that is, theories which imply that biological features are morally relevant or which involve using biological features which are relevant in some contexts in a way in which they are not relevant. Now, we should ask whether this claim can be justified. Is it the case that the only ways for a person to justify the claim that confinement rearing is morally acceptable would logically commit that person to accepting some form of speciesism?

I don't think that this claim can be justified. Indeed, I think it is mistaken. In the first place, it may be that confinement rearing is morally acceptable (for animals but not for human beings) but that we do not have a moral theory by reference to which we can establish this claim. In other words, the theory which I called "explanatory rationalism" may be false. At any rate, we do not yet have knowledge of a complete moral theory, that is, a theory by reference to which all moral questions should be resolved. Thus, even if there is some true moral theory which explains why it is acceptable morally to treat hens and humans differently, we do not yet know what that theory is. Sometimes, it looks as if Rachels and others who accept explanatory rationalism are assuming we are now in possession of a complete and adequately justified set of moral beliefs. Such an assumption is, in my view, mistaken.

It should not, of course, be assumed that I am arguing that confinement rearing is morally acceptable because we do not have knowledge of a complete moral theory. To argue in that way would be to argue fallaciously. That would be a simple case of the fallacy known as "argument from ignorance." I am not claiming to know that confinement rearing is morally acceptable, and consequently I am not claiming that it is morally acceptable because of our ignorance of moral principles. However, I am claiming that the charge of speciesism, understood as I have explained it here, has not been established either.

In the second place, as we have argued above, some form of confinement rearing may be morally justifiable on utilitarian grounds. Conceivably, in light of the species differences between hens and human beings, there is a type of cage production system such that hens reared in that cage production system have a quality of life which is as good or better on the whole than hens raised in a free-range or aviary type of system. Given that human beings tend to have a higher quality of life if they are not confined in cages, whereas this may not be the case of hens in improved cage production systems, we could say that the differences between hens and humans which explain why a hen's quality of life in an improved cage could be as good as it would be in an aviary, etc., but why that is not the case for humans, is a morally relevant difference.

SUMMARY

In this chapter we have considered two definitions of "speciesism" and have considered whether intensive confinement rearing is necessarily speciesist in either sense of the term. We have examined the views of Peter Singer and James Rachels and have argued that, for all we know, some forms of intensive confinement rearing may not be speciesist. However, given that we can envision forms of confinement rearing which would improve the quality of hens' (or other farm animals') lives considerably, with only relatively minor harms to human beings, we have strong reason to suspect that some forms of intensive confinement rearing, which have been and continue to be used in the United States, Canada, and elsewhere, are probably morally unacceptable because they are speciesist (in the sense of the term as defined by Peter Singer).

NOTES

1. Peter Singer, *Animal Liberation: A New Ethics for Our Treatment of Animals*, 6.

2. Regan's theory of value is expressed in Regan, *The Case for Animal Rights*, 235. Regan assumes that individuals who are subjects-of-a-life have value of this distinct type. He calls such value "inherent value."

3. Singer, *Animal Liberation*, 7.

4. Given these two definitions, a person could be a speciesist while his actions are not speciesist. This would occur if the person was prejudiced against other species but if his actions, perhaps unwittingly, were such that there was no way for him to produce a greater sum of values by performing some alternative action which would better satisfy the interests of members of other species.

5. Singer, *Animal Liberation*, 25.

6. R. G. Frey in trying to raise questions concerning the alleged benefits of people becoming vegetarians calls attention to a large number of costs that would result from such a move. See R. G. Frey, *Rights, Killing & Suffering*, 197.

7. Tom Regan, "Do Animals Have a Right to Life?" in *Animal Rights and Human Obligations*, ed. Tom Regan and Peter Singer, 203.

8. James Rachels, "Darwin, Species, and Morality," in *Animal Rights and Human Obligations*, 2d ed., ed. Tom Regan and Peter Singer, 98. Rachels also says, "It is a point of logic that moral judgments are true only if good reasons support them: for example, if there is no good reason why you ought to do some action, it cannot be true that you ought to do it." James Rachels, *The End of Life: Euthanasia and Morality*, 139. Many questions might be raised about this alleged point of logic.

9. James Rachels, "Why Animals Have a Right to Liberty," in *Animal Rights and Human Obligations*, 2d ed., ed. Tom Regan and Peter Singer, 122.

10. These ideas are explained in Rachels, "Darwin, Species and Morality," 95.

13. Technoanxiety and Agriculture

RECENTLY WES JACKSON started a paper by posing the question, "How long did it take chemists before they were finally able to come up with a substance that would destroy the ozone?" He went on to remark, "It matters little whether the most satisfactory answer to my question is a century or a half a century... Now the question might be, 'How long will it take the biotechnolgists to come up with the equivalent of the ozone hole?' Surely they won't let the old style chemists hold the record."[1] This is an attention-getting way to remind us of matters that are giving rise to anxiety in many quarters. The application of technology, while often yielding many benefits for human beings, has also produced results which are very harmful. We can already expect increased incidence of skin cancer and cataracts as a result of the ozone hole. There may also be damage to crop production systems, to oceanic organisms which contribute to production of oxygen for the atmosphere and food for other organisms, etc. It is premature to make confident assertions as to how widespread and serious the damage from this cause will be.

What is "biotechnology" and how, if at all, should we proceed with its deployment? "Biotechnology" (new style chemistry), even "agricultural biotechnology," are rather broad terms. "Technology" may be understood as the application of knowledge in activities of living. So understood, we may speak meaningfully of the technology used by humans in prehistoric times. The earliest agricultural technologies emerged in such times. Given a distinction between scientific knowledge and other knowledge, we may speak of scientific technology. Probably, even today, there are many agricultural practices which were not developed either by agricultural scientists or on the basis of knowledge developed by scientists. Such practices would constitute "agricultural technology" but not "scientific agricultural technology." "Agricultural biotechnology," being the application of biological knowledge, is a form of scientific technology. It includes such practices as the use of growth hormones, chemical fertilizers and pesticides, and genetically engineered organisms, such as herbicide-tolerant plants and bacteria developed to prevent frost damage.

People are expressing anxiety concerning technology.[2] However, given the broad significance of the term "technology," outright opposition to technology, to any possible form of technology, is not rationally defensible. Any manner of living involves some form of technology. I suspect that most of those people who are anxious about technology in modern times are alarmed by certain forms of technology. The use of certain technologies is perceived as threatening to the existence of all life on Earth, whereas use of other technologies is perceived as threatening to the existence or nature of our humanity. Further, the use of some technologies is perceived as threatening to objects which are cherished or highly valued. Possibly, some of those anxious about technology are alarmed more by the increasing rate of change of technology than by any specific form of technology. In this chapter I try to address this anxiety. Wes Jackson has alleged that the biotechnologists' world view is presumptuous. In part one of this chapter I try to explain that world view as, I think, Jackson sees it. In part two I discuss an argument which I call the "argument from horrible consequences." If, as Jackson suggests, biotechnologists claim to have adequate knowledge that deployment of agricultural biotechnology will not lead to horrible consequences, there are grounds for saying that they are presumptuous. To avoid this criticism, biotechnologists must accept that their knowledge is not perfect knowledge. In consequence, they are not entitled to be certain that deployment of biotechnology will have no horrible consequences. This, in turn, forms the basis for an argument for the cautious deployment of technology. Finally, in the third part of this chapter, I consider possible criticisms of the argument for cautious deployment.

THE BIOTECHNOLOGIST'S WORLD-VIEW

Our answer to the question of how we ought to proceed in regard to the deployment of agricultural biotechnology will depend, at least in part, on very general assumptions we make concerning the nature of reality, of human knowledge, of values, and of ethics. The network of assumptions to which we subscribe in these regards may be called our "world-view." We certainly shall not undertake the arduous task of spelling out completely the world-view of biotechnolgist's. However, since Jackson is critical of the world-view of biotechnologists, we shall consider some aspects of that world-view.

What is a rational attitude toward the deployment of technology? Conceivably, a person could advocate rigorous maintenance of contemporary technology. However, such a policy involves commitment to the preservation of the flaws which characterize present technology, and so does not recommend itself to a rational person. Such a person could reasonably ask why we should not try to replace contemporary technology with an improved technology, a technology in which some of the flaws in contemporary technology are eliminated. Another possibility would be to replace contemporary technology with a technology used in earlier times. In conversations, agricultural scientists often suggest that critics of agriculture advocate a simple-minded return to the agricultural technology in use in some earlier period. Indeed, some of Wendell Berry's remarks, referred to in a previous essay in this work, suggest that the introduction of small tractors and associated farm machinery is good, but that the increasing size of such implements contributes to a worsening of our farming methods. While Berry does not appear to advocate this, some agricultural scientists might infer that he is recommending a straightforward return to the use of technology available early in the twentieth century. As with the above objection, there is much to be said against this recommendation. However, we should note that those who compare contemporary technology unfavorably with earlier forms of technology are not necessarily advocating a straightforward return to the older technology. They might be recommending that we modify the new technology to make it more like the older technology in some respects.[3]

Jackson does not single out a specific form of technology for condemnation. He differs from those who have condemned outright the use of synthetic pesticides such as atrazine. Agricultural scientists have responded to those who object to the use of synthetic pesticides by affirming that "natural" chemicals are often just as toxic as synthetic pesticides. Such a reply has some validity. The use of an agricultural chemical is not necessarily wrong. However, the extent or manner of its use may be open to criticism. Jackson suggests that the real problem underlying inappropriate applications of synthetic pesticides or other chemicals is the mind-set or world-view which directs the development or use of such technologies. He called that worldview the "knowledge-as-adequate" world-view and attributed it to Descartes.[4] (In his *Meditations*, Descartes suggested that if we were to use the proper method to establish our beliefs, then our beliefs would be true; further, that we would be entitled to subscribe to those beliefs with the greatest confidence.[5])

What is the knowledge-as-adequate world-view? Jackson does not say.[6] I shall try to characterize a world-view which could be described as the knowledge-as-adequate world-view. I believe this may be that view that Jackson has in mind, and further, I believe some serious criticisms of this world-view are justified. I shall start by considering the way that agricultural scientists view their social role.[7]

Agricultural scientists view their work as helpful to producers of agricultural products. They see the producers as trying to earn a decent living through the use of agricultural technologies of one sort or another. The scientists believe that, with appropriate knowledge of the production process, the producer will be able to modify the production technology so as to increase production and thereby earn more. The scientist views his or her role as consisting in the development of such knowledge—knowledge which is adequate to the realization of the producers' objectives. In the scientist's eyes, the producer who utilizes traditional methods of production is acting on beliefs which are, in some respects, incomplete or mistaken. The gaps and errors in the producer's understanding lead to reduced productivity. The scientist sees his or her work as leading to a set of beliefs to supplement or replace the producer's opinions. Following Jackson's suggestion, we may say that the scientist sees the revised beliefs as constituting adequate knowledge of the production processes. This view may be called the "knowledge-as-adequate view." After listening to informal discussions of agricultural scientists, one often gets the impression that they think they know the correct ways to go about the business of farming; that is, that they have adequate knowledge of appropriate farming methods.

Presumably, the person who holds that he or she has adequate knowledge of how to farm need not hold that he or she knows all there is to know about proper farming methods. Typically, the scientist will recognize that his or her understanding of farming processes is incomplete in significant ways, that there is more valuable research to be done to add to what is known. The idea that one's knowledge is adequate can readily be distinguished from the idea that one's knowledge is perfect. In principle, someone who holds the knowledge-as-adequate view would allow that some of his or her beliefs are mistaken and that the knowledge is incomplete. Given that the scientist recognizes that his or her knowledge is incomplete and, in part, erroneous, one may ask, what is wrong with the knowledge-as-adequate view?

Jackson's remarks suggest that what is wrong is the presumption to know—to know anything. He says, "When we spread atrazine all over Iowa and Illinois, we presume to know!"[8] His use of these words suggests, first, that we don't really know, that our beliefs about how to farm may be mistaken; and second, that we are being presumptuous in thinking that we know. This interpretation of his remarks is buttressed by some further remarks of his. In describing the objectives of The Land Institute, of which he is a leader, he says, "We have said at The Land Institute that we are working on 'perennial polyculture' for grain production. I have never been quite comfortable with that expression because it. . . emphasizes our clever agronomic arrangement which forces us to feel more informed than we deserve to be."[9] He goes on to say that nature is "the reservoir of intelligence" and that he regards his objective as to imitate nature. These remarks may be taken to imply that it is a mistake to assume that we have even adequate knowledge of what we have to do. Further, in saying that we presume to know, he is implying that we are being overconfident, that we would have been wiser had we been more cautious in applying agricultural biotechnology, and that the anxiety that many people feel with respect to the increasing deployment of agricultural biotechnology is warranted.

Were we to agree that it is a mistake to think that our beliefs concerning the use of agricultural biotechnology do not constitute adequate knowledge, what should we think concerning such beliefs? Jackson suggests that we should regard natural ecosystems as having knowledge and that, in our agricultural practices, we should strive to imitate such natural systems. This suggestion, whatever its validity in other regards, is not satisfactory as an answer to the question raised here, namely that if we do not have adequate knowledge, what do we have? Jackson's suggestion that we regard nature as a repository of knowledge does not really provide an alternative to the knowledge-as-adequate world view. Let us see why this is so.

We could say that the sort of ecosystems which Jackson seems to have in mind do not literally believe anything. Thus such systems have no knowledge. They cannot literally teach us. However, this objection is misguided. We can imagine how Jackson might reply to such a claim. He might observe that he is well aware that natural ecosystems don't have beliefs and don't literally know anything. Nonetheless, he could say, such systems manifest the correct principles for sustainable living. He might even characterize those principles by saying that in natural systems one finds valuable resources being conserved and recycled, as well as a great diversity of forms of life which are interrelated in mutually supporting ways, etc. In saying that we should strive to imitate nature, he is saying that we should try to develop agricultural systems which instantiate these same principles.

We might agree with Jackson, were he to say this namely so that we could acquire valuable beliefs by studying the structure of natural ecosystems which are sustained over long periods of time. Suppose that we studied natural systems in that light. After a time we would begin to have complex sets of beliefs about how to attain sustainable systems. Very likely, given human predispositions in the past, we would come to think that we had adequate knowledge concerning what is necessary to succeed with such systems. Indeed, agricultural scientists could say, with some accuracy, that they have been trying to uncover the principles which govern the behavior of natural phenomena in order to learn how to farm well. In other words, we can accept Jackson's suggestion that nature is the repository of knowledge and still hold that we have adequate knowledge. To suppose that nature has knowledge is metaphorical. When the metaphor is explained, we see that Jackson has not really provided an alternative to replace the knowledge-as-adequate world-view. Given that the knowledge-as-adequate world-view is presumptuous, what attitude toward our beliefs will be acceptable? So far as I can see, Jackson does not say. In the end, we shall argue that the knowledge-as-adequate world-view is not presumptuous. However, some advocates of the use of biotechnology may be presumptuous in thinking that they currently have more than adequate knowledge regarding such technology.

ARE ADVOCATES OF AGRICULTURAL BIOTECHNOLOGY PRESUMPTUOUS?

Is Jackson's contention that advocates of the use of agricultural biotechnology are presumptuous correct? It might be argued that it is not correct, since advocates of the use of such technology need to claim only that their scientific knowledge is adequate. They can allow that it is not perfect. Yet there is an argument, implicit in Jackson's remarks, which can serve to challenge the validity of this distinction. Though he does not spell out this argument, Jackson may be taken as offering the following argument against the further deployment of agricultural biotechnologies. Let us call this argument the "argument from horrible consequences":

Further deployment of agricultural biotechnology will lead to some horrible consequences, consequences comparable to or worse than the emergence of the ozone hole. The benefits obtained through the use of such technology will not compensate for the harm which will be generated. Thus, we should not develop or deploy such technology.

This argument may appeal to many people who are opposed to the deployment of agricultural biotechnology, and we shall subject it to critical assessment shortly. However, agricultural scientists, in responding to arguments such as the argument from horrible consequences, may be claiming to have more than adequate knowledge.

In defending the deployment of agricultural biotechnology, some scientists appear to give the impression that it is quite irrational to object to the use of scientific technology. In giving this impression, they appear to imply that they know that use of such technology will not have horrible consequences. Thus they may be taken as arguing that adequate knowledge regarding technology would be knowledge which, if deployed in practice, is known not to lead to horrible consequences comparable to the production of the ozone hole. However, it may be argued that whenever our knowledge contains gaps or errors, then we do not know that application of such knowledge will not lead to such horrible consequences.[10] Thus, only knowledge which is complete and error-free is adequate. But knowledge which is complete and error-free is perfect knowledge. In other words, advocates of technology may be taken as claiming to have perfect knowledge. Given that the claim to have perfect knowledge is presumptuous, it appears that Jackson's contention that advocates of the use of scientific agricultural technology are indeed presumptuous is warranted.

Is this contention which we have attributed to Jackson correct? To evaluate it we shall clearly have to reflect on the notion of adequate knowledge. Let us turn briefly to that task. Jackson suggests that advocates of agricultural biotechnology claim to have adequate knowledge. But characterizing some knowledge as "adequate" suggests that it is relevant to ask what the knowledge is allegedly adequate for. The use of the term suggests that the biotechnologists think that they have knowledge which is adequate to realize some purposes. However, any reasonable advocate of the use of biotechnology will admit that he cannot guarantee that deployment of such technology will have no horrible consequences. There are always unforeseeable consequences, and some of these could be horrible. Nonetheless, the advocate of the use of biotechnology will not agree that his or her knowledge is not adequate simply by virtue of the fact that such a guarantee cannot be given. The advocate of technology will point out, quite reasonably, that not deploying the biotechnology could have horrible consequences also. Thus, he or she will maintain that adequate knowledge does not require such a guarantee, and further, that the distinction between adequate and perfect knowledge is valid. In this way the advocate of using agricultural biotechnology will resist the charge of presumptuousness.

What about the argument from horrible consequences? Must we agree that we ought to halt further deployment of agricultural biotechnologies? In my view, in its present form the argument is open to serious criticism. As stated, the argument is so general that the premises are open to serious challenge. We are not in a position to justify the claim that deployment of any agricultural biotechnology which is developed will (or will probably) lead to such horrible consequences. Use of genetically engineered bovine growth hormone to enhance milk output of dairy cows would have consequences for dairy cows, milk producers, and consumers. While some dire warnings have been offered concerning this product, they are controversial. Conceivably it could be used, and would, on the whole, be beneficial.[11] However, there are similar arguments to which we can appeal in support of the conclusion that at the present time, we should be especially cautious in regard to the introduction of certain new forms of biotechnology in agriculture. Let us consider one of these arguments. We shall call it the "argument for cautious deployment."

Technologies based on developments in molecular biology which involve transplanting genes from one species into another and utilizing the chemical or biological processes which occur as a result of the expression of those genes rely on areas of scientific knowledge which are undergoing rapid development. That is, such technologies rely on principles developed in a rapidly changing area of science. Given that this area of science is changing rapidly, it is not unlikely that many beliefs currently accepted among scientists will be modified or rejected in the near future. Further, given the relative newness of many of the principles currently accepted in this developing area of science, we have not had time to thoroughly investigate many implications of these principles. These considerations should incline us to be more than normally skeptical in regard to our predictions concerning the consequences of implementing technologies based on these principles. In a word, we should expect to be surprised. Judgments that such technologies are acceptably safe in the long as well as the short term are justifiably viewed with increased skepticism.

Further, given the capacity of living organisms to replicate themselves rapidly, surprising consequences of the applications of technologies based on genetic principles could readily have very far-reaching consequences. If such consequences were very undesirable and had been extended widely in agricultural applications, then disaster, for example, environmental disaster, could occur on a large scale.

Finally, in many cases the benefits to be expected from the development of new agricultural biotechnologies are not great. The expected benefits of a small increase in efficiency in milk production are marginal. This premise, taken in conjunction with the above two premises, supports a conclusion to the effect that deployment of new agricultural biotechnologies based on application of knowledge of genetic processes should be deferred until we have far greater assurance that such deployment will not cause serious harm to individuals.

The rapid expansion of pesticide use over the last fifty years or so has given us some nasty surprises in regard to environmental damage. The rapid expansion of the use of chlorine compounds, which we thought we understood well, has led to an even nastier surprise. Judging from these cases, we might argue that deployment of agricultural biotechnology based on genetic engineering should proceed at a much slower pace. Except in cases where there is a great benefit to be gained, a benefit comparable to medical benefits contributing to significant extensions in human lifespans, major environmental improvements, or improvements in health, it is arguable that such technologies should be restricted to laboratory testing or to testing in small, carefully monitored situations for the next fifty years or so. In this way long term consequences could be analyzed. Further, in this way the effects of the interactions of specific technologies with other technologies could be studied. Then, if we have not uncovered any unavoidable nasty consequences which could result from the use of the technology, and if the basic molecular biology has stabilized, a more rapid expansion of the technologies which could be developed would be warranted.

This argument may be stated briefly as follows: In light of the potentiality for surprise, due to the reliance on a rapidly changing area of science, and in light of the potentiality for harm on a large scale, due to the speed of development resulting from genetic processes in living organisms and the widespread use of technologies involved in agricultural practices, and in light of the fact that in many cases the benefits to be derived from deployment of agricultural biotechnology are marginal, we should continue to carefully test and evaluate such technologies for a relatively long time prior to permitting them to be deployed on a large scale. Exceptions to this principle would be warranted only where exceptional gains can be expected from a more rapid deployment of the technology. Significant benefits to human health, increases to human lifespans, or major contributions to undoing some of the environmental problems we have created are some cases in which exceptions might be allowed. Improvements in production efficiency in cases where there are alternative agricultural means of satisfying human needs would not be a sufficient reason to make an exception to this principle. If the argument for cautious development is sound, then we are entitled to conclude that those who advocate deployment of agricultural biotechnology at the present time are indeed presumptuous.

CRITIQUE OF THE ARGUMENT FOR CAUTIOUS DEVELOPMENT

We shall not undertake here a thorough critique of the argument for cautious deployment. Rather, we shall indicate several possible critical challenges that might be made. One sort of criticism would be, of course, to challenge the truth of the premises. Some scientist might maintain that the principles of molecular genetics are more secure than we have suggested, or that the long range implications of the sort of modifications introduced in gene transplants or other sorts of genetic engineering are already well-analyzed and understood. I would not agree with this sort of challenge. I believe that many molecular biologists also would agree with me in this regard. As evidence for this, I would note that in regard to potential gene therapies for human illnesses, many medical researchers want to proceed very cautiously. To the best of my knowledge, there is nearly universal rejection, at this time, of any therapy which would involve inserting genes into human germ plasm.

I want to briefly indicate two mutually opposed bases of criticism of the argument for cautious deployment. The first sort of criticism might come from people opposed to any development which involves modification of environments found on Earth, unless such developments can be shown to be compatible with principles of "deep" environmental ethics. Such theories postulate that certain supra-individual forms of biological entity have some intrinsic value or even basic moral rights.¹² Such theories are often expressed in ways that leave great obscurity in regard to concrete moral obligations. How are we supposed to balance the alleged intrinsic values of human lives and species or ecosystems in order to arrive at the greatest overall sum of values? Could it really be the case that in totally eliminating a species from the Earth we are necessarily violating some basic moral right of that species? Suppose that species is the microorganism which causes smallpox.

Many general ethical or value theories contain obscurities, and we cannot cite obscurity as a conclusive objection to deep environmental ethics. Nonetheless, it may well be some time before clear implications regarding our obligations can be derived from such theories. Let us briefly indicate one minimal type of implication which, I believe, would be common to any deep environmental ethics. To explain this let me first distinguish a special class of human moral obligations. This class consists of those moral obligations which are essentially associated with obligations to individual human beings or animals. Some people would characterize these obligations by saying that failures to respect these obligations involve violations of individual human or animal moral rights, such as the right to life, to liberty, to own property, etc. Other people might characterize roughly the same class of obligations by saying that failures to respect these obligations involve reducing the well-being of individual humans or animals in ways that are not compensated by enhancements of individual welfare of other humans or animals. Let us call such moral obligations "obligations derived from individual welfare or moral rights."

Now we can say that what the deep environmental ethical theories have in common is the view that human beings are subject to moral obligations that go beyond any obligations derived from individual welfare or moral rights. Such obligations would place limits on the ways that humans are entitled to modify or dispose of various natural objects such as species, varieties, ecosystems, etc., in addition to the limits that derive from consideration of individual welfare or moral rights. Such a view of environmental ethics is hinted at by Wes Jackson when he says that "If all agricultural species. . . are regarded as the property of humans . . . then the best we can hope for is to become 'smart resource managers.' From my point of view, that is too limiting to prevent soil erosion, or, for that matter, any other desecration of the agricultural landscape. . . ."¹³ People who accept a deep environmental ethic and, if I am correct in identifying this common element in virtually all such theories, who thereby accept additional restrictions on what human interventions in our environment are acceptable, would criticize the argument for cautious deployment for suggesting that once we have been sufficiently cautious in regard to long-term harms or harms resulting form complex interactions of many substances, then use of agricultural biotechnologies is acceptable. Such thinkers will maintain that this implication of the argument for cautious deployment does not take account of obligations which go beyond such obligations as derive from individual welfare or moral rights.

Let us now briefly mention two criticisms of the argument for cautious deployment from points of view which imply that the argument is mistaken due to its claim that the development of agricultural biotechnology should be substantially delayed. Probably the first criticism which many advocates of the use of technology will make is that the conclusion of the argument for cautious deployment is impractical, idealistic, or unrealistic. While some people take such a criticism very seriously, they should not do so. It is not well-formulated. Expressions of this criticism are very obscure. I suspect that such criticisms are virtually always an indication of shoddy and shallow thinking on the part of the critic.

Why is the claim that the conclusion of the argument for cautious deployment is impractical or unrealistic obscure? First, this claim is obscure because, in one sense of terms such as "practical" or "realistic," the recommendation to defer deployment of such technologies is clearly possible and so, in that sense, the recommendation is realistic. Presumably the critic has some alternative notion of what is realistic. However, he or she never (to my knowledge) explains what that notion is. Alternatively, we may say that the charge that deferring deployment of agricultural biotechnology is obscure because the critic rarely or never spells out the principles by reference to which we are to determine what the limits of practicality or realism are. We need such principles spelled out if we are to be able to judge whether deferring development of agricultural biotechnology is realistic or not. Rather than pursuing this line of criticism further, let us consider a more serious basis for criticism.

Whereas the advocates of deep environmental ethics maintain that we have moral obligations to certain supra-individual entities or systems, many thinkers have maintained that all our moral obligations derive from a far more restricted set of basic moral assumptions. Some thinkers, such as John Locke or Immanuel Kant, have suggested that we have moral obligations only to human beings. Such views derive this implication from theories of natural moral rights (in the case of Locke) or from other very complex considerations (in the case of Kant).[14] On the basis of such theories concerning the moral entitlements of individuals, it will be argued that to restrict human activity in the way implied in the conclusion of the argument for cautious deployment would be a violation of obligations owed to those individuals. They will say that deploying agricultural technology properly will not necessarily cause people's premature death, injury, or illness; thus, to restrict such deployment is a violation of obligations owed to people who wish to develop the technology. Advocates of deploying this technology will allow that where such deployment is known to cause such harms, then it may be prohibited.

I believe that the defenders of deploying agricultural biotechnology who would argue as I have suggested they might are making an unwarranted claim, namely that careful deployment of such biotechnology will not cause premature death, injury, or harm. I suggest, for reasons spelled out in the premises of the argument for cautious development, that they do not know that careful deployment of this technology at the present time will not cause premature death, injury, or illness. We do not have the scientific knowledge to substantiate such a claim. Just as deployment of chlorofluorocarbons will cause such consequences, not only to living people but also to people yet unborn (to whom we have or will in time have moral obligations), immediate deployment of genetic agricultural biotechnologies will probably cause such harms as well. Acceptance of the conclusion of the argument for cautious deployment does not commit us to being total skeptics (as Jackson comes close to suggesting but ultimately denies). However, it does not appear to be presumptuous either. If having adequate knowledge of the implications of using agricultural biotechnology implies that we are entitled to be confident that such use will not give rise to serious injury, illness, or premature death to human beings, now or in the near future, then, in my judgment, we do not yet have adequate knowledge of such implications. However, this does not imply that we cannot have such knowledge at some time in the not-too-distant future.

SUMMARY

Wes Jackson has charged that in light of commitment to the knowledge-as-adequate world-view, biotechnologists are presumptuous. In this chapter we made a distinction between adequate knowledge and perfect knowledge. While some scientists give the impression of claiming perfect knowledge and thus of being presumptuous, most biotechnologists would agree that their knowledge is not perfect. We have argued that biotechnologists may eventually be entitled to claim that they have knowledge adequate for the safe deployment of agricultural biotechnology. On the basis of these considerations, we have argued that agricultural biotechnology should only be deployed with great caution.

NOTES

1. Wes Jackson, "Our Vision for the Agricultural Sciences Need Not Include Biotechnology," 207.

2. I have heard students and others express such concerns.

3. This appears to be the message of E. F. Schumacher. He advocated modifying technology so as reduce the size of organizations and units of production so that humans might feel more comfortable in dealing with them. He suggested that modern technology has directed violence against nature and humanity and should move toward some non-violent form. One place these ideas are expressed is in E. F. Schumacher, "The Age of Plenty: A Christian View," 159.

4. Jackson, "Our Vision for the Agricultural Sciences," 208. It is interesting to note that several trends in contemporary thought are anti-Cartesian. Besides Jackson's objections, Descartes has been criticized for maintaining that animals are merely machines. (See the excerpt in Tom Regan and Peter Singer, eds., *Animal Rights and Human Obligations*, 2d. ed., 13.)

5. Descartes expresses this suggestion both in his *Discourse on Method* and in his *Meditations*.

6. He does not say in the essay cited in note number one. He may have spelled this out elsewhere.

7. I have no sociological studies to refer to in order to document these claims about the views of agricultural scientists. Based on conversations I have had and remarks I have heard, I suspect that this is the way that such scientists view their role.

8. Jackson, "Our Vision for Agricultural Sciences," 208.

9. Ibid., 213.

10. Philosophers will rightly object to my speaking of knowledge as containing errors. I apologize for this way of speaking here. I believe that it is harm-

less in this context. I believe that reformulation of my language here to avoid this locution would increase wordiness but would not increase clarity for non-philosophers. Many people's understanding of the term 'knowledge,' is not incompatible with allowing that some of what is "known" is false.

11. For some discussion of this see J. L. Burton and B. W. McBride, "Recombinant Bovine Somatotropin (rBST): Is There a Limit for Biotechnology in Applied Animal Agriculture?" 129.

12. One such theory has been expressed in Homes Rolston III, *Environmental Ethics: Duties to and Values in The Natural World*. For a persuasive defense of such a theory see Mark Sagoff, "Zuckerman's Dilemma: A Plea for Environmental Ethics," 32.

13. Jackson, "Our Vision for Agricultural Sciences," 213–14. Readers not familiar with ethical theory may wish to consult John Locke, "An Essay Concerning the True Original, Extent, and End of Civil Government." Kant's ideas are expressed in a number of works. The simplest is Immanuel Kant, "Fundamental Principles of the Metaphysic of Morals."

Bibliography

Allen, Patricia, and Carolyn Sachs. *What Do We Want to Sustain? Developing a Comprehensive Vision of Sustainable Agriculture*. Sustainability in the Balance Series. Santa Cruz: University of California Agroecology Program.

———, Debra Van Dusen, Jackelyn Lundy, and Stephen Gliessman. *Expanding the Definition of Sustainable Agriculture*. Sustainability in the Balance Series. Santa Cruz: University of California Agroecology Program.

Bacon, Francis. *Novum Organum: True Directions Concernng the Interpretation of Nature*.

Berry, Wendell. *The Gift of Good Land: Further Essays Cultural and Agricultural*. San Francisco: North Point Press, 1981.

———. "A Defense of the Family Farm." In *Is There a Moral Obligation to Save the Family Farm?* edited by Gary Comstock. Ames: Iowa State University Press, 1987.

———. *The Unsettling of America*. San Francisco: Sierra Club Books, 1977.

Broad, C. D. "Egoism as a Theory of Human Motives." In *Problems of Moral Philosophy: An Introduction to Ethics*. 2d ed., edited by Paul W. Taylor. Belmont: Dickenson Publishing Co., 1972.

———. *Five Types of Ethical Theory*. Patterson: Littlefield, Adams & Co., 1959.

Brown, Lester R. "Sustaining World Agriculture." In *State of the World: 1987* A Worldwatch Institute Report. New York: W.W. Norton, 1987.

Brunk, Conrad, Lawrence Haworth, and Brenda Lee. *Value Assumptions in Risk Assessment: A Case Study of the Alachlor Controversy*. Waterloo: Wilfrid Laurier University Press, 1991.

Buchler, Justus, ed. *Philosophical Writings of Peirce*. New York: Dover Publications, 1955.

Burton, J. L., and B. W. McBride. "Recombinant Bovine Somatotropin (rBST): Is There a Limit for Biotechnology in Applied Animal Agriculture?" *Journal of Agricultural Ethics* 2, no. 2 (1989): 129–160.

Butler, Joseph. *Sermons on Human Nature*.

Callicott, J. Baird. "Agroecology in Context." *Journal of Agricultural Ethics* 1, no. 1 (1988): 3–10.

Campbell, R., and L. Sowden, eds. *Paradoxes f Rationality and Cooperation: Prisoner's Dilemma and Newcomb's Problem*. Vancouver: University of British Colombia Press, 1985.

Carson, Rachel. Preface to *Animal Machines*, by Ruth Harrison. London: Vincent Stuart Ltd., 1964.

Churchland, Patricia S. *Neurophilosophy: Toward a Unified Science of the Mind/Brain*. Cambridge: The MIT Press, 1988.

Clark, E. Ann. "Resolving Conflicting Priorities in Ontario Agriculture." *Journal of Agricultural Ethics* 1, no. 4 : 275–89.

Cochrane, Willard W. "Beliefs and Values Underlying Agricultural Policies and Programs." In *Farm Goals in Conflict: Family Farm, Income, Freedom, Security*. Ames: Iowa State University Press, 1963.

Comstock, Gary. "Genetically Engineered Herbicide Resistance." *Journal of Agricultural Ethics* 2, no. 4 (1989).

———. "Genetically Engineered Herbicide Resistance, Part Two." *Journal of Agricultural Ethics* 3, no. 2 (1990).

———, ed. *Is there a Moral Obligation to Save the Family Farm?* Ames: Iowa State University Press, 1987.

Crews, Timothy, et al. "Energetics and Ecosystem Integrity: The Defining Principles of Sustainable Agriculture." *American Journal of Alternative Agriculture* 6, no. 3 (1991): 146–149.

Dennett, Daniel C. *Brainstorms: Philosophical Essays on Mind and Psychology*. Cambridge: The MIT Press, 1978.

DeVita, Vincent T., Jr., and Harriet Kennedy. "Of Mice and Men: What Animal Tests of Carcinogens Mean to Us." *Connecticut Medicine* 44, no. 9 (Sept. 1980): 581–583.

Descartes, René, *Discourse on Method*. Indianapolis: The Liberal Arts Press, Inc., 1960.

———. *Rules for the Direction of the Mind*. Indianapolis: The Bobbs-Merrill Co. Inc., 1961.

Douglass, Gordon K. "The Meanings of Agricultural Sustainablilty." In *Agricultural Sustainability in a Changing World Order*. Boulder: Westview Press, 1984.

Earman, John, and Wesley Salmon. "The Confirmation of Scientific Hypotheses." In *Introduction to the Philosophy of Science*, by Wesley Salmon et al. Prentice Hall: Englewood Cliffs, 1992.

Fentress, John C. "The Covalent Animal: On Bonds and Their Boundaries in Behavioral Research." In *The Inevitable Bond: Examining Scientist-*

animal Interactions, edited by Hank Davis and Dianne Balfour. New York: Cambridge University Press, 1992.

Frankena, William K. *Ethics*. 2d ed. Englewood Cliffs: Prentice Hall, Inc., 1973.

Freud, Sigmund. "Group Psychology and the Analysis of the Ego." In *The Freud Reader*, edited by Peter Gay. New York: W. W. Norton & Co., 1989.

Frey, R. G. *Interests and Rights: The Case Against Animals*. Oxford: Clarendon Press, 1980.

———. *Rights, Killing & Suffering*. Oxford: Basil Blackwell, 1983.

Garnett, A. Campbell, "Conscience and Conscientiousness." In *Moral Concepts*, edited by Joel Feinberg. London: Oxford University Press, 1969.

Gauthier, David P., ed. *Morality and Rational Self-Interest*. Englewood Cliffs: Prentice Hall, 1970.

———. *Morals by Agreement*. New York: Oxford University Press, 1986.

Gewirth, Alan. *Reason and Morality*. Chicago: University of Chicago Press, 1978.

Gips, Terry. "What is Sustainable Agriculture." In *Global Perspectives on Agroecology and Sustainable Agricultural Systems*. 1986.

Graubard, Mark. *Circulation and Respiration: The Evolution of an Idea*. New York: Harcourt Brace & World, Inc., 1964.

Griffing, Donald. *Animal Thinking*. Cambridge: Harvard University Press, 1984.

———. *The Question of Animal Awareness: Evolutionary Continuity of Mental Experience*. New York: The Rockefeller University Press, 1976.

Harman, Gilbert. *The Nature of Morality: An Introduction to Ethics*. New York: Oxford University Press, 1977.

Hobbes, Thomas, *Leviathan: Or the Matter, Form and Power of a Commonwealth Ecclesiastical and Civil*. 1651.

Holton, Gerald, and Duane Roller. *Foundations of Modern Physical Science*. Reading: Addison-Wesley Publishing Co., 1965.

Hull, David. "The Effects of Essentialism on Taxonomy." *British Journal for the Philosphy of Science* 15-16, nos. 60, 61 (1965).

———. *Philosophy of Biological Science*. Englewood Cliffs: Prentice Hall, 1974.

Hume, David. *An Enquiry Concerning Human Understanding*. LaSalle: The Open Court Publishing Company, 1955.

———. *A Treatise of Human Nature*. Edited by L. A. Selby-Bigge. Oxford: The Clarendon Press, 1888.

It's Everybody's Business: Submissions to the Science Council's Committee on Sustainable Agriculture: A Discussion Paper. Science Council of Canada, 1991.

Jackson, Wes. "Our Vision for the Agricultural Sciences Need Not Include Biotechnology." *Journal of Agricultural and Environmental Ethics*. 4, no. 2 (1991): 207.

James, William. *Pragmatism and Four Essays from the Meaning of Truth*. New York: Meridian Books, 1955.

———. "The Will to Believe." In *Essays in Pragmatism*. New York: Hafner Publishing Co., 1948.

———. *The Will to Believe, Human Immorality, and Other Essays on Popular Philosophy*. New York: Dover Publications, Inc., 1956.

Kant, Immanuel. *Fundamental Principles of the Metaphysic of Morals*. New York: Liberal Arts Press, 1949.

———. *Critique of Practical Reason*. Indianapolis: The Liberal Arts Press, Inc., 1956.

———. *Critique of Pure Reason*. New York: Macmillan & Co. Ltd., 1958.

Kuhn, Thomas. *The Structure of Scientific Revolutions*. Chicago: University of Chicago Press, 1962.

LeBaron, Homer M. "Herbicide Resistance in Plants." In *Biotechnology and Sustainable Agriculture: Policy Alternatives*, edited by June Fessenden MacDonald. Report 1 of National Agricultural Biotechnology Council, 1989: 92–102.

Lee, Linda K. "The Impact of Landownership Factors on Soil Conservation." *American Journal of Agricultural Economics* 62, no. 5 (December 1980): 1070–1076.

———, and William H. Stewart. "Landownership and the Adoption of Minimum Tillage." *American Journal of Agricultural Economics* 65, no. 2 (May 1983): 256–264.

Lehman, Hugh. "Anthropomorphism and Scientific Evidence for Animal Mental States. In *Anthropomorphism, Anecdotes, and Animals*, ed. Robert W. Mitchell et al. Forthcoming.

———. "Are Value Judgements Inherent in Scientific Assessment." *Journal of Agricultural & Environmental Ethics* 6, special supplement 2 (1993): 60–67.

———. Review of *The Unheeded Cry: Animal Consciousness, Animal Pain and Science*, by Bernard Rollin. *Journal of Agricultural Ethics* 2, no. 3 (1989): 253–256.

———. Review of *Value Assumptions in Risk Assessment: A Case Study of the Alachlor Controversy*, by Conrad Brunk, Lawrence Haworth, and Brenda Lee, *Journal of Agricultural & Environmental Ethics* 5, no. 1 (1992): 110–12.

———. "What is Animal Welfare." *Newsletter of The Centre for the Study of Animal Welfare* 3 (Summer 1992).

———, and Frank Hurnick. "The Disappearance of the Family Farm." *Journal of Agricultural Ethics* 1, no. 4 (1988): 237–40.

———. Ann Clark, and Stephan Weise. "Clarifying the Definition of Sustainable Agriculture." *Journal of Agricultural & Environmental Ethics* 6, no., 2 (1993): 127–143.

Leslie, John. *Value and Existence*. Oxford: Basil Blackwell, 1979.

Lewis, Clarence Irving. *An Analysis of Knowledge and Valuation*. LaSalle: The Open Court Publishing Company, 1946.

Locke, John. *An Essay Concerning Human Understanding*. New York: Dover Publications, Inc., 1959.

Lowrance, William. *Modern Science and Human Values*. New York: Oxford University Press, 1986.

Masterman, Margaret. "The Nature of a Paradigm." In *Criticism and the Growth of Knowledge*, edited by Imre Lakatos and Alan Musgrave. Cambridge: Cambridge University Press, 1970.

McEwen, F. L., and L. P. Milligan. "An Analysis of the Canadian Research and Development System for Agriculture/Food." A report prepared on contract for the Science Council of Canada.

Mill, John Stuart. *Utilitarianism*. In *The English Philosophers from Bacon to Mill*, edited by E. A. Burtt. New York: The Modern Library, 1939.

Midgley, Mary. *Animals and Why They Matter*. Athens: University of Georgia Press, 1983.

Montmarquet, James A. *The Idea of Agrarianism: From Hunter-Gatherer to Agrarian Radical in Western Culture*. Moscow: University of Idaho Press, 1989.

Moore, G. E. "A Defense of Common Sense." *Philosophy of Recent Times*, edited by James B. Hartman. New York: McGraw-Hill Book Company, 1967.

"The Morality Behind Sustainability." *Journal of Agricultural Ethics* 2, no. 2 (1989): 113–128.

Myers, Norman. *The Primary Source: Tropical Forests and our Future.* New York: W. W. Norton & Company, 1985.

Narveson, Jan. "Animal Rights Revisited." *Animal Regulation Studies* 2, no. 3 (August 1980): 223–236.

———. *The Libertarian Idea.* Philadelphia: Temple University Press, 1989.

Nef, Jorge, Jokelee Vanderkop, and Henry Wiseman, eds. *Ethics and Technology.* Toronto: Wall & Thompson, 1989.

Partridge, E., ed. *Responsibilities to Future Generations.* Buffalo: Prometheus Books, 1981.

Peirce, Charles S. "The Fixation of Belief." *Popular Science Monthly* (1877).

———. "A Theory of Probable Inference." In *Studies in Logic.* Baltimore: Johns Hopkins University Press, 1883.

Perry, Ralph Barton. *Realms of Value: A Critique of Human Civilization.* Cambridge: Harvard University Press, 1954.

Pimentel, David, and Hugh Lehman, eds. *The Pesticide Question: Environment, Economics and Ethics.* New York: Chapman and Hall, 1993.

———, et al. "Environmental and Economic Impacts of Reducing U.S. Agricultural Pesticide Use." In *CRC Handbook of Pest Management in Agriculture.* 2d ed. Boca Raton: CRC Press Inc., 1991.

Pluhar, Evelyn. Review of *The Unheeded Cry: Animal Consciousness, Animal Pain and Science*, by Bernard Rollin. *Journal of Agricultural Ethics* 2, no. 3 (1989): 256–259.

Popper, Karl R. *The Logic of Scientific Discovery.* New York: Basic Books, 1959.

Price, Henry H. "Our Evidence for the Existence of Other Minds." In *Meaning and Knowledge: Systematic Readings in Epistemology*, edited by Ernest Nagel and Richard Brandt. New York: Harcourt, Brace & World, Inc., 1965.

Proceedings of the First European Symposium on Animal Welfare. Köge, Denmark, June 9–12 1981.

Proceedings of the Second European Symposium on Animal Welfare. Celle, Germany, June 10–13 1985.

Quine, W. V., and J. S. Ullian. *The Web of Belief.* 2d. ed. New York: Random House, 1978.

Rachels, James. *The End of Life: Euthanasia and Morality.* Oxford: Oxford University Press, 1986.

Rawls, John. *A Theory of Justice.* Cambridge: Harvard University Press, 1971.

"Referential Communication with an African Grey Parrot." *Harvard Graduate Society Newsletter* (Spring 1991).

Regan, Tom. *The Case for Animal Rights*. Berkeley: University of California Press, 1983.

———. "An Examination and Defense of One Argument Concerning Animal Rights." *Inquiry* 22, nos. 1–2 (Summer 1979): 189–220. Also in *All That Dwell Therein: Essays on Animal Rights and Environmental Ethics*, pp. 184-205.

———. *All That Dwell Therein: Essays on Animal Rights and Environmental Ethics*. Berkeley: University of California Press, 1982.

———, and Peter Singer, eds. *Animal Rights and Human Obligations*. Englewood Cliffs: Prentice-Hall, Inc., 1976.

Rescher, Nicholas. *Risk: A Philosophical Introduction to the Theory of Risk Evaluation and Management*. New York: University Press of America, 1983.

Rollin, Bernard. *The Unheeded Cry: Animal Consciousness, Animal Pain and Science*. Oxford: Oxford University Press, 1989.

———. *Animal Rights and Human Morality*. Buffalo: Prometheus Books, 1981.

Rolston, Holmes III. *Environmental Ethics: Duties to and Values in the Natural World*. Philadelphia: Temple University Press, 1988.

Russell, Bertrand. "Mathematical Logic as Based on the Theory of Types." In *Logic and Knowledge: Essays 1901–1950*, edited by R. C. Marsh. London: George Allen & Unwin Ltd., 1956.

Sagoff, Mark. *The Economy of the Earth*. Cambridge: Cambridge University Press, 1988.

———. "Zuckerman's Dilemma: A Plea for Environmental Ethics." *Hastings Center Report* 21, no. 5 (Sept.–Oct. 1991).

Salmon, Wesley. "The Foundations of Scientific Inference." In *Mind and Cosmos: Essays in Contmporary Science and Philosophy*. Pittsburgh: University of Pittsburgh Press, 1966.

———, et al. *Introduction to the Philosophy of Science*. Englewood Cliffs: Prentice Hall, 1992.

Sapontzis, S. F. *Morals, Reason and Animals*. Philadelphia: Temple University Press, 1987.

Scheffler, Israel. *The Anatomy of Inquiry*. London: Routledge & Kegan Paul, Ltd., 1964.

Schumacher, E. F. "The Age of Plenty: A Christian View." In *Valuing the*

Earth: Economics, Ecology, Ethics, edited by Herman E. Daly and Kenneth N. Townsend. Cambridge: The MIT Press, 1993.

Shrader-Frechette, K. S. *Risk Analysis and Scientific Method*. Dordrecht: D. Reidel, 1985.

———. *Risk and Rationality: Philosophical Foundations for Populist Reforms*. Berkeley: University of California Press, 1991.

———. "Pesticide Toxicity: An Ethical Perspective." In *Environmental Ethics*. Pacific Grove: Boxwood Press, 1991.

Singer, Peter. *Animal Liberation*. London: Jonathan Cape Ltd., 1976.

———. "Animals and the Value of Life." In *Matters of Life and Death: New Intruductory Essays in Moral Philosophy*. 2d ed., edited by Tom Regan. New York: Random House, 1986.

———. *Practical Ethics*. 2d ed. Cambridge: Cambridge University Press, 1993.

Sontag, F., M. Beckner, and R. Fogelin, eds. *Approaches to Ethics: Representative Selections from Classical Times to the Present*. New York: McGraw Hill Book Co., 1962.

Spencer, Herbert. *The Data of Ethics*. London, 1879.

Stevenson, Charles L. *Ethics and Language*. New Haven: Yale University Press, 1944.

Stich, Stephen. "Do Animals Have Beliefs?" *Australian Journal of Philosophy* 57, no. 1 (March, 1979).

———. *From Folk Psychology to Cognitive Science: The Case Against Belief*. Cambridge: The MIT Press, 1983.

Sustainable Agriculture: The Research Challenge. Science Council of Canada, Report 43 (July 1992).

Swartz, Robert J., ed. *Perceiving, Sensing and Knowing*. Garden City: Anchor Books, 1965.

Tax, S., and C. Callender. *Evolution After Darwin*. Vol. 3. Chicago: University of Chicago Press, 1960.

Taylor, Paul W. *Problems of Moral Philosophy: An Introduction to Ethics*. 2d ed. Belmont: Dickenson Publishing Co., 1972.

Thompson, Paul B. "Risk: Ethical Issues and Values." In *Agricultural Biotechnology, Food Safety and Nutritional Quality for the Consumer*, edited by June Fessenden McDonald. National Agricultural Biotechnology Council, Report 2, 1990.

———. "Risk Objectivism and Risk Subjectivism: When are Risks Real?" *Risk: Issues in Health and Safety* (Winter 1990): 3.

———. "The Philosophical Foundations of Risk." *The Southern Journal of Philosophy* 24, no. 2: 285.
———. "Collective Action and the Analysis of Risk." *Public Affairs Quarterly* 1, no. 3 (July 1987): 23–42.
———. "Agricultural Biotechnology and the Rhetoric of Risk: Some Conceptual Issues." *The Environmental Professional* 9 (1987): 316–26.
University of California, Berkeley: *The Wellness Encyclopedia*. Edited by the editors of the University of California, Berkeley, *Wellness Letter*. Boston: Houghton Mifflin Company, 1991.
Vallentyne, P., ed. *Contractarianism and Rational Choice: Essays on David Gauthier's Morals by Agreement*. New York: Cambridge University Press, 1991.
Wilbur, Charles K., and Kenneth P. Jameson. *Beyond Reaganomics: A Further Inquiry into the Poverty of Economics*. Notre Dame: University of Notre Dame Press, 1990.
White, Morton. *What Is and What Ought To Be Done, an Essay on Ethics and Epistemology*. New York: Oxford University Press, 1981.
Woodward, J. "The Non-Identity Problem." *Ethics* 96, no. 4 (July 1986): 804–31.

Index

ad hoc adjustments, 74
ad hominem, 112
affection, 77
aflatoxin, 15
Alachlor, 12, 28–30
Alar, 11, 12, 14, 15, 17, 20
Allen, Patricia, 161
analogical argument, 59, 60
analogical theory, 59, 60
anger, 36
animal feelings, 52
anthropomorphism, 52–54, 67
appetites, 36
a priori, 41
argument: for cautious deployment, 200, 206, 208–12; from horrible consequences, 200, 205, 206; from ignorance, 194
Aristotle, 128; Aristotelian, 120
atrazine, 201, 203
aviary, 187, 188, 194
axiom of comprehension, 113
axioms, 103

Bacon, Francis, 75
basic desires, 43–45,
battery cages, 86, 87, 124, 186–88
begging the question, 53, 54, 66
Berry, Wendell, xiii, 89, 94, 129–42, 201
beneficial insects, 25
benevolence, 39
bias, 27, 28, 30, 31, 74, 81; speciesism, 186ff
Bible, 168, 172
boredom, 77
Brantas, G. C., 68
Broad, C. D., 94

Broom, D. M., 68
Brown, Lester, 142
Brunk, Conrad, 33, 34
Buchler, J., 67
burden of proof, xii, 29, 30, 71, 76, 77
Burton, J. L., 214
Butler, Joseph, 94

Callender, C., 67
Callicott, J. Baird, 128
Campbell, R., 114
Carruthers, Peter, 66
Carson, Rachel, 142
Cartesian, 120, 213
categorical imperative, 112
Churchland, Patricia, 94
Clark, E. Ann, 134, 142, 162
Cochrane, Willard W., 142
Comstock, Gary, 19, 20, 32, 141
concept of self, 86, 90–92,
confinement rearing, 183, 186, 187, 193–95
conscious, 52, 62, 73, 86, 174, 175
conscience, 90
consequentialism, 174, 175
consequentialist, 99
contentment, 79
contractarianism, 109, 110
Copernicus, 120
Crews, Timothy, 162
Culliney, Thomas, 19
cumulative argument, 70–77
curiosity, 77

debeaking, 125
deep environmental ethics, 209, 210
degree of confidence, 22, 23

Dennett, Daniel C., 81
Descartes, Rene, 75, 116, 119, 127, 128, 202, 213
de Sousa, Ronald, 50
DeVita, Vincent, 19
discomfort, 77
Douglass, Gordon K., 162

Earman, John, 19, 32
economically viable, 147–50, 161
ecosystem integrity, 155, 162
efficiency, 97, 131, 133–35, 142, 150, 151, 165, 207, 208
emotion, xiii, 35–50, 77–79, 98–100, 111, 114, 131, 133; emotional as a pejorative term, 129
emotive theory of ethics, 37, 49
emotivist theory, 98–100
empirical: research, 133; scientific studies, 129; testing, 136
entropy, 153
equal consideration of interests, 183–87
essentialism, 53, 54
essential traits, 53, 54
expected value, 12, 13, 15, 16
explanations, 25, 61–63, 69, 71–75, 166, 168; belief-desire explanation, 69, 71, 73, 74; explanatory rationalism, 190, 193, 194; explaining observational data, 8, 105, 106; moral relevance, 191; reductive, 120, 123

faith, 100, 104
fallacy, 53, 54, 112; fallacious arguments, 98, 194; fallacious moral theory, 192; fallacious reasonings, 102
farm workers, 25
fascist, 135
fear, 77
feelings, 77–79

Fentress, John C., 75, 80
Frankena, William K., 113
Freud, S., 95
Frey, R. G., 68, 76, 196

Galilean-Newtonian, 120
Garnett, A. Campbell, 94
Gauthier, David P., 95, 114
generic: consistency, 101; features, 101; rights, 101
genetically engineered bovine growth hormone, 206
Gewirth, Alan, 101, 102, 112
Gips, Terry, 161
God, 168
Graubard, Mark, 67
Griffin, Donald, 62, 66, 68, 73, 74

Harmon, Gilbert, 113
Harrison, Ruth, 89, 142
Hathaway, Janet, 19
Hobbes, Thomas, 114
holism: methodological, 118, 127; ontological, 118
horrible outcomes, 13, 15
Hull, David, 66
human embryos, 179
human traits, 53, 54
Hume, David, 36–40, 42, 94, 102, 103

illusions, 21, 41
impartial, 27
incommensurable, 26, 185
instrumentally valuable, 174
intentional states, 78
interest: economic, 86, 87; positive, 184; self-, 47, 92, 96
interests, 183–87, 196
interpretation, 55, 56, 68, 70, 85
intrinsic goodness, 174, 180
intrinsically good, 172, 180
intuitionists, 32; intuitionism, 103, 104

Jackson, Wes, 199–205, 209, 211, 213, 214
James, William, 20, 49, 66, 67
Jameson, Kenneth, P., 128

Kant, I., 101, 104, 112, 180, 210, 211, 214
Kennedy, Janet, 19
Kite, V. G., 68, 81
knowledge-as-adequate world view, 202–4, 211
Kuhn, Thomas, 143

Land Institute, 203
LeBaron, Homer, 32
Lee, Linda K., 142
Leslie, John, 32
Lewis, Clarence Irving, 33
LISA, 149
Locke, John, 112, 210, 214
logical possibilities, 7
love, 36, 174; of truth, 39; self–, 90, 92
Lowrance, William, 32

marginal humans, 175
Masterman, Margaret, 143
McBride, B. W., 214
McEwen, F. L., 128
methodological principles of science, 74, 75
Mill, John Stuart, 163
Milligan, L. P., 128
Montmarquet, James A., 142, 162
Moore, G. E., 72
moral cynicism, 85–89, 92
moral reasons, 83, 85, 90
moral relevance, 190, 191, 193
moral right, 166, 191, 209
Myers, Norman, 179

Narveson, Jan, 95, 114
Nef, Jorge, 94

objective, 10, 26–31, 32
observable, 25, 33, 54, 55, 67
observations, 25, 29, 37, 55–58, 61, 85, 102, 105, 107, 108, 111

pain, 78, 79
paradigm disagreement, 139
Partridge, E., 163
passion, 39, 40, 46, 49
Peirce, Charles S., 67, 104
Pepperburg, Irene, 68
perennial polyculture, 203
perfect knowledge, 200, 205, 206, 211
Perry, Ralph Barton, 33, 113
pesticide, 5–11, 13–15, 18, 23, 25, 26, 28–30, 40, 42, 97, 119, 138, 207; natural, 16, 17; synthetic, 13, 16, 17, 44, 45, 201
philosopher–scientist kings, 135
Pimentel, David, 19, 20, 163
Pimentel, Marcia, 19
Plato, 36, 38, 40, 49, 100, 112, 135
Popper, Karl, 112
Price, H. H., 68
principle of contradiction, 103, 104, 111
principle of parsimony, xii, 70, 74, 75
principle of utility, 157–60
probability, 7–10, 12, 13, 18, 22–24, 26, 32
problem of induction, 102, 113
producers, 29, 30, 83, 87, 93, 138, 157, 188, 189
psychological egoism, 84, 94

Quine, W. V., 67

Rachels, James, 183, 190–94, 196
rational action, 42
rational belief, 42–46, 51, 52
rational desire, 42–46
Rawls, John, 113

real, 4, 7, 32; possibility, 7; risk, 22–26, 28, 31
reductionism: metaphysical, 115, 116; methodological, 115, 116
Regan, Tom, 63, 68–81, 113, 167, 175, 178, 185, 190, 191, 196, 213
relative frequency, 23, 24, 26, 32
religious belief, 43, 46
Rescher, Nicholas, 32, 33
risk, xiii, 6, 10, 15–17, 20–34, 37, 131; assessments, 26–31; perception, 21–23, 26
Roller, Duane, 67
Rollin, Bernard, 66, 72, 178
Rolston, Holmes, 181, 214
Russell, Bertrand, 113
Russell's paradox, 113

Sachs, Carolyn, 161
Sagoff, Mark, 87, 94, 214
Salmon, Wesley, 19, 32, 245
Sapontzis, S. F., 68, 178
Scheffler, Israel, 67
Schumacher, E. F., 213
scientific criteria, 19, 29, 76
scientific method, 19, 25, 38, 39, 57, 102, 129, 136–40
self-defense, 177
self-evident, 103
selfish reasons, 83, 90
self-sufficient community, 149
sentient, 52, 66, 78
Shrader–Frechette, K. S., 19, 20, 34
Singer, Peter, 163, 178, 183–87, 194–96, 213
skeptical, 60

slave of the passions, 36
Sowden, L., 114
speciesism, 177
Spencer, Herbert, 105, 106, 113
spirited part of the soul, 36
Starr, Chauncey, 32
Stevenson, Charles L., 49
Stewart, William H., 142
Stitch, Stephen, 55, 66, 76
subjective, 27, 41, 55, 73, 108
subjects-of-a-life, 80, 175, 196
super-ego, 90

Tax, S., 67
Taylor, Paul W., 180
theoretical assumptions, 56, 57
Thompson, Paul, 32
Tinbergen, N., 55, 59

Ullian, J. S., 67
unobserved entities, 57–60
utilitarian, 99, 157, 158, 166, 169–75, 180, 184, 185, 188, 189, 194
utilitarianism, 112, 157, 166, 169, 172, 174, 178, 179, 185, 186, 193

Vallentyne, P., 114
values, 11, 12, 22–33, 87, 139–40, 157, 172, 174, 184–86, 189, 201, 209; knowledge of, 24, 25; negative, 22, 23, 25, 26, 31
value theories, 174, 175, 185, 209

Weise, Stephan, 162
White, Morton, 113, 114
Wilber, Charles K., 128
Woodward, J., 163